D0715923

THE
TEACHER
AND
COUNSELLING

Douglas Hamblin

second edition

CHICHESTER INSTITUTE OF HIGHER EDUCATION LIBRARY		
AUTHOR HAMBLIN	WS 2108114 X	
TITLE TEACHER	CLASS NO. 371.4	

JUL 95

Text © Douglas Hamblin 1993
Design and artwork © Simon & Schuster Education 1993

All rights reserved

First edition published 1974 by Basil Blackwell Ltd.

This edition published in 1993 in Great Britain by
Simon & Schuster Education
Campus 400, Maylands Avenue
Hemel Hempstead, Herts HP2 7EZ

British Library Cataloguing in Publication Data
available on request from the British Library

ISBN 0 7501 0192 X

Typeset by Columns Design and Production Services Limited
Printed and bound in Great Britain by Butler & Tanner, Frome and London

Still to: Ursula and Rosemarie
Geoff and Phil

Contents

Introduction

In the 1974 edition of *The Teacher and Counselling* I presented the 'active model' of counselling which made counselling a joint enterprise involving other teachers, with the counsellor a mobiliser of resources for students. Developments such as TVEI and NVQs suggest that it is now time to extend and develop the active model.

The 1974 volume ended by claiming that counselling is only fully meaningful when we use students themselves as agents for change and development (p. 327–8). Failure to do so deprives us of the most potent agency for achieving our educational aim of preparing young people for a technological, post-industrial society. Initiative, imagination and enterprise have to be facilitated, at least partially, through counselling integrated into the daily life of the school. The school is a community where positive identity is fostered and mutual respect is the norm. Counselling is not to be confused with benevolent maternalism or paternalism, nor is it (as many older students believe) 'Nosy-Parker teachers asking questions no teacher has a right to ask'. Counsellors are not in the business of producing the barren of spirit, or those who will be the passive recipients of the non-wisdom of politicians or alleged 'experts'. They try to enable young people to ask relevant questions, seek answers and, in an informed way, take responsible action.

The thesis that counselling is a co-operative undertaking involving all teachers is now extended to give students an equal part in developing a systematic approach to counselling which equips them to meet the legitimate demands of home, peers, school and work. The movement towards flexible learning – still in its infancy – and the growth of negotiation inherent in TVEI and other developments, makes this a reasonable, perhaps inevitable, position. Counselling therefore is education for responsibility rooted in self-respect: the indispensable ingredients being active participation by students in planning and implementing their own guidance and counselling.

A debilitating separation of the pastoral and curricular has long existed in certain schools, reducing such counselling and guidance as is given to emotional first aid, 'mopping-up' after the event rather than preventive work, and the giving of ineffective reprimands for trivial offences. None of which does much to facilitate adolescent development positively. Even in 1974 I argued for linking 'the activity of counselling and guidance to curriculum development'. It is pointed out that, 'as soon as we treat them as an integral part of the school, we cannot evade the task of critically examining the relationship of teaching method and classroom regime to the attitudes and behaviour of pupils' (p. 297). If students are actively to affiliate with the school, and engage with teachers to achieve their full potential, preparing to live constructive lives, then they must assimilate the values and skills of counselling. This is most likely when they are involved as equal partners in the counselling process.

We are also tackling alienation from school: neither a trivial nor an easy task! Those suffering from it may well be justified sometimes by the failure of school to adapt to their needs. Just as likely can be an emotional stunting which inhibits positive commitment to current social roles. Unless the school tackles the problem through allowing counselling to inform the curriculum, this susceptibility to alienation is carried into family and work roles. The resulting poverty of emotions harms us all.

My debt to Frances Wood, Mary Hollyman, Jane Phillips and Leslie Morgan, the librarians of the Education Department at Hendrefoilan, is great. Not only have they given me great help, but I have noted for many years the massive support they have provided to those taking my courses.

For the second time, I offer sincere thanks to Letty Johns for her excellent typing, careful presentation of the manuscript, and unfailing good humour. Letty: I'm deeply grateful.

Swansea
New Year's Day, 1992

1 Counselling skills:
A practical perspective for the secondary school

'Counselling is a necessity, but counsellors are not.' This statement opened the 1974 edition. It should now be amended to, 'Counselling skills are vital, but they are an integral part of many roles.' This extends the then near-heretical active model which argued that counselling is only effective when it is part of the everyday life of the school. The counsellor was seen as a mobiliser of resources for the pupil, making counselling a joint enterprise between teachers. Today, I go further, arguing that if it is to complement trends in curriculum development, counselling should be a joint enterprise between teachers and students. The argument is stark. If schools are to foster responsible identity and self-respect in students, preparing them for the anxiety and challenges of a largely unpredictable future, then pupils have to play an important part in negotiating and carrying out their own guidance and counselling.

To return to the initial statement: what evidence is there of the importance of counselling skills in education? It is readily available, although it would be tedious to give more than a few examples. Jones (1987) shows that counselling skills employed to understand group behaviour form an important sub-set of management skills. Special needs provide another example. We now accept they are usually best met in the ordinary classroom, often requiring the use of a support teacher well versed in the sensitive application of counselling skills. Ainscow and Florek (1989) usefully reveal the complexities of this curriculum-based approach, whilst Thomas and Feiler (1988) highlight the necessity for the support teacher to negotiate working behaviours in the classroom. This applies to the pupil as much as to the support teacher. Counselling skills enable support teachers to engage in constructive interaction based on accurate understanding of the pupil's perception of the classroom, and of pupils' views of his or her client and the situation. This facilitates fruitful collaboration with the subject teacher.

The primacy of counselling skills emerges in a number of areas that preoccupy both teachers and pupils: discipline, learning, assessment and peer relationships. The Elton Report (1989) on discipline stated that initial training should include counselling situations. The recommendation that a sense of community should be promoted through pupils' involvement in negotiation of rules and evaluation of disciplinary policy adds weight to the thesis advanced in this book. Effective communication, rooted in accurate listening and the ability to take the other's perspective will be required on both sides. Active co-operation in areas where pupils traditionally have been, at least ostensibly, passive, albeit reluctant, recipients of their teachers' decisions, calls for the exercise of maturity. Peer counselling, through which impetuous and unwise reactions are tempered by consideration, will also be necessary (see Hamblin, 1974; 1986).

Other forces compel us to give students counselling skills. Advice-giving is no longer acceptable as the main tool of guidance. The demands for initiative and decision making in learning; the probable growth of self-supported study, eg SCET (1988); coupled with students' rejection of anything savouring of benevolent paternalism or maternalism shifts responsibility to the student. Time-honoured adolescent reactions persist: advice may be taken to prove the giver wrong; or defensive reactions stimulated by 'Just look at what you made me do!'. We may think we are sources of wisdom: in fact, we are more likely to be viewed as having a precarious hold on reality, or as peddling outdated platitudes.

The long-term strategy of counselling is to build a network of co-operative relationships in tutor groups and classrooms. These co-operative relationships are anchored in learning and achievement tasks meaningful to adolescents. They are not personally intrusive, nor do they invite 'psychic striptease'. The argument is that counselling skills be given to pupils as tools for achievement and task-orientated co-operation. They are applied to problem solving, eg in formulating hypotheses or in work experience. This is on par with the consumer research and involvement of pupils in the pastoral programme that I believe to be vital.

Levels of counselling

For the purposes of exposition the concept of levels of counselling is useful. In practice, the boundaries between them may be blurred. Different levels of counselling carry no connotations of superiority or inferiority; all are equally valuable. The threefold classification of immediate, inter-mediate and intensive given in the 1974 volume still applies. The year or house head has taken over some of the responsibility for the intensive counselling, previously the responsibility of the counsellor.

The immediate level

This is the classroom level. Counselling skills are used to promote a positive climate for learning, and realistically to promote pupils' sense of self-worth. Success and failure are at the forefront of both teachers' and pupils' preoccupations. The reasons attributed for both are enlightening: often a focus for constructive intervention. Beliefs about what can be controlled and modified in pupils' behaviours, and what has to be endured significantly influence judgements and subsequent reactions (see Levine and Wang, 1983). Teachers' expectations conveyed through low-level behaviours can enhance or erode pupils' sense of mastery. Put simply, the classroom is a signal system in which pupils are bombarded with messages – some intentional, some unwitting – about their identities which shape the behaviour of the vulnerable, and alienate the more resilient.

Counselling skills stimulate awareness of feelings in their possessor. They also convey acceptance, and are used to help the student think about learning in ways which suggest the steps that can be taken to resolve problems. They encourage sound order through early positive interventions in negative sequences of behaviour. Commitment to learning is induced because the pupils' sense of mastery is strengthened. The immediate is just that: reinforcements, adaptations and supports embedded into classroom interaction where individuals are easily damaged by loss of face, and in which they cannot escape the reactions of peers.

Lindsay (1985), in exploring problems of adolescence in the secondary school, reminds us of the intimate connection between the way the school operates and pupils' behaviour. Mittler (1988) cautions that adolescent development can only be comprehended through understanding the environments which impinge on young people and the transactions within them. The classroom, with its peer groupings, is a highly significant environment to which the counselling principle that problems must be considered in their context is all too relevant. Yet even skilled counsellors have not always appreciated how counselling skills can enhance interaction within it. When counselling skills are excluded from the classroom, time and energy has to be expended on 'mopping up' after the event, and in providing emotional first aid. Difficulties are perpetuated because the causes of tensions are left unmodified, and teacher exhaustion remains high.

This first level of counselling is part of a preventive policy, eg anticipating the dissociation from school which develops as certain individuals and groups work their way through the school. Developing *this* level of counselling is no easy task: it is tempting to see the problem as located within the individual pupil who is then subjected to 'counselling' of a different order. Failure to change the state of affairs can then be blamed on the intransigence of the pupil. Some teachers resolutely hold to misconceptions of counselling as esoteric or outside the responsibility of the teacher: for them it can never be part of the everyday life of the school.

The intermediate level

This could well be the initial area for development of counselling, although the difficulties created by current devaluation and misunderstanding of tutor work are formidable. Sharp critical thinking about providing continuity of concern as a *prerequisite for pupils' school success* is more noticeable for its absence than presence. This level of counselling builds on the strengths pupils possess, rather than labouring the negative. As a developmental activity it is about positive identity; about activity rather than passivity, which does not preclude reflection on behaviour; about independence rather than habitual reliance on others for direction.

At this level, the basic concern is with longer-term adolescent development: the individual's coping with the extensive tasks and transitions of this major growth period. The pastoral system – the latter word implying co-ordination, which unfortunately is not always present – is the locus of intermediate counselling. When professionally, and systematically, carried out through the medium of well-designed activities, it provides stable relationships, which act as anchors in a period of sometimes bewildering change. These relationships are essential when the young person feels beset by conflicting or contradictory expectations and demands. These sustaining relationships take two forms.

1. With a concerned tutor who, *over the years*, garners insights and knowledge which allow her or him to relate therapeutically to a pupil, *when, and only when*, circumstances require it.

2. As a member of a form, or sub-group within it, in which the tutor, under the leadership of the year or house head, systematically has encouraged a network of co-operative relationships.

Intermediate counselling is largely conducted through group activity. Misgivings must be expressed: group work conducted with integrity and discipline is excellent; but sometimes it is best described as a bad case of loose concepts. The well-trained drama specialist is an excellent source of advice on the development of group work. I find their focus is practical: related to the goals of the school, and pupils' 'all-round development'. (The cautions which follow also apply to the later chapter on group counselling.)

The warnings given in 1974, taken from Thompson and Kahn (1970), are still relevant. They emphasise:

● the danger of 'reliance upon the untrammelled operation of group forces' *and*

● that 'confidence in the group's capacity to solve its own problems can be a rationalisation for incompetent leadership and an abdication of responsibility'.

Neither making counselling a joint enterprise between teachers and students nor the use of group work implies rejection of professional responsibility or abandoning one's role as a leader. They make this more imperative.

These reminders are necessary because the arrogance and omnipotence of some adolescents is only matched by their vulnerability. Caution is necessary: we have to guard against over-enthusiasm. Fiehn (1989) claims that PSE programmes which overstress personal development in a group context could have unexamined implications, and constitute an illegitimate invasion of privacy. The enthusiastic, but partially-informed tutor, impressed by the importance of group work, could develop some kind of 'amateur psychiatric world view' which they try to foist on their students. Fortunately, adolescents usually have sufficient *nous* to reject it with good humour.

Fiehn provides an interesting illustration which alerts one to the possibility that activities may stimulate adolescents to attribute intent to, and make personality judgements about, their peers, unbacked by evidence. This is a self-indulgent, pseudo-therapeutic approach, damaging to both the originator and recipient of these attributions. One could say they do this in their peer groups anyway, or that psychological aggression is common among adolescents. Psychological aggression can be profoundly damaging and is very difficult to deal with. To give less obvious variants of it legitimacy in counselling situations seems a little odd. Be clear that such tendencies are not an acceptable or inevitable concomitant of group work: they reflect misunderstanding, inadequate leadership and training.

Counselling skills in the service of positive mental health

A corrective to the misconceptions discussed above is to link counselling firmly to positive mental health. Allport (1955), Jahoda (1958), Klein (1960) and Maslow (1970) constitute valuable reading on the topic. Wisely used, counselling skills function to enhance positive mental health which is marked by sensibly confident attitudes to oneself and realistically positive attitudes to others. Tutors should employ them to reinforce a valid conception of self-worth in their students. The above, and the latter part of the previous section, remind us that counselling is a disciplined process in which the onus is on those who counsel to know *why* they say what they say, and do what they do. To give false reassurances to avoid the anxiety of facing reality, or to ladle out undeserved praise, almost certainly arouses suspicion in the recipient, diminishing one's credibility. We need constantly to anticipate the potential impact of our statements and deeds on their recipient. The emphasis on studying problems in their context creates awareness of how the transactions between tutor and form; between the individual and the wider school environment; sharpen, modify, or even create identities at this vulnerable life stage.

The next element in this self-respect building process is stimulation of judicious attempts to master one's environment rather than resort to negativism, eg blaming others indiscriminately for one's failures and problems. There is constructive acceptance of one's limitations, while using what one has to the full, and using environmental resources effectively. A striking feature of some self-fulfilment theories was the emphasis on the social environment as a hindrance. We must not deny, however, that there are occasional insuperable difficulties and intolerable circumstances in which the adolescent is almost powerless, or has little room for manoeuvre. The pursuit of positive mental health requires us to help the adolescent react in a less costly way and defend himself or herself against the self-erosion inherent in their predicament. Facing the facts may mean deciding such cases are better helped by outside agencies with better training and greater resources.

The thrust of counselling skills applied consistently over the secondary years is to build pupils' capacity for responsible self-management. Young people are therefore equipped to cope with frustration and loss of face; they discover how to use mistakes and minor crises as occasions for learning and informed decisions. More importantly, they should be building their capacity to recognise and explore opportunities for mastery. Students should be encouraged to analyse situations, rather than respond instantly on the basis of unverified assumptions about the motives of others or the nature of the situations. Hargreaves (1979) demonstrates the importance of reflective decisions for teachers: they are equally as important for students who have to learn to assess their own contribution to that which they deprecate.

Finally, counselling skills should be employed to build the sense of efficacy which derives from the ability to deal with immediate and episodic pressures; and, in certain cases, to maintain oneself in the face of long-term stress. Counselling helps eliminate unnecessary anxiety, but its crucial function is to equip adolescents to contend with the inescapable anxieties of resolutely striving to be the best that one can be.

Tutor work often seems to be drifting aimlessly. Facilitating positive mental health through a disciplined use of counselling gives the second level – tutor work – a sense of energetic purpose that too often is lacking. It meets students' needs for respect, achievement and dignity; among the fundamental developmental objectives of education. Thorough consideration of this thesis, followed by its reasoned and adapted introduction, would revitalize trivial or sterile tutorial activity.

Challenging it is: but teachers meet challenges with determination and integrity. It 'stretches' students and teachers alike; demanding the best from both, yet this is part of the pride of teaching. Counselling and teaching both strive to bring out the best in adolescents. A question: much has been said and written about the resistance of some teachers to pastoral work; but is the lack of dynamism and irrelevance of some tutor work responsible; rather than the personality of the resisters? Does a conflict of standards exist? In the last year I have acquired some evidence that objections to tutor work by caring, zealous teachers stem from the feeling that they are expected to accept lower standards of work than they would tolerate in their subject teaching. Perhaps worth pondering on?

The more intensive level of counselling

This constitutes the more intensive help proferred by a pastoral head to a relatively small number of pupils. In this, he or she occupies a position similar to that of the head of a large department who works indirectly with most pupils through the subject team. Criteria for referral to head of house or year have to be established to prevent waste of time or effort. One must guard against the possibility that the tutor's lack of the focused observational skills which permit detection of less obvious difficulties will prevent referral to the pastoral head. Unsuspected possessive protection of what the tutor regards as her or his territory, may preempt more considered investigation by year or house head. Training and open-minded discussion help alleviate such hazards.

The conditions given in the first edition for deeper investigation and prolonged support still apply. Where, after careful exploration of behaviours *and* their contexts, causation appears primarily to reside within the individual rather than in the environment, then more intensive and lengthy counselling is indicated. This is also the case where investigation reveals a number of complicating factors, probably located within the family. Here the year or house head has to decide, on the basis of the likely time involved, the possible outcomes and repercussions from the family, whether or not to offer counselling. The pastoral head's crucial function may well be informed referral and liaison with the relevant agency. Conditions which merit the pastoral head's intervention include a marked discrepancy between high intellectual ability and social/emotional competence, problems of poor communication with peers or adults, erratic and unpredictable behaviour.

Year and house heads are gradually escaping from the effectiveness-destroying burden of administering reprimands for trivial behaviours and giving emotional first aid. Many have acquired a fund of expertise about interpersonal interaction, but this should be made manifest through their use of group counselling. Form tutors are tempted to say, 'They tell us to do it, but can they do it themselves?' Group counselling is an extension of tutor work: an adjunct which ensures that tutors feel supported, and that additional help is being given to pupils. It has the virtues of being economical of the pastoral heads' time, and less threatening to many students than individual counselling.

Group counselling should be a carefully structured process through which students learn about themselves: vitally, about the way they defeat themselves or indulge in the psychological equivalent of banging their heads against brick walls. The experience aids acquisition of new modes of coping. Hence revised and extended repertoires for grappling with problems should be the outcome of carefully designed programmes. Typical themes of the groups are disruptive tendencies, learning about learning, acquiring productive assertiveness, vocational choice or coping with examination or social anxieties.

Counselling skills at this level are resourcefully exercised in the leadership of tutors to increase their efficiency and job satisfaction. They also play an important part in staff appraisal, not only in the interview, but in target-setting and follow-up. The conclusion is that their harnessing in areas relating to system development are as important as in direct work with students.

Developmental applications of counselling skills

The foregoing discussion of the three levels provided a structure; within it a developmental process is at work. In 1974 it was necessary to point out that counselling meant many things: at one extreme, heavy emphasis on advice-giving; at the other, a non-directive process scarcely distinguishable from psychotherapy. In 1993 it may be almost devoid of precise meaning. We apparently can be counselled for beauty – a prospect which fills me with grim amusement – to cope with debt; to escape from drug or alcohol dependence; to invest wisely; to cope with job change, unemployment or retirement. Our world seems crowded with those who claim they are qualified to assist us resolve our problems. Questions abound about this. Does this plethora of alleged counsellors stem from our desire for dependency and inability to cope with the challenge of rapid change? Is it reflecting our desire to escape from responsibility? If so, it has little in common with the work of Rogers (1942, 1951, 1961), Tyler (1969) and Blocher (1966) which stimulated early attempts at introducing counselling into British schools. Constructive independence coupled with social responsibility has always figured prominently in adolescent counselling.

Developmental counselling is necessary when a discrepancy exists between the individual's current capacity to cope and the legitimate demands of home, school and peer group. Later, developmental tasks will be examined more closely: for the moment Tyler's (1969) statement that, 'the purpose of counselling is to facilitate wise choices of the sort on which a person's later development depends' gives an excellent orientation. Transitions, especially that from primary to secondary school, reveal startling differences in possession of coping skills, communication, and the ability to make new relationships. Developmental counselling encourages the growth of controls from within, and discourages reliance on external controls and coercive checks. Self-respect causes the adolescent to say, 'I am not the kind of person who does that.' Self-knowledge aids the acquisition of relevant and effective coping strategies which are right for that person. Principles may be provided as broad guides to action, but there is no place for global prescriptions about coping behaviours. Note what was touched on earlier: initiative and foresight are required from the counselled; Krumboltz (1966) argued from a behaviourist standpoint that the counselled should be enabled to 'solve *future* problems more independently and efficiently.' (Italics not in original.)

Martin (1987) extends this theme. He provides an educational model of counselling which helps the achievement of personal developmental goals. Ivey (1986) embodies a forward-looking stance into counselling, utilising Piaget's stages of thought as a guide to moving individuals from confused illogicality to thinking rationally, employing hypotheses as aids to decisions, and surveying their situation from different perspectives. Such techniques mirror the cognitive growth teachers work to induce in students, therefore they seem particularly suited to schools.

Techniques will be explored in later chapters. The basic task here is to explore aspects of adolescent development. Failure to appreciate their significance could lead to hasty, impulsive responses and techniques which bear little relation to underlying developmental issues of which the specific problem is a manifestation.

Adolescence is a time of reorganisation of the past. Erikson (1959) claims that the adolescent is taking charge of his or her past. Livson and Peskin (1980) make a statement that encapsulates the essence of developmental counselling of the adolescent: adult development 'transforms the individual's particular past into a well of resources to be drawn from to meet the ever-changing demands of the present'. But this is the nub of adolescence, where young people are engaging in decisions about their potential strengths and preferences socially and vocationally. This process of reorganisation is, for the most part, undetectable: identity formation is submerged in, yet sharpened by, a constant flow of small and apparently paltry decisions.

The first developmental task

Erikson's (1968) view of adolescent developmental tasks should be at the forefront of pastoral thinking. The first is that of attaining a sense of identity – a task in which young people free themselves socially and emotionally from dependence on parents. In Wall's 1948 and 1968 seminal work, adolescents are seen as building philosophical, vocational, social and sexual selves: a long-term enterprise of which they are largely unaware in any coherent way. Uncertainty is rife: trial roles are adopted in a clumsy and exaggerated manner. Vulnerability is often present: all too often, adults and peers seem to threaten; defensive bravado results. Swings between crude assertion and dependency are familiar to parents at this stage. The mechanisms are touchingly simple: unruly parents are supposed to be quelled by 'Well, I didn't ask to be born, did I?' With timely and discriminating support from parents and significant adults all will be well. Even so, perceived lack of acceptance may produce a pervasive sense of malaise, exemplified in the statement, 'We are the people our parents warned us against.' Badly handled, the outcome is that they are clearer about what they will not do than that to which they are committed; what they are not assumes predominance over what they are.

Marcia (1980) produces a helpful typology of adolescent statuses related to identity. Those offering counselling will find them thought-provoking.

1. Some individuals seem to be clear about their identity, and have a sense of direction moving towards self-chosen goals.

2. Parents appear to have imposed major life goals, but this seems acceptable to the adolescent who seems comfortable with this.

3. Identity is diffuse, if not confused: there is little evidence of clear values or of vocational direction.

4. Anxious effort currently is invested in the resolution of value and vocational issues.

All of us are concerned with how others evaluate us – this is a force for social cohesion – but where identity is uncertain, there may be undue susceptibility to such comparisons. They may then derive identity through opposition. Worse, the vulnerable and unsupported adolescent adopts a façade identity based on their *interpretation of the expectations of others.* This makes them awkward in relationships, compounding their difficulties.

A weakness of the first edition of this book was the implicit assumption that the needs of both sexes in adolescence are identical. Marcia raises a challenging question: is the position to be perpetuated in which females are expected to be 'carriers of the culture' because of their traditional role as the inculcators of values in the basic socialisation of children, or should they be urged to take a change-oriented, even iconoclastic stance? Counselling is not value-free and such issues have to be clarified. Women may be well placed to breach monolithic structures of social class and privilege.

In comparison with males, little work has been done on female identity formation. Miller (1978) states, 'Not only is the process of identity formation qualitatively different for women than men, but the very nature of female identity is not the same.' Much has been achieved by the feminist movement, yet it seems probable that there are forces in the secondary school which strengthen the identity of the male, and which weaken, or render ambiguous, the status of female identity.

Much therefore remains to be done. Freud, cited in Rosenberg and Sutton-Smith (1972) asked 'What does a woman want?' I fear he remained too patriarchal to have any real chance of finding an answer to his question. I suspect that, like me, many male teachers have given little thought as to how girls come to terms with their own bodies. Girls are well aware that in relationships they will be judged and valued largely in terms of male perceptions of the ideal female body. Erikson (1968) remarked that 'Anatomy is destiny', but should schools perpetuate this?

In *Womanhood and the Inner Space* (1968) Erikson obviously wants females to make greater contributions to commerce and politics. He claims that women 'might well contribute to a new kind of vision in the differential application of scientific thinking to humanitarian tasks.' He goes on to argue that 'women's vision and creativity may yet lead, not to new laws of verification, but to new areas of enquiry and application.' Yet even Erikson seems to find it difficult to shed outworn conceptions. His supposition is that woman is different from man, but most certainly not inferior. Yet there still is emphasis on alleged feminine qualities of passivity, pacifism and lack of aggression which reflects the romantic, near delusory, stereotypes of middle class men. Even this civilised and profoundly insightful man was in danger of a subtle version of blaming the victim. He chides woman for allowing herself to be 'exploited, prostituted and infantilized' as if she determined it, rather than society's pressures and expectations. Sadly, it will be at least several decades before the undertones of such ambivalences cease to reverberate in education and counselling.

The just verdict should be 'equal but different'. This book cannot explore in any depth the nature of those differences or disentangle the reasons for them. But a crucial one may be girls' greater susceptibility to anxiety. Sunderland (1983) explored this succinctly, arguing that unless it is recognised, and responded to, girls' 'aspirations will be self-protectively low'. Attempts at achieving equality of opportunity are sabotaged by this. The problem is compounded by many factors in the school, especially the confusion of equality of opportunity *into* courses with equality of opportunity for experiences *within* them. (No in-depth discussion of anxiety is offered here, although the outline of an appropriate framework for coping with it is provided. Levitt (1968), Ruebush (1963) and Spielberger (1966) are recommended for the theoretical and research backgrounds.)

Sunderland draws attention to girls' sensitivity to, and probable dependence on, feedback. But do they receive the same kind of feedback as boys? Stanworth (1982) in a study of A-Level classes, highlights the differences in feedback received by boys and girls. Differences in the manner of addressing, responding and reprimanding led Stanworth to conclude that girls in these classes were seen as different and unequal. Teachers, male and female, tend to give more attention to boys who assume they have a legitimate right to leading roles in the classroom, whilst girls become marginalised. Stanworth is definite that classroom interaction functions, not merely to reflect common beliefs about boys' superiority, but 'actively serves to give such beliefs a concrete foundation in personal experience.' Logically, this would reinforce differential anxiety, but does it create it? Exploration of the problem with younger girls may well hold important implications for counselling.

Are younger girls' exploratory behaviours more restricted than boys? Maccoby and Jacklyn (1975) report that after the age of eight, girls tend to be more restricted in the freedom given to them to carry on activities outside the home than boys. But there is no evidence as to how such constraints transfer to the school, and produce anxiety in learning situations. Girls may be more ready than boys to conform and please, which despite some teachers' aversion to 'creeps' is likely to bring approval and rewards which are anxiety-reducing. Sunderland also shows how certain girls manipulate the mores of society to legitimise their evasion of competition and achievement. Other and deeper factors are at work: Licht and Dweck illuminate the problem when they remark that, 'girls and boys differ in how they interpret or incorporate the expectations that others hold for them.' The key words, 'interpret' and 'incorporate', may go a long way in explaining the problem.

From the above it is clear that anxiety and achievement are related, indeed almost inseparable. It reminds us that achievement motivation is surprisingly subjective. The model put forward by Atkinson and Feather (1966) included the *incentive value* of success and *predictions* of success. Both are crucial: if success is seen as having little value, or as bringing personal and social punishments, then the people holding such perceptions may avoid it, even if they maintain a façade of effort. If failure is predicted, active striving for success is seen as futile; attempts to induce it provoking anxiety, rebellion or a sense of a hostile world full of threat. Both values and predictions are susceptible to individual interpretations.

Next, Weiner (1972; 1980) and Weiner and Litman-Adizes (1980) put forward an attribution theory of achievement concerned with the individual's perceptions of their responsibility for success. The major causes assigned for success are ability, the effort invested, the difficulty of the learning task, and the contribution of luck. Other causes of success or failure include the teacher's dislike of the pupil or biased treatment of him or her, tiredness or mood. A crucial question is: which factors leading to success are within the control of the student? Effort and perseverance are; ability, task difficulty, and to a large degree, the attitudes and behaviour of the teacher, are beyond his or her influence. Certain factors persist over time, eg ability, whilst others such as mood and fatigue are relatively transitory. If the reasons given for failure – by teachers or the pupil – habitually focus on those outside the control of the pupil (which are also permanent) then self-confidence is almost certainly diminished.

Counselling therefore takes seriously the causes pupils give for success or failure. We should also ask if gender-related patterns of attribution exist; if girls attribute their failure to a lack of ability, whilst boys dismiss it as due to their laziness, 'not bothering' or rejection of teacher's demands, this should be brought to the forefront of counselling efforts. Anxiety – or worse, depressed resignation – may come from girls' disbelief in their capacity, interacting with acceptance of the legitimacy of pressures on them to achieve. They then work conscientiously, probably relying on rote learning where possible, building up their personal theory of the 'impossible task'.

Are girls therefore more susceptible to learned helplessness? That is a sense of powerlessness: the belief that one's efforts will not influence the outcome of the learning endeavour. Put simply, 'Even if I do try, it won't work!' Seligman (1975) and Garber and Seligman (1980) have researched the phenomenon usefully. The work of Dweck and Licht in the latter volume is particularly useful. They argue that girls seem more likely to resort to lack of ability as explanation of failure: causation is therefore seen as immodifiable. Boys attribute their successes to their ability, and are reluctant to accept failures as evidence of intellectual inadequacy. In counselling, I have noted, however, that both sexes who have acquired a mastery orientation, regard their mistakes as rectifiable: sometimes as opportunities for strengthening their skills as learners; certainly not as immutable or predictors of future performance. The task of counselling may be action research into the forces which constrain girls' sense of mastery and push them towards over-dependence on external evaluations.

Developmental counselling is alert to the longer-term changes of adolescence. What is happening to the girls who were confident and eager achievers in the primary school? Even in the early years of the secondary school they usually appear balanced and mature in comparison with boys of the same age. Obviously, exaggeration has to be avoided. The differential anxieties may operate more strongly in certain subjects, especially the sciences, and also be related to teaching methods. For individuals the gender of the teacher may be an important variable. A possibility to be explored is that girls' readiness to interpret negative feedback as evidence of lack of ability varies with the context in which it is received, therefore it may be stronger in the sciences. Familial and sub-cultural expectations may create a climate in which doubts about their scientific ability are reinforced. Feedback is not only received from teachers; a more potent source of feedback for girls in middle adolescence is their male counterparts. The brash confidence of many boys and their stereotyped views about the nature of girls' ability can enable them to push girls towards the marginal position described by Stanworth. I believe the best way to tackle such deeply-embedded distortions of reality is by raising awareness of the forces at work in the classroom. Action research within the form, to identify the vulnerabilities of both sexes in relation to achievement is essential. Much that shapes learning behaviour remains as a hidden agenda. Action by students and teachers must be planned, implemented and evaluated. Note that equity requires equal consideration of the feedback sent by females to males in, for example, modern languages.

We must also recall that explanations appertaining to large groups gloss over the fact that differences *within* the group are often greater than the differences *between* the groups. In this matter of differential anxiety, aspiration and achievement, certain girls are at high risk because of family background, long-term conditioning, health, body chemistry and psycho-logical insecurity. The combination will be unique in each case, and include idiosyncratic features of peer group and school. Even so, Dweck and Licht's work is valuable and enlightening. They see girls as receiving ostensibly more favourable treatment which is actually debilitating as the years pass. Boys receive more reprimands, almost certainly directed at their behaviour, which they interpret as evidence of the teacher's unpleasant personality and prejudice towards them. Therefore they tend not to associate the feedback with their ability. Indeed, Dweck and Licht claim boys *learn* to interpret reproof in a way which boosts their confidence in their ability. The conforming, approval-seeking behaviours of girls bring them fewer reprimands: inevitably, those received incorporate censure about their achievement. Because of their history of positive relationships with teachers – at least, in a significant number of cases – they do not reject it as suspect or biased. It is taken as a valid assessment of their ability.

One explanation, however valuable, is insufficient. The positive approach of counselling urges study of adolescent girls marked by confidence in their ability, and who refuse to be influenced adversely by teacher and peer feedback. Could they act as models for others or as initiators of action research within the form?

Sunderland notes that girls hide their anxiety, therefore teachers may not recognise the gravity of the problem. She suggests that peer groups should evaluate their members for anxiety. More could be asked of them as part of making counselling a joint enterprise between teachers and students. The work of Lazarus (1966) and Lazarus and Folkman (1985) provides a guide. This work again stresses that people interpret events differently, and that each has her or his pattern of vulnerability. The first step in coping is to appraise the threat. It is easy to mystify anxiety unnecessarily, failing to see that it is a signal of danger: a response to some perceived threat. Peer groups, with their tutors, might well design a piece of action research in which they scan the school environment detecting sources of threat. Once detected, they evaluate their reactions to them. This self-observation is crucial: in both individual and group counselling, I have found that self-observation often induces some behaviour change, increasing the student's sense of control. Ranking the sources of threat in an order of importance, and then justifying it increases clarity – vital, for anxiety flourishes in conditions marked by ambiguity and uncertainty. The study of attributions of threat and their reality is demanding. Pupils should be trained to ask, 'What is the evidence?' and submit it to critical scrutiny. Note too, that this is about perceptions of threat common in the school and does not involve speculations about personality. Secondary appraisal is concerned with the behaviours used to deal with threat. Judgements have to be made about the coping behaviours, their effectiveness, and the costs entailed. Mandler and Sarason (1952) showed how students develop characteristic responses to anxiety in a specific situation: coping behaviours that all-too-quickly become automatic and rarely questioned. Once they have identified threats accurately, students benefit from discussing the viability and costs of the way they cope. What works for one person will not work for another, therefore recipes are not useful. Each student has different levels of skill in problem-solving, degree of determination, and beliefs about what will work. They have to accept ownership of their difficulty and not spend energy in blaming others for it.

Primary and secondary appraisal do not necessarily follow in the sequence given above. They may occur together, or assessment of the costs of coping may occur first, to be followed by examination of the nature and reality of the threat.

Tutors help by distinguishing two factors in coping, and encouraging discussion of them.

1. Controlling and managing the source of threat;

2. Evaluating, and if desirable, altering one's emotional response to it.

Case studies of a number of potential coping responses to an anxiety-provoking situation can be offered for discussion. Pupils' discussion can focus on detecting the barriers that prevent control and management of threat. It would be naïve of the tutor or pastoral head to create the impression that every threat is amenable to control: indeed it could damage pupils' self-respect. Open discussion in a climate of support will reduce the sense of isolation and difference stimulated by frequent experience of anxiety. Extended discussion can be found in Hamblin (1978; 1984).

Classroom situations and learning provide the framework for joint projects by tutors and pupils. Dissociation from the objectives and values of the school, and avoidance of challenge, flourish if key anxiety-provoking situations are ignored. A start may be made by tackling the following sources of anxiety found in pupils aged nine to 14 by Phillips (1978).

1. Almost 75% of his sample wished the teacher would slow down so that she or he could understand better.

2. More than 50% were worried about making a mistake when reading aloud. Related situations are answering the teacher's question incorrectly or making an error when translating.

3. Having a report which met parental expectations was a source of anxiety for 60% of the sample.

4. Meeting teachers' expectations in class appeared to be threatening for over 50%.

Counselling stresses anticipation and preventive intervention. The first six weeks after entry to the school is a period when pupils are particularly receptive to teacher influence. Constructive challenges to already established ideas about achievement and gender are likely to be received positively. Firm ideas are already held about what girls and boys are likely to be good at. Families have contributed to expectations of likely success in certain areas, eg 'Dad says none of his family were ever any good at maths!' Such prophecies cannot be left to run their course. False conceptions about the nature of subjects, and the kind of people good at them, have to be brought out into the open and modified.

Year seven pupils may lack the flexibility to adapt to the different teaching styles and approaches to classroom management and discipline they meet. Discussions of this have helped to maintain confidence and positive attitudes to learning. Each year has its own source of anxiety. Year eight brings awareness of the demands the school is making; pupils may be uncertain whether they can, or want to, meet them. Girls *may* find coping with this ambivalence a source of anxiety, due to the near emotional blackmail sometimes used to induce conformity. Boys *may* enjoy their psychological truancy – present in the flesh, but absent in the spirit – because they believe they will catch up if they do decide to employ themselves in school work. The commonly-operating expectations that girls like making neat notes, and will give correct responses to factual recall questions, must be openly explored if girls are not to be confined to a regurgitative style of learning, which anxiety and uncertainty prevent them from discarding.

Those offering counselling must attend to questions which involve parents. Despite the many overt changes relating to equality of treatment, are we at a latent level still tied to an image of girls as concentrating on relationships rather than vocational preparation? Are boys expected to make choices and decisions that free them from their family backgrounds? Is conflict and assertiveness seen as acceptable and desirable for boys, but regrettable for girls?

Counselling and guidance which does not recognise differences in developmental rates could be accused of denial of the obvious. Girls are, *on average*, two years ahead of boys in early and middle adolescence. This maturity should be welcomed and used to the full. In classroooms where interaction is geared to the needs of boys is this maturity a handicap? Is girls' identity then disconfirmed? Counselling as currently practised in schools has not tackled the situation in mid-adolescence where awareness of the subtle punishments society applies to the able woman leads to motivation to avoid success. Ambivalence then produces unwitting sabotage of ambition. This is related to, but different from, the points made on anxiety. More positively, are we neglecting a vast potential for raising the level of interaction and maturity in the secondary school by not harnessing different developmental rates and intellectual orientations? Year nine boys would gain from perceiving and applying the value orientations girls hold about science. Counselling skills should validate girls' style of thought and processing of knowledge.

Counselling may need to produce psychological androgyny, giving both sexes the intellectual and emotional characteristics traditionally associated with the other. Counselling should not canvass dichotomies! Individuals can be ambitious and caring, dominant and gentle, independent and co-operative without being at war within themselves. For both sexes the cardinal principle must be that they have the opportunity to decide what they want.

Counselling takes the standpoint of those being served: yet the body image still may not receive sufficient consideration, although it is a key element in identity, and a major preoccupation for both sexes, even if anatomy should not be destiny. Girls experience more overt pressures to influence others through their body: many find this distasteful and derogatory. Boys are easily wounded by bodily comparisons with others, especially if this makes their masculinity questionable. As teachers we forget the far-reaching changes induced by puberty; even the eyeballs change, hence the onset of myopia in adolescence. Doubts about identity are intensified by late entry to puberty: unfortunately the adolescent does not know about the completely normal wide range of entry! For those in a counselling position it is crucial to recognise the sharp impact of idealised norms interacting with physiological factors. Both sexes are forced to undertake a thorough-going revision of physical evaluations of themselves. Caring tutors are alert to the consequent dangers of self-deprecating comparison and face-saving defensive manoeuvres. For example, the obese may cope by adopting clowning roles or other self-belittling tactics to ensure marginal acceptance within a group. Pupils coming from backgrounds where the physical looms large in acceptability, need coping tactics if they are markedly different physically from their perceived 'norm'.

Perspective has to be maintained: adolescence is a life stage notable for precise motor coordination, agility and grace. The stresses derive from the adolescent's subjective perceptions of that most intimate possession – his or her body – and their interpretations of others' reactions to it. A final point: stereotyping about gender and physical activities persists. Sport is seen as an arena dominated by males: could it become the last bastion of male prejudice against females?

The second developmental task

This is learning to make a truly intimate relationship of integrity. It is dependent on the way the earlier task was resolved. Inadequate resolution often means defensiveness, awkwardness in social relationships and superficiality. This is poor preparation for a task in which fears of manipulation, eventual rejection, or exploitation, are easily aroused in those whose sense of identity is fragile. Again, the greater maturity of girls may be costly; keener awareness of risks and sensitivity to nuances of relationships in comparison with the males involved provoke insecurity and consequent anxiety. The issues reduce to what can be given and taken in a relationship. Questions condense to the danger that if one reveals oneself honestly, this can be used to exploit or deride. Both sexes are aware of the danger of investing the other in the relationship with qualities he or she does not possess, bringing eventual disillusionment and hurt. Tensions between trust and mistrust are strong: there is a tendency for the 16–19 age group simultaneously to be cynical and yet look for women, men and ideas in which to have faith. Counselling them requires elements of caution and courage. They are alert to any hint of patronage or attempt to impose a solution to their problem. One has to have the ability, with humility, to earn their trust, and achieve credibility. Above all the tutor has to work to create a climate of safety and mutual respect. A curious feature of counselling this age group is that the tutor has to learn to work within a context riddled with contradictions and ambivalences, eg humility and acting as a model of competence have to be combined, or at least placed in juxtaposition. No mean task.

For a more extensive coverage of this discussion, see *The Teacher and Pastoral Care* (1978) and *Guidance 16–19* (1983).

The importance of the self-concept

Why is the self-concept seen as important in counselling? The preceding work indicates that girls may be particularly liable to evaluate themselves negatively, but for both sexes the school presents challenges to self-esteem. Transitions and disjunctions, such as entry to the secondary school, going from year 11 to sixth form college, or moving from education to work bring threats, indeed do damage, to self-esteem. Physical puberty can be seen as a transition which has profound implications for the young person's view of himself or herself, bringing revision of their self-evaluations.

What is the self-concept? In essence – indeed it is a gross simplification – the self-concept can be seen as our attitude to ourselves which incorporates more or less accurate evaluations. James (1910) explored the 'I' and the 'ME'; the self as object and the self as subject. The former refers to our capacity to view ourselves in a detached way – as distinct from our bodies and environment. Self as subject means we are referring to ourselves as experiencing, although it is difficult to disentangle what belongs to 'self' from conditioning and physiology. Gordon and Gergen (1968) indicate that the crucial thing is the way people interpret themselves, and counselling certainly gives this pride of place.

Cooley (1922) produced the useful concept of the 'looking-glass self'. The mirror provides feedback as to whether or not one is acceptable to others. Counsellors, however, are alert to the possibility that in matters of gender or alleged deviance those looking glasses may be cracked or distorting. From Mead (1925) we take the idea that the self-concept is a socially derived product of significant communication with those who matter to us in some important way. It is an artifact of the way we are treated by others: we learn to respond to ourselves as others respond to us. This is not absolute, for we may have the courage to refute their evaluations.

To summarize: by the age of entry to secondary school pupils have a perspective about themselves, which is partially the residual aggregate of what the individual has learned about herself or himself from others, and from important life situations. This characteristic mode of viewing himself or herself is organised and provides continuity with the past. Even adolescents undergoing rapid, maybe intensive, change, can be locked into outworn conceptions of themselves, stemming from the past but constricting in current circumstances. For those offering counselling the crucial realisation is that the self-concept is not solely about self-esteem, but is a process which gives a general orientation to other people; a process through which an adolescent interprets, and allocates meaning to his or her relationships. Developmental counselling examines the portent of those meanings for future tasks and challenges.

But is talking as if there is a single self misguided? Are there a number of selves which for the facilitation of development can validly be considered? A self seems to be present in every major life area. Wall (1948; 1968) discussed the philosophical, sexual, social and vocational selves. There is also the self as a learner and the self within an organisation. The danger is that of reification: acting as if an explanatory or diagnostic concept is a concrete entity. It is meaningful to diagnose the difficulties relevant to one 'self', or ask whether the content of two 'selves' are incompatible with one another, provided we never forget that these 'selves' are expository tools.

Horrocks and Jackson (1972) agree that self-interpretation is the most salient aspect of human life. They emphasise process and change, seeing people as building a wide range of identities or 'selves' which are measured against reality, and then changed, discarded or extended according to their productivity and the satisfaction derived by the individual trying them out. It helps to take Kelly's (1955) view about constructs, ie regarding them as pathways into the future.

To condense: it is vital to explore the meaning that adolescents assign to themselves in important situations. Equally, we must not forget that the environment sets limits to identities. What identities does a particular group setting, family or neighbourhood endorse, even permit? Tutors would benefit from discussion of such questions as part of a training programme led by a pastoral head.

Counselling begins by clarifying the problem *and* its context, which does not mean over-simplifying it. Interaction exists between the young person's potential, his or her actual skills, the expectations of others, their valid or invalid perceptions of him or her, and what is valued in the group or context. Simple analysis of this interplay through diagrams or drawings can help pupils see what is happening, revealing previously unapprehended possibilities for coping. Realistic counselling looks critically at the accuracy of perception on every side. Pupils may have fallacious views of themselves, and of the attributions of others, whilst those others may be just as inaccurate.

Part of adolescent growth is achieving a satisfying balance between acceptability and independence. Those taking a counselling stance in the school know that adults also face tensions from this task. Hamblin (1989) shows that colleagues' expectations restrict pastoral heads' desire to innovate and develop their role in the way they feel right. An example is the year head who said 'I agree with the need for something different, but I can't change. My colleagues expect me to lam into pupils . . . and if I don't they will think I've gone soft'. Here, the need for acceptability inhibits desirable and desired change. Expectations take compulsive hold and are perhaps seen as immutable. Pastoral heads come to believe that they are tied to unproductive versions of their role; that they are powerless to modify the situation. Counsellors will find many examples of this conflict between acceptability and independence operating in adolescents. It must not be assumed that these situations are always resolvable. If groups or people of major significance to the adolescent are involved then sometimes the best that can be done is to help the young person manage the tensions they experience and achieve some sense of freedom.

The ideal and actual selves

Ideals are necessary for constructive living. Counselling reinforces self-respect and supports young people in the pursuit of their self-set ideals. Sometimes people do not appreciate that counselling is about standards of excellence in living, which includes compassion for others, tolerance for those who are different, and a constructive tough-minded evaluation of one's own motives and behaviour.

The actual self is one's perceptions of oneself. This sounds delightfully simple, but self-perceptions are notably inaccurate, even delusory. Any experienced counsellor knows that an adolescent's self-perceptions may be coloured by guilt, especially sexual guilt, or omnipotent fantasy. Socialisation within certain families promotes denial of reality, blame-pinning, evasion of challenge, arrogant dismissal of the judgement of others, an almost automatic attribution of malicious intent to those in authority, or a pervasive sense of the 'rightness' of their own attitudes and actions. Such things cocoon the young person against the evaluations of others, and inhibit self-evaluation. The task of encouraging adolescents to question their self-evaluations therefore cannot be evaded without loss of integrity. Respectfully, but firmly, we help them examine possible discrepancies between what they say they are, and do, and what they actually are, or do. Failure to tackle this puts a counsellor into a position of collusion with the adolescent. *Collusion can be defined technically as the maintenance of a false definition of reality.* Obviously, this rather stern approach is only used when necessary, and without rejection of the pupil. Challenge of self-perceptions should come into many activities, eg study skills programmes do not lead automatically to confirmation of the actual self as currently perceived. Some individuals find they are more competent than they thought; others discover that they had over-assessed their competence. Counsellors soon learn that the actual self as judged by its owner is far from accurate.

The ideal self is, at least partially, culturally or sub-culturally determined. Courtesy and respect are imperative: one may not agree with the content of the ideal self inherent in certain cultures, but to indulge in condemnation alienates. There is a duty on the counsellor to understand the social groups from which young people draw their values, and against which they compare themselves. More sensible than rejection is the question, 'What function does this group serve for the individual?' To ignore the influence of such reference groups and their relationship to the ideal self is to render onself incompetent. We must not forget, however, that there is the personally-determined element of the ideal self which becomes more influential as counselling proceeds. It should be valued and fostered: certainly counselling at all levels should clarify the personal ideal, and reduce dependence on the external.

What is the relationship between the ideal and actual selves? May too great a discrepancy between them over a long period of time result in poor adjustment, inadequacy and underfunctioning? The rather unsatisfactory answer is 'sometimes, in some people'. Three factors urge caution in assessment of the actual/ideal discrepancy. First, it has proved difficult to quantify the discrepancy: actual/ideal self scales have proved more effective as stimulators for discussion than as measures. Second, adolescence is a stage of rapid intellectual change (see Piaget and Inhelder, 1958). The orientation in later adolescence is on what could, or should be, rather than anchorage in what is. Possibilities fascinate the adolescent! Accelerating changes in social relationships – both in range and type – are coupled with growing awareness of an exciting technological and vocational world. All three interact to encourage the lively adolescent to extend her or his horizons and lift her or his ideals. A wide gap between the ideal and actual may well be a healthy phenomenon in later adolescence. Third, all this is highly subjective and fundamentally relative. A discrepancy which is stimulating and creative for one person is beyond the tolerance of another, creating confusing dissonance.

My experience suggests that the critical factor is often, although far from certainly, whether the high ideal is self-set or imposed by others. A self-set ideal can, however, damage. There are young people who cannot take a rationally objective view of their ability, and impose punishingly high targets and unrealistic work schedules on themselves. This seems to me even worse than parental imposition of unrealistic aspirations on the wretched adolescent. In both cases reactions are multifarious. Some students display harsh, self-condemning attitudes, punctuated by periodic depressions or quite violent outbursts. Some opt out, apparently happy in their evasion of academic demands. Some adopt a sullen or solid front of passive aggression, responding to almost everything with 'Don't know', as a means of blocking the teacher's attempts to activate them. They are well-practised in passive aggression with both parent and teacher – indeed occasionally I have detected a cynical amusement at the powerlessness of the teacher.

McCandless and Trotter (1977) remind us that the possession of ability does not automatically entail a positive perception of oneself: able pupils felt teachers expected too much of them, and had significantly lower self-concepts than those of lower ability. This, and other work, suggests that the able are more aware of pressures and threats, but manage them better. In counselling, I find they have often internalised the schoolmaster's old dictum, 'Could do better': one target fulfilled means another to be reached. They manifest self-respect rather than complacency, although they can be intolerant of peers not sharing their orientation. Enough has been said to show that the relationship between self-esteem and the ideal and actual selves is complex. It is unwise to try and apply one formula to explain it, or make advance predictions about the connections between them, in relation to an individual causing concern. Provided that warning is held in mind, Thomas' (1973) careful review of the trends will be useful.

The self as a learner

Developmental counselling helps adolescents sharpen their sense of direction in life. It is about acquiring a realistic sense of mastery, a belief in their capacity to make wise choices, and the ability to take responsibility for their futures. It is about achievement, and learning to make an impact on a malleable world. Of all the selves mentioned earlier, the self as a learner integrates counselling and the mainstream task of the teacher. It is a major element in the output of the secondary school, shaping pupils' responses to higher and further education, work and training. Yet, as Hamblin (1978; 1981) comments, it is sadly neglected. Schools teach study skils (often forgetting that 'skill' acquisition implies controlled practices) but also neglect personality factors and their contribution to success or failure. Personality, following Sherman (1979) is seen as 'the characteristic pattern of behaviours, cognitions, and emotions which may be experienced by the individual and/or manifest to others'. It can be seen from the learning perspective as an accumulation of learning experiences, the impact of background influences, conditioning and stable tendencies such as extroversion and introversion. Note Sherman's inclusion of emotions. Record of Achievement interviews will include helping pupils understand feelings which hamper learning, and develop ways of coping with them. Through exploration, discussion and thoughtful application of counselling skills, pupils are assisted to build a style of learning effective for *them* in particular learning situations. This is very different from the usual attempt to impose a template of *the competent learner*. Therefore at the immediate and intermediate levels, counselling contributes to the 'production of a trained mind which works efficiently because it has grown out of the student's idiosyncratic learning style which he or she has consciously extended', (Hamblin, D, 1978 *The Teacher and Pastoral Care*). GCSE, TRIST, CPVE and TVEI have provided the context and opportunity for this, but much remains to be done.

Techniques of counselling make planned reflection on learning effective. Purpose is given by Kolb's (1984) cyclical process of: classroom experience, reflection on that experience, abstract conceptualisation and testing out of the ideas formulated. Learning should be the centre of active debate, not only between teacher and pupil but between pupil and pupil. The aim is to encourage pupils to develop an effective cognitive style. Hamblin (1981) argues that this is based on the assumption that the individual brings a particular structure or style of thinking to different curriculum areas. It is therefore a characteristic mode of functioning appearing in different contexts, although it can be modified by coercive forces within a specific situation, and also by the student's perception of what is required of him. Even so the student has a style of attributing meaning to the learning process, and organising facts and ideas, which to a large degree determines his success or failure.

This sounds a little intimidating; in fact it is very practical. Just consider the importance of students' perceptions of what teachers require of them. The teacher may be hoping for independent thought, while the pupil sees learning as regurgitation of what he or she has been told or read. Does the student's style consist of immediate imposition of meaning on the problem and task with a refusal to admit further evidence? Is it unduly limited so that all learning tasks are tackled as if they were similar, with consequent failure? Broadfoot *et al*'s (1988) splendid analysis of the pilot work in Records of Achievement gives the impression that teachers have no option but to be directive and dominant in interviews because a significant number of pupils lack the language, concepts and skills essential for productive, independent self-evaluation.

Loss of face and frustration are ever-present threats in learning: yet a counsellor would see them as presenting opportunities for mastery. Awareness of the strengths and weaknesses of one's tactics in demanding learning situations contributes to building up an effective cognitive style. One can train pupils to check their own contribution to the learning difficulty of which they complain, rather than blaming others. The cry, 'They don't teach you properly here', should receive a suspicious glance from pupils as well as staff. Phares (1976) points out that general expectations of success and failure accruing from the past have a powerful impact on how the new situation is tackled. The prediction, 'I can never do that sort of thing', creates a frame of mind which outweighs the impact of good teaching. Failure sometimes *is* caused by external circumstances, but a prevalent tendency to see success as lying outside one's control is a gross handicap. Inner resources are built up when pupils are encouraged to identify threats in learning, and find ways of coping for which they, and not their teachers, take responsibility.

Processes and personality in counselling

The Home Office (1976) pointed out that we can pay too much attention to personality and not enough to the situations in which the behaviour occurs. A proper caution, although counselling goes beyond it to assess the processes operating in the situation. Matza (1966) shows how people get caught up in a process which steadily emphasises their difference from others, until they finally accept this definition of themselves. Three weeks ago I began counselling a young man who claimed that he was 'a pathological liar'. (What seemed pathological to me was the readiness with which he had accepted this identity.) As individuals are identified as being different, they begin to react to the signals of disapprobation coming from family, peer group and school. In schools, as in other organisations, a labelling process is at work which casts a student eventually into a deviant role from which they cannot escape. Initial reactions from the student will probably be distress, coupled with protest, but as reinforcing incidents occur over time, he or she has little option but to accept the identity as a failure, inadequate or aggressor. As the identity is accepted, the behaviours associated with it become more meaningful. At the crudest level the response is, 'All right, if they think I'm like that, I'll really be like it.' To be cast in a negative or deviant role, compounds and hastens the process of becoming that very thing. Labelling excludes the student from other identities and opportunities, making her or his chances of perceiving herself or himself in positive terms progressively smaller. There sadly is a tendency to treat a person, once we have identified them as different in some unacceptable way, as if he or she were generally deviant. Acts of punishment, reprimand and exclusion feed the negative identity. Students are then held fast in the web of expectations which have built up. Tutors or year heads who counsel will be concerned with building self-respect and resistance to temptation, especially that of meeting the negative expectations.

What of the personality of those who counsel? The first edition cited research which claimed that certain personality qualities are essential for counselling to be effective, eg Truax and Carkhuff (1967). Three core conditions were listed. First was the ability to empathise accurately with the person receiving counselling: a deep understanding that allows one to comprehend the thoughts and emotions of him or her; the skill of taking, for the purposes of counselling, the student's standpoint about the problem situation. Empathy, of course, does not eliminate the need for thought about the causes and consequences of the perspective held by the student.

Next came spontaneity and genuineness. The former may be misunderstood. In practice, it means that we do not adhere to some rigid conception of a counselling role or the correct approach to the problem. We cannot indulge in defensive manoeuvres to maintain a *false* position of authority or bolster our authority. We must honestly confess when answers to pupils' questions elude us: adolescents have well-attuned ears for the evasive or phoney. Answers have to indicate that other viewpoints exist, and if necessary, spell them out impartially. Adolescents need a model of competence from those who counsel: this means openness to new evidence rather than clinging to one's initial viewpoint; above all, the capacity to admit one's mistakes is a pre-requisite for credibility.

Teachers sometimes fear that counselling is another name for loose permissiveness and abdication of authority. Authority lies in the model of competent analysis and concern presented by the teacher; the fact that he or she sets limits to the encounter, and initially, the agenda. Pupils are well aware of the status of the teacher, and his or her greater knowledge and ability in problem solving. Authority is reinforced because the pupil's statements are received with attentive respect; it is always present, but in a mature way, and not coercively. There is a powerful form of authority inherent in mutual respect.

Lastly, there is the capacity to show a non-threatening, safe and non-possessive warmth. The first edition warned against an undiscriminating use of praise: to ladle it out unthinkingly to an adolescent with a very negative self-picture is to arouse suspicion that they are being manipulated for some reason or risk the loss of credibility. Galloway (1990) usefully draws attention to cultural and sub-cultural reactions to warmth. From my viewpoint the stress should be on sending judicious signals of acceptance, and establishing the climate of mutual respect.

Today, I see it as more realistic to see these well-researched requisites for counselling, not as personality qualities *per se* but as skills to be acquired. Personality probably operates to set limits to competence in their use, or slows down the rate of their acquisition. Natale (1972) showed that empathy can be developed through training in critical thinking. Training of tutors should incorporate problem-solving exercises related to counselling which encourage flexibility of approach and questioning of the validity of the assumptions and viewpoints brought to them. To impose one's view of what 'that sort of problem is about', is to render oneself impotent.

Pupils, especially in the upper forms, do not necessarily welcome teacher's attempts at counselling. Some view it as intrusive and beyond the legitimate role of the teacher: others as a more subtle form of discipline against which it is difficult to argue because it is couched in a language of caring; and some as imposing a deviant identity on them. Such perceptions have to be acknowledged and subjected to rational debate. Teachers attempting counselling have to be prepared to be challenged and justify themselves. Some will be startled at this statement, but what was always desirable has now become a necessity with Local Management of Schools which is creating far-reaching changes in the ethos of schools. Fidler and Bowles (1989) argue that schools are moving from 'being professionally-driven institutions' to having to adjust to clients' views of their needs and the purpose of the school. Parents and pupils have increased their power, although few have yet realized this.

Even if challenged, the purpose of the interaction should always be positive, eg calming down an angry pupil who is reacting to some real or imagined slight from a peer or adult, or helping an offender in a disciplinary position take the standpoint of those he or she has injured. Counselling skills equip one to cope with aggression without replying in kind. The counsellor is aware of the need to read situations accurately, assessing their meaning for the participants. If one acquires skill at this, then there is a reasonable chance of avoiding actions which 'boomerang'.

Let us apply these considerations briefly to the Record of Achievement interview which can be problematical for both student and tutor. The insistence in counselling that problems have to be considered in context and not in isolation, alerts one to the need to understand a pupil's possible reactions to a face-to-face interview with an adult. Previous experience of them may arouse anxiety or feelings of inferiority. For some, 'interviews' are contaminated by associations of trouble. Such things create a framework for anticipating what may happen, and interpreting what actually happens. The former activates defences, whilst the latter may distort the meaning of the actions and statements of the tutor. Students insulate themselves against the whole process by adopting a passive role, and not committing themselves. The well-meaning tutor is unaware of the above, and the possibility that other views are held by the pupil: perhaps that the teacher's job is to tell them exactly what to do. The tutor remains unaware of this and other misconceptions, and faced by the passivity of the pupil, makes suggestions which have a superficial validity when considered in isolation, but in practice will fail, because the student sees no point in them. The tutor will then feel the need to look for new suggestions, but the student has by now decided that the whole process is a 'load of rubbish' or a curious foible of that quite nice person, the tutor. This humorous caricature, which is not totally divorced from reality, underlines the need to look at the less obvious features of the situation, preparing the reader for the next chapter.

Traditionally, most approaches to counselling stressed the importance of the relationship between the counsellor and the client as the major tool for change. I endorsed this in 1974, but now feel that current approaches to counselling require a shift of emphasis. It is now creating a climate of warmth and acceptance which removes the hindrances of communication. The relationship is best anchored in the tutor role, acquiring significance as the student comes to appreciate the tutor as a reliable person in whom she or he realistically can have confidence.

Activities

1 Aim

1.1 To provide activities which pastoral heads can use in their own training programmes. Modification and elaboration of them will be necessary. In selecting, heads of year or house should consider the level of knowledge, the needs for structure and the attitudes of their group of tutors.

1.2 The activities are intended to stimulate discussion which leads to situational self-awareness.

1.3 The training group hopefully will gain a sense of cohesion through participation and collaboration in the activities.

2 The general orientation

2.1 Basically it is that of developmental counselling, ie helping adolescents achieve effectiveness. The focus is on building strengths and facilitating pupils' ability to meet the proper demands of home, school and peer group.

2.2 It draws tutors' attention to the crucial skills of standpoint-taking, decision making and problem solving so that pupils can acquire them as tools for successful living.

2.3 Activities will encourage deeper exploration of the attributional and interpretational processes touched on in Chapter One.

3 Leadership of the training group

3.1 This wil obviously vary, although it is desirable that pastoral heads lead their team of tutors where possible.

3.2 Year or house heads may productively work as a team under the leadership of a deputy head to develop materials and structure their training programmes. This will ensure consistency of approach and possibly result in co-ordinated effort.

Activities related to Chapter One

1 Step one: preparatory activities

1.1 The subsequent activities relate to the major themes of the preceding chapter. The aim is to orientate those using them to some of the issues, give relevant experience of problem exploration and encourage situational self-awareness.

1.2 Methods: partner, small group and whole group work can be used. Leaders will have to incorporate any activities they select into:

a a structure that fits the time available;

b the readiness and skills level of the group.

2 Situational self-awareness

2.1 Draw a line down the middle of a piece of paper. On the left-hand side list the characteristics of the kind of pupil you enjoy teaching, and to whom you relate well. On the right-hand side, list the characteristics of the kind of pupil who arouses negative feelings in you – somehow 'gets up your nose' – and who you would rather not teach.

With a partner discuss what this seems to tell you about yourself. In groups of four discuss:

a the less obvious difficulties of interaction with the liked pupil;

b how your feelings about the other type of pupil might influence any attempt to offer him or her guidance, eg would you lean backwards in order not to let your dislike take any obvious form?

c is there a possibility that the same behaviours will have different meanings according to the gender of the pupil?

2.2 Fill in each of the four sections of the grid (Figure 1.1) trying to imagine yourself in a counselling situation. Try to be as concrete as possible in identifying the circumstances which might evoke the response.

Figure 1.1 *Guidance and counselling situations with adolescents*

Situations in which I might feel anxious.	Situations in which I probably would feel confident.
Situations in which I might feel embarrassed.	Situations in which I might feel angry.

In discussion with a partner examine the causes for possible anxiety and embarrassment. Are they connected? If so, in what ways? How would you cope with the anger? Are there costs attached to not expressing it? Would it be possible to give vent to it constructively?

This activity allows participants to approach the possibility that there are areas of guidance and counselling they should approach warily or avoid. End with a whole group discussion of this.

3 Exploring the application of counselling skills

3.1 In small groups 'map' or diagram the areas of school life where you think counselling skills could be applied with profit for pupils, parents and teachers. As you build your diagram try to make the justifications for your decision clear.

Next, examine the sources, nature and form of stress on groups within the school, eg senior management, heads of year or house, the teachers of certain subjects, probationary teachers, departmental heads and ancillary staff.

Compare the two analyses, discussing the implications of what you find. Apply the old 20/80 rule: on what 20% of all the situations where counselling appears desirable would it be profitable to expend 80% of the time and available effort in the next three terms? Discuss the implications of your priorities.

3.2 In a small group, develop job descriptions for both year or house heads (heads of lower and upper school if appropriate) which specify the counselling skills they need, and the situations in which they should be employed. What changes need to be made in the official job specifications?

3.3 Consider the form you tutor or a class you teach. List the needs of that form or class as you conceive them to be. Now, imagine you are a pupil who appears to enjoy your tutoring or teaching. Describe what he or she gets out of it. Next take a pupil who seems to reject the tutoring or subject teaching, and try to describe it from his or her point of view. Consider the needs of both pupils. How do these specific, and extreme, examples relate to your initial assessment? Discuss the implications with others in the group.

4 Counselling skills and learning

4.1 In groups of five undertake a preliminary assessment of the relationship of low self-esteem to learning. Do not assume that it always has a negative influence. In what circumstances might it raise the level of learning? Two group members then marshal the evidence available to them that low self-esteem hampers learning; two look at the opposite viewpoint. They then debate it. The fifth member makes notes, assessing the evidence offered, giving a balanced appraisal. (This can be undertaken in groups of three if more convenient.)

4.2 In small groups assess the forces which operate to constrain or facilitate learning, eg

- teachers' judgements and expectations of pupils;
- pupils' perceptions of an effective teacher;
- pupils' responses to praise and criticism;
- differential treatment of the sexes.

Chart them, and then compare your findings with those of another group.

Next, work out ways in which counselling skills could contribute to building a positive climate for learning. Again, compare ideas with another group.

4.3 Some teachers see counselling and pastoral care in limited terms as 'emotional first aid' or 'a shoulder to cry on', and as necessarily in conflict with their mainstream task of teaching. Attempt to assess in groups of four to six.

a the reasons why some teachers hold this viewpoint;

b its validity.

Should this viewpoint be accepted, or challenged? If the latter, how would you avoid alienating them, or more importantly, making their viewpoints more extreme?

5 Pupils' and parents' reactions

5.1 In pairs assess the reasons for some pupils' beliefs that counselling and pastoral care is about, 'Nosy-Parker teachers asking questions no teacher has a right to ask.' Then in groups of four work out ways of preventing this occurring.

As a staff development group explore year 11 pupils' perceptions of counselling: looking carefully at the possibility they have little time for teachers' claims of caring when they examine the mode of resolution of teacher/pupils' differences, and find them unjust. Consider

a the accuracy of these perceptions;

b reasons for not tackling them which seem to be operating in your school.

Then look for ways of boosting positive conceptions of discipline and making the purposes of counselling explicit to pupils.

5.2 Each member of the training group thinks of a pupil with whose parent(s) they would like to talk. They write a letter inviting that parent to come to the school. When written, the letters are read aloud to the group. Members evaluate the different styles and likely impact on the recipients.

5.3 How would you create rapport:

a when dealing with a parent visiting the school for the first time;

b dealing with a resentful year 11 pupil who has not completed his homework?

Share ideas in small groups.

5.4 As a pair try to obtain precise answers to the question, 'What might a pupil learn at home which impinges directly on performance in school?' Do not concentrate on the negative alone; identify the positive learnings, and work on ways of extending them. End with a whole group discussion.

5.5 Before the exercise, the group leader consults a group of year 11 or sixth form students about the support pupils need from their teachers. The ensuing discussion is recorded on tape.

Each member of the training group initiates a discussion with their tutor group about the areas of school life with which they would welcome help. A summary of each discussion is prepared on a large sheet of paper, displayed on the walls of the room in which the training is held. Participants read them and make notes.

The tape recording is played to the group. On the basis of this, their notes and the posters, the group consider the implications for tutor group and classroom interaction.

6 Decision making: preparatory activities

6.1 Work out individually the criteria you employ for asking a parent to come to the school. With a colleague evaluate your criteria, looking closely at the underlying assumptions about the purposes of parental contact with the school.

6.2 Take the following situation: *A year eight pupil shows fatigue and signs of tension at morning registration and in tutor periods. She has been noticed hanging about the school playground at the end of the day. The tutor has talked to her, but the response was silence or a grudging, 'Don't know'.*

Is this sufficient to justify calling the parent to school? Do you feel the need for further information? If so, about what and how is it to be obtained? What are, if any, the potential dangers of inaction?

6.3   The problem: *A year 11 student apparently has difficulty in planning and self-management. His GCSE course work projects are in a muddle, and urgent action is necessary if he is to meet the deadlines.*

a Step one
In groups of three generate ideas about the possible causes that could be present, eg parental unawareness of the demands of GCSE projects and the need for parental support, inconsistency in parental attitudes to achievement, the pupil's dependence on adults for structure. Explore the situation's ramifications in depth.

b Step two
Construct a plan for dealing with the situation. Begin by building a bank of ideas through Osborn's (1963) brainstorming approach. Record them, deferring judgement on them until later. Then select the most promising ones, looking at their feasibility, costs and relevance to the student. (Bear in mind Osborn's warning that a creative group should be an evaluative group.) Organise your plan or recommendations as clearly *and* economically as possible, eg listing the sequence of actions as a flow diagram.

c Step three
One person explains the plan from the standpoint of the tutor. The second person evaluates it, taking the perspective of the student.

The third person observes, recording important points, adding any new ideas which spring to mind. After the other two have finished, he or she provides a balanced appraisal of their position.

If time permits, groups should compare ideas.

2 Communication and understanding the problem

The intent of this chapter

We now explore the principles of counselling of which pastoral heads and tutors should be aware. They should, of course, apply them in their daily work with students. The next step is not so immediately obvious. The almost irrational resistance of many older students to counselling, guidance and pastoral work will only modify when these principles are discussed with them, *and* they are seen to be operating in tutor-pupil transactions. Failure to engage in this dialogue will strengthen students' suspicions that counselling is a devious form of discipline and denial of their maturity. Put in the words of some students, it is seen as 'Treating us like kids' or a 'Way of seeing we don't step out of line'.

Salient aspects of communication and perception are then explored. The content of this section can also be embedded in tutor group discussions as tools for learning and living. Developments in learning, eg flexible learning and self-supported study (TVEI, 1990; Waterhouse, 1990), make demands for initiative and maturity, but also for effective communication, analytical thought, problem solving and co-operation. This is relevant to traditional examinations. I visited a girls' grammar school with strikingly high performance in GCSE and A-Level examinations. The headmistress felt this had been achieved through the emphasis on pastoral work in the last few years. I argue that failure to appreciate that the skills and knowledge used in personal development are equally essential for learning, reduces students' chances of success irrespective of the particular approach to the curriculum.

Next, the importance and limitations of attitudes are discussed. Attitudes, in conjunction with predictions, determine the way students approach or try to avoid areas of achievement and interpersonal relationships. Understanding of the nature and functions of attitudes, and the ways in which they promote or stifle efficacy, is a potent weapon in the struggle for positive mental health.

The final section investigates methods of clarifying and comprehending problems, assessing their dimensions and significance accurately. Students need the orientations and willpower which allow them to question their original definitions of problems, and detect less patently obvious causation. Exploratory and self-assessment skills are a prerequisite for viewing situations more accurately, and tackling them constructively. The final section presents simple frameworks for assessing what has to be done in the corrective action-based stage of counselling.

The principles of counselling

Counselling skills applied to brief interventions and sustained interactions make them rewarding. The basic principles of counselling should inform these transactions whatever they are about – discipline, personal problem solving, learning, dealing with anxiety or peer relationships. Briefly:

1. The dignity of the individual requires that, except in grave situations of danger, we do not take the responsibility for dealing with the problem away from him or her. Implications have to be assessed, the consequences of actions explored, but the decision as to action has to be the individual's own. Without this, there is the danger of manipulating the person; treating him or her as an object to be acted on in the most convenient manner.

2. Problems always have to be studied in their contexts, from which part of their meaning is derived. The most crucial element of the context is the student's perceptions of the problem, his or her beliefs about the nature of a problem or situation, and assumptions about the motive and intent of those involved. How we see things determines what we do. The old Helmholtzian position that behaviour is a function of assumptions still obtains: the assumptions of others are a crucial part of the context, always needing to be taken into account. Counselling is not conducted in a vacuum!

3. From the above we see that suspension of initial judgements is imperative. We cannot impose our view of what the situation *ought* to be about on the student. This would tell us something about ourselves, but grossly handicap us in working with the reality of the situation; possibly leading us to deal, not with reality, but with our own invention.

4. Certainly, a basic principle is that the best interests of the student have to be predominant in our actions. But this does not endorse prejudgement as to what they are, or the application of simple formulae without thought. What is in the best interests of the pupil may not easily be detectable: indeed it may have to be negotiated, only

gradually becoming clear. Conflicts of values become apparent as situations are explored. Those who offer counselling have to be prepared to evaluate their own values and justify them to students, allowing them the same opportunity.

5. Reliability is a key principle: in this respect those who offer counsel should strive to be exemplars. Trust is not derived from status or age. It has to be earned. A salutary question is, 'Why should this student have confidence in me?' What is taken for granted, then becomes questionable.

6. The power of realistic adaptation to the needs of the student is crucial. Reliance on the same approach implies that everyone is alike, which is patent nonsense. Some students will need structure, some freedom to tackle things in an idiosyncratic way; some flourish when warmth is offered, and some appreciate a detached questioning approach. Styles therefore differ between students, and also with the same individual over time, eg initial acceptance may be followed by facilitating challenge.

These maxims are the background to helping students detect and analyse the problem situations, decide on the outcomes they desire, and take the steps which lead to the chosen goal. They build the climate in which young people resolutely set about finding how they defeat themselves, and go on to develop new patterns of behaviour.

Communication

Sapir (1930) defined society as 'a highly intricate network of partial or complete understanding between the members of organizational units of every degree of size and complexity ...'. From this viewpoint, a school should, as a small scale society, be a complex of shared meanings which allow students and teachers to orient themselves to each other and function effectively in a common environment. But what is the reality of these shared meanings in the school? Are they confined to sub-groups, possibly acting as impediments to co-operation, and leading to antagonistic communication? Hamblin (1989) explored the different meanings of pastoral work held by groups of teachers in the school, finding differences which, unless dealt with, rendered pastoral work abortive. The shared meanings held within sub-groups may block communication as easily as they facilitate it. The same applies to counselling: Dryden (1989) argues that client and counsellor bring entrenched attitudes and behaviour into counselling which shape what happens.

Communication therefore cannot be take for granted. We must pay close attention to it. Lorac and Weiss (1981) see communication skills as the ways in which 'information about facts, feelings, judgements, concepts or whatever is passed from one person or group to others.' This process will be aided, I believe, if the communicator possesses counselling skills. These authors also remark on the need 'to recognise and eliminate confusion and irrelevancy' and 'to express feeling sensitively'. That is a good description of what counselling is about.

Communication has five basic factors: the source of the message, its recipient, the message, the medium through which it is conveyed, and the impact it has on the recipient. We want our messages to have some effect on the recipient, but this does not take into account the possibility that the meaning of the statement depends on the student's beliefs about our intentions. Our expectations of its effect may differ sharply from his or her actual reactions. Then, if we are not careful, we begin to make judgements of the recipient based on flimsy evidence. Teaching and counselling are both intimately concerned with interpersonal perception. We are engaged in a search for meaning, whilst building an orderly and coherent view of our environment, especially of individuals with whom we need to interact. To achieve this, we have to go beyond the surface behaviour of others, and attribute to them motives and intention. Heider (1958) claims that in everyday interactions with others, our perceptions are based on a naïve or implicit psychology which allows us to identify relatively stable dispositions and intentions lying behind their behaviour. Our focus therefore often is on temperament and motivation rather than overt behaviour.

This inferential process of attributing motives and purpose to students and colleagues is open to unsuspected distortion stemming from our inner needs, and sometimes deep-seated anxieties. Be that as it may, identification of one strongly rewarding or threatening characteristic in the other person is often sufficient to trigger off a sequence of largely implicit, and almost certainly unquestioned, judgements. We give meaning to students' actions more often than we would care to admit, on the basis of minimal cues.

Other processes are at work. In the traditional report form, precautions were taken to prevent the 'halo' effect operating. Without them, pupils perceived as good in one important area were also rated as good in another, or knowledge of a particular good performance predisposed the rater to judge them more positively in other aspects of performance. Halo effect may be seen as an implicit theory held by the assessor about which personality or performance characteristics go together. It is an unquestioned 'psychologic' which assumes that if someone possesses Attribute A, she or he probably has Attribute B. We may therefore be ready to believe that a student known to be aggressive is likely to be guilty of bullying. In fact, these characteristics are not necessarily associated. A not uncommon association is that of ability and moral goodness. The student may have the capacity to make complex, discriminating moral judgements but this does not inevitably influence her or his behaviour. Readers may recall a colleague's surprised reaction when some peccadillo is uncovered, 'But he/she is a good A-Level candidate!'

We have to 'read' situations accurately. The teacher in a helping interaction 'reads' the student's behaviour and responses to make sense of them. This is the equivalent of reading the spaces between the words. At the same time the student is assessing the teacher's behaviour and statements, attributing intent or motive to him or her. Opportunities for misunderstanding are legion on both sides. Mismatches operate between what each individual convinces himself or herself that he or she is doing, what is actually being done, and the perceptions of the other person as to what is occurring. I may see myself as attempting to be supportive whilst in reality I am arousing anxiety, and the student perceives me as indulging in coercive, guilt-producing tactics. The student believes I am classifying her or him as an incorrigible nuisance when in fact my perception is of someone reacting understandably to pressures from parents who hold unrealistic aspirations for their son or daughter. Students in middle and later adolescence are capable of analysing interaction, assessing the impact of such misconceptions. Discussion of them is essential preparation for boosting co-operation in group work, work experience and assessing the validity of judgements of others.

Perceptions of what we say or hear are highly selective. We bring to interaction 'inferential sets' as Jones and Thibaut (1958) call them, which limit our perceptions. We pick up or respond to only those signals to which we are attuned. Over-concentration on verbal ones brings the risk of ignoring contradictory non-verbal messages. Even with verbal signals we discard or fail to recognise certain sentences or phrases because they do not fit our expectations or concepts of what is salient. The more experienced we are, the wider should be our range of responsiveness and our openness to information. Even so, we are still engaged in a search after meaning, selecting from the manifold of signals impinging on us, those which fit our hypotheses about the situation. The room for error is intimidating: some information has not been registered; the translation of the unfamiliar into the familiar carries the risk of over-simplification. Interpretation is at work because the helper cannot escape from the attribution of significance to what a student says. The only safeguard is continuously to question the validity of our judgements and to have the humility to revise them.

Osgood *et al* (1957) working on the semantic differential, drew attention to the pervasive elements of good versus bad, strong versus weak, and passive versus active in judgements of self and others. The dimensions may be universal, but the content is variable. Many adolescent difficulties spring from what they misguidedly allocate to the negative poles of bad, weak and passive in particular. Teachers may well profit from examining their allocation of adolescent attitudes and behaviours to these categories. Students should undertake such examination seeing the linkage of their discriminations to sources of threat. Remember that threat makes judgements more rigid and less accurate: also when self-esteem is threatened, perception becomes rigid and narrow.

The focus therefore should be on systems of personal meaning which mediate young people's interaction with the tasks of development facing them. They contain predictions which shape behaviour: we have already seen that there is little point in advocating striving for success if the learner's prediction is that nothing will change and failure is inescapable. It would be a waste of time helping a pupil change his or her behaviour at home if he predicts that any attempt at improvement will be interpreted by his or her mother as evidence of 'being up to something'. Change for this pupil means more blame.

Predictions explain why adolescents resist courses of action which seem eminently sensible from our viewpoint. The world view of an adolescent contains sets of expectations which, because they have been confirmed, have become self-maintaining. It is encapsulated in the phrase, 'We get what we expect!' People work unwittingly to make their expectations come true, even when they do not like the results. Practical helpers are therefore alert to a student's expectations.

Kelly (1955) argues that everyone is a scientist, for the key quality of the scientist is to make predictions about the course and consequences of events. As we live, we build up systems of constructs that are predictive. Through them we are not confined to responding to our environment: we can *represent* it, thereby being able to anticipate and gain some control over situations. These constructs or predictions are validated continuously in everyday living, determining our future behaviour through anticipation of rewarding or self-diminishing consequences. We may know people whose lives seem dominated by predictions of success, failure or rejection. Close study of the way these predictions influence their perceptions and thinking helps one understand less obvious instances.

The important fact is that current interpretations can be revised or replaced, but first they have to be clarified. Many adolescents have never been given the opportunity to stand back and assess the predictions which underlie their actions; occasionally trapping them in self-restricting and uneconomical patterns of behaviour. Guidance as exhortation is less effective than guidance as planned consideration of such fundamental issues. Helpers orientated towards developing positive mental health and efficacy are alert to evidence of predictions, assisting students to confront the negative and build on the positive. Keen observation is needed, but there is nothing esoteric about the process. Simple questions, eg 'What do you think will happen if ...?' are sufficient to begin to thaw the frozen matrix of behaviours.

Working with adolescents means their world of subjective meanings has to be understood and respected. Brusque dismissal of it would bring loss of credibility for the alleged helper, even creating a hiatus which makes what we say devoid of significance for the recipient. What is the significance of this for developmental counselling? Kelly's work is valuable because it demonstrates that the determination of behaviour comes, *not* from external events as such, *but from self-created mental structures*, which not only form the lens through which the adolescent interprets those events, but also determines her or his reaction to them. The model of personality that is subscribed to is one where an adolescent is not seen merely as a reactive being, but as somebody potentially able to control her or his environment.

There is no anarchy in this: there is recognition that individuals are disposed to act in an orderly and predictable way. But the laws of action which guide his or her behaviour are self-erected, springing from a construct system developed over time. The outlook it produces is a very real phenomenon, and part of the basic data of helping. The fact that it does not represent reality accurately from the perspective of tutor or pastoral head is not the point: it determines the student's reactions to major life challenges. If the viewpoints and predictions produced by the construct system are not apprehended, the communication essential for co-operation and purposeful change will be absent.

Attitudes

Overlapping with the concept of prediction is that of attitudes. Guidance, pastoral care and counselling discussions call out frequent references to attitudes. Frequency of reference is matched by imprecision in the use of the term. Indeed it *is* an imprecise term. Rokeach (1968) provides an initial definition: 'a relatively enduring organization of beliefs around an object or situation predisposing one to respond in some preferential manner.' Fishbein (1967) stressed attitude as assessment: it is 'the evaluative aspect of a belief'. Allport (1954) also emphasised the readiness to respond in a particular kind of way. To summarise: attitude is a learned disposition to react to some person, event or idea in a consistently favourable or unfavourable way. At heart an attitude is about approach and avoidance: the disposition to aid or harm the object of the attitude. The most crucial object to which attitudes are oriented is oneself. (This was touched on in Chapter One.)

Let me raise a simple question. Why should tutors and pastoral heads include attitudes in their work with students? Perhaps because we rely on imputed attitudes as a basis for predicting how a student will behave in different situations. Attitude therefore is equated with the probability of recurrence of a certain type of behaviour directed towards specific people or situations. Note, however, we must take into account the possibility that forces – especially social disapproval or approval – may inhibit or strengthen behavioural manifestation of the attitude. The assumption is that some inner process underlies the consistent behaviour we observe. Change of behaviour may therefore require the student to examine the attitude as a prerequisite for change. This is a point to which we shall return.

Counsellors have learned that it pays to ask *functional* questions rather than speculate on origins. What purposes does this attitude or behaviour serve for the student? Questions of this type centre on the 'here and now', and protect one against illicit attribution of causation or loose speculation involving personality. They also encourage careful observation. This does not mean one is not interested in causation. Indeed, if an attitude with its approach/avoidance behaviours can be seen to serve a purpose, that itself is a cause. What is pertinent is the current utility of the attitude. Indeed, whatever its genesis, it is possible that the attitude serves a current purpose which has little to do with its origins; it has acquired some kind of functional independence from them. It is on the current significance that the helper concentrates.

Katz (1960) helpfully shows that attitudes serve four functions for their holder. They can function adaptively or contribute to a disordered and ineffective style of life. First, there is the instrumental function. Attitudes are held because they increase rewards, especially social approval; they also help us avoid the punishment of disapproval and social rejection. Adolescence is a time of rapidly increasing social relationships which, with the insecurity caused by other areas of development, makes the need for social approval and affiliation urgent. Some might laugh cynically at this. The helper needs to ask, 'Affiliation with whom, and for what purposes?', or 'Approval from whom, or on what conditions?' Hamblin (1981) in a study of year eight found that pupils were afraid of being laughed at by their peers, and would brave sanctions from adults to prevent this. Psychological truancy – present in the flesh and absent in the spirit – was found in a sizeable number. Their affiliations were with their peers whose approval was prime for them, and they seemed largely to have rejected the values of the school.

The purpose served by attitudes differs from student to student, and with the same individual as the years pass. Our suggestions for change of behaviour may be sincerely made in the best interests of the pupil, seem reasonable; yet present a severe threat because they violate valued parts of his or her self-picture. If a boy sees smoking as tough and adult, and these qualities are a prime part of his self-conception, then he is unlikely to give it up. To attack smoking directly, is also unwittingly to bring into question an important part of his self-image. Misguidedly, he may feel he is being asked to affiliate with a group who are unattractive because they lack these crucial qualities. His positive attitude to smoking functions to reinforce his self-image, and also brings the reward of approval from peers with whom he wishes to identify.

Next, there is the knowledge function. Attitudes help their holder carve up their world and see it consistently, or as Rokeach puts it, 'give(s) adequate structure to his universe.' Attitudes function to help the adolescent build his or her own charts so that interaction and the environment become predictable. They may also, unfortunately, cover complexities that need to be faced because they encourage pre-categorisation. One of the delights of the traditional Western film was the clear distinction between the 'goodies' and 'baddies': the evaluative dimensions were clear and left us untroubled by doubt. Adolescent attitudes may be based on such simple dichotomies, leaving their possessors baffled in the face of social and relational complexities.

Third, ego-expressive or, more accurately, value-expressive attitudes serve to signal to others the kind of person one is. We construct on the basis of these attitudes an 'identity kit' which expresses our need to tell others about ourselves, and helps us find a self-confirming social anchorage. Rewards are derived from keeping a favourable self-image on the individual's own terms; identity is bolstered through comparisons with others.

Finally, ego-defensive attitudes protect a person from seeing her or his undesirable qualities and facing unpalatable facts. None of us are free from the inclination to deny our weaknesses, but if as Katz suggests, self-protection is achieved through prejudice, or projecting on to those who are convenient scapegoats what we cannot accept in ourselves, the social costs are too high. Yet the fact that these attitudes defend us against internal conflict and external dangers makes them resistant to change. Where the adolescent's environment is permeated with threat to self-esteem, unpredictability and contradictory demands, ego-defensive attitudes are frequently called into play and rewarded.

Attitudes serve important purposes for their holder, but often the helper feels that change would benefit the student and those who interact with her or him. Research on attitude change (eg Insko, 1967; Petty and Cacioppo, 1986) shows it to be intimidatingly complex. A few remarks only can be made here with a pragmatic intent. The first point is whether there is any real incentive to change existing attitudes. The tutor or pastoral head may lead the horse to water but find it reluctant to drink what has a bitter taste. Brief interventions individually may have little impact, but a climate of respect and caring over the years may be potent.

The credibility of the source of the attempts at attitude change influences acceptance of persuasive messages. Self-esteem is the value an individual places on herself or himself. This does not exist in a vacuum: it flows from groups whose members' approval or disapproval is valued by the student. If the group norms support the attitudes which are causing concern, and the young person wants to belong to that group, then change is unlikely. The tutor, however, probably has knowledge of the group values and can adjust his or her change messages. Each individual has a latitude of acceptance or rejection for messages impinging on group norms and behaviour. Initial messages must fall within the latitude of acceptability. Messages pitched into the latitude of rejection diminish the credibility of the communicator, and cause the recipient to polarise her or his attitudes.

We are suspicious of those we believe to be attempting to change us. Perceptions of intent are accompanied by evaluations of the source of the message as trustworthy and concerned, or as arbitrary and coercive, determining to a significant degree the meaning of the message. Studies of dogmatism (Rokeach, 1960) show that dogmatic individuals may pay more attention to the source of the message than its content in evaluating it. Adolescents who are gaining identity by opposition are obviously likely to respond to attempts at influence by stubbornly digging in their heels. The only sensible thing for the tutor or pastoral head to do is to explain the reasons for his or her intervention, otherwise future communication will be contaminated by suspicion.

Tutors and heads of year or house have to see that attitude change is a chancy matter. Although people vary in their reactions, threat or the use of fear generally provoke defensive reactions which include dismissal both of the message and the sender. Students have to feel *they* are making the decisions, and those decisions will be respected. The helper allows them to formulate the changes, breaking the process down into small, manageable steps. Difficulties are anticipated, and the student equipped to cope with them, building his or her sense of effectiveness.

Two possibilities exist: attitudes determine behaviour or behaviour determines attitudes. The likelihood is that both apply because attitudes and behaviour dynamically inter-relate. There is some evidence that making the wearing of seat belts compulsory resulted in more favourable attitudes to them. The original work on cognitive dissonance (Festinger, 1957) implies that attitudes are more likely to change when individuals engage in behaviours at variance with their conception of themselves. They then experience tension and psychological discomfort which they reduce by modifying their attitudes to the behaviours. The crucial element was shown by Brehm and Cohen (1962) to be keeping any pressure to behave in the new way minimal. If the student feels that heavy pressure to comply has been brought to bear, then she or he absolves herself or himself from responsibility for the behaviour. No dissonance is experienced, therefore attitudes are not revised.

What does all this mean to those who counsel? First, it will be profitable developmentally to teach students about the nature and functions of their attitudes, giving them a suspicious glance rather than blindly endorsing them. Second, direct attempts at attitude change will arouse resistance. In particular, the authoritarian black and white thinkers react by immediately closing their minds and clinging more determinedly to their existing viewpoints. However, the well-known sleeper effect may operate: eg the message has some effect four to six weeks later when the source has been forgotten. But it would be unwise to take this for granted! Third, it may be most sensible to remember that attitude changes are likely to follow new behaviours which bring the reward of success. Engagement in them with the support of peers is probably the most potent source of attitude change available to the tutor or pastoral head.

This reminds us that the influence of the group must not be underestimated. Earlier, its role in maintaining existing attitudes was stressed, yet it is also a vehicle for promoting change. What is learned in the presence of peers is more likely to be applied in other situations. Activities in small groups which require a student to examine a situation or problem from different perspectives, or take the standpoints of those occupying contrasting roles in it, will assist the unfreezing of rigid perceptions. The basic principle of role play is that taking, not a single role, but all the roles in turn, allows deeper appreciation of the tensions and significance of a particular participant's behaviour. Also peer judges may be attached to each group who provide a considered evaluation of the various viewpoints. Peer judges normally take their responsibilities seriously, whilst they have credibility with their fellows; which is not saying that they are never challenged, but that they contribute to both flexibility, and appreciation of the fact that no single viewpoint holds a prerogative on legitimacy.

Although easy generalisations about attitudes and their change are best avoided, action research by subject departments on how pupils acquire negative attitudes to the subject would be rewarding preventive work, fostering achievement and positive mental health as described in Chapter One. We know, for example, that students bring into the secondary school misconceptions about the nature of subjects and the kinds of people who are good at them which contribute to underfunctioning; but how does this impinge on classroom behaviours? Tutors under the leadership of house or year heads could analyse the processes through which students affiliate with, or dissociate from, the values and objectives of the school. Even more vital is the image of teachers created in the eyes of pupils and their parents. Not only must teachers be caring, they must also be *seen* to be caring. This image is in effect an emergent attitude which needs careful monitoring: even more so since the introduction of LMS when, as Fidler and Bowles (1989) point out, schools changed from 'professionally driven institutions to being more client oriented'. Power has shifted towards parents; we can no longer afford to discount the need to understand how parents acquire negative attitudes to the school. Students 'switch themselves off' about pastoral care and counselling after year nine. It would be simple-minded to think they do not convey this disregard to their parents.

These issues should be adventures in action research in which pupils are deeply involved. From what I have seen in my M.Ed. and other students' work in recent years, it is likely that when pupils grasp the nature of these processes, they are halfway to changing them.

Discovering the nature of the problem

In the limited opportunities for talking and listening to students, time has to be used wisely. A teacher's concern for students has to be expressed in situations where interruptions are likely and other urgent matters compete for attention. A number of contacts may be required to reveal the nature of the problem, for often the student does not fully comprehend it. We want to help and support, but this is not achieved by giving advice before we know what the problem is. It cannot be assumed that the student's perceptions of it are accurate or that he or she understands its ramifications. This reminds us to inhibit our almost automatic reaction of asking, 'Why?' Almost always, the reply will be, 'Don't know.' Then we are tempted in an omniscient way to tell them what they ought to know without evidence or precise understanding. Adolescents tend to be baffling creatures: they have a problem they wish to resolve; but ask them what their problem is, and they deny they have one. Problems, as such, are something others have; to admit ownership of one puts its possessor into a special category. Saving face seems to be operating.

Therefore we have to listen rather than question at first; suspending immediate judgements, allowing the dimensions and nature of the difficulties as seen by the student to emerge. False assumptions of similarity with, or difference from, our view, have to be discarded. The student may not see the situation as the tutor does; but neither does he or she *necessarily* see it differently because of generational or cultural influences.

Questioning and listening

We can over-rely on closed questions which can be answered by a simple 'Yes' or 'No', for example, 'Do you frequently lose your temper?' or 'When you are told off do you argue with the teacher?'. Munro *et al* (1989) point out that they merely confirm or disconfirm. What they support or discount comes from the helper, who through the closed questions is imposing his or her framework of meaning on the student. Open questions, employed as part of active listening, evoke information, for example, 'How do you feel when . . .?' 'Could you tell me about that?'.

In active listening we train ourselves to look for the feelings, and having identified them, reflect back that part of the statement. For example, 'It sounds as if you worry a great deal, is that right?' or 'Feel like giving up?'. Here the counsellor draws attention to what the student has said. Reflecting back means that instead of asking a direct question, a phrase, word or sentence containing the feelings is repeated by the helper. This elicits further information which clarifies the meaning. Feelings shape behaviour, therefore they must be taken into account straight away.

Closed questions force the tutor to ask yet another question, risking two dangers. Social desirability can be stimulated: the student then begins to provide what he or she believes to be the desired answers. Persistent use of closed questions may cause the student to retreat to defensive use of 'Don't know', anticipating that the well-meaning tutor will tell him or her what they ought to know. The student then withdraws from what has become an unsatisfying encounter with good face. Nothing of value has been achieved on either side.

Probing is an ever-present temptation when one is pressured by time. For the student it is a painful experience, akin to a patient in a Western film having a bullet extracted without an anaesthetic. One does not blame the patient for kicking the surgeon! Students 'kick' tutors or pastoral heads by complaining to friends that she or he, 'Doesn't understand: keeps on at you; asks too many nosey questions.' Credibility is then eroded and passive resistance by students grows.

Any fundamental activity has mythologies attached to it. Listening is no exception. We have assumptions about the importance of eye contact, ignoring its cultural and idiosyncratic meanings. Naïve assumptions that it is an indicator of honesty and straightforwardness have to be challenged. The conman or conwoman knows this: earnestly looking their victim in the eye as they manipulate him or her. Eye contact may evoke strong feelings about dominance or submission; it has different meanings in certain cultures; whilst its significance varies with, and between, the sexes. The meanings conveyed vary: between two members of the same sex in relation to a third, it may have the quality of 'knowingness', the equivalent of the derogatory wink; chance eye contact makes one aware of the limits to social interchange. Accidental eye contact on a train results in the fellow passenger looking hastily away as if an indecent proposal was imminent. We need to be aware that some pupils need eye contact as a requisite for communication: others find it inhibiting.

We would endorse encouragment of the student to continue speaking if they feel lost for words. Yet this may be self-defeating. Unwitting resort to assumptive statements occurs, eg 'What you are saying . . .', or 'What you mean is . . .'. Such responses are remarkably unhelpful if the student is struggling to explain an embarrassing event or deciding whether or not to trust the helper with something shameful. The encouragement actually given through assumptive statements is to acquiesce with the irrelevant or escape from the anxiety of self-revelation. Thus do helpers defeat their objects. After all, it is a little odd to set about understanding a problem by telling someone what he or she will say.

Another source of distortion is interruption. Cutting the student off in the middle of a statement redirects his or her flow of thought, imposing our idea of what is relevant. It controverts our intent to look at the situation through the eyes of the student, who then suspects us of hypocrisy, doubting our genuineness. Students, however, can produce an unending spate of words intended to obscure the problem. The motive may be to prevent action being taken or hide specific details. The tutor must intervene firmly, stemming the flow of verbiage. The principle that counselling is concerned with the 'here and now' is then activated. Attention is given in a non-judgemental way to the functions of this behaviour, and why the student finds it necessary.

Listening implies observation: indeed it is a form of it. We listen to register hesitations or changes of topic. The gentle statement, 'Perhaps we can return to this when you feel ready', signals that it has been noted. This is done when non-verbal signs of anxiety – foot-tapping, tense hand movements, facial expressions of strain or bodily restlessness are present. Sometimes the hesitation is a prelude to introducing a more disturbing element or used to decide whether to bring it into the open. The meaning of these things can only be assessed in context.

Congruity has to be achieved between the verbal and non-verbal. It is alarming for the student when I say, 'Don't worry', but my voice conveys stress, my knuckles are clenched until they are white and my posture tense. The student reads my bodily signals as carefully as I read his or hers.

Perceptual sensitivity has to be developed through attention to detail: inaccuracy in recall of what occurred at an earlier encounter could be interpreted as indifference. Adaptation to the student's mood and the severity of the problem is paramount. For a highly anxious, depressed or crisis-engulfed student to be confronted by a teacher presenting a front of determined heartiness or brittle cheerfulness is intolerable.

When we talk about listening we forget that the listener responds. We abstract the student's statements as if they had been made in isolation. The diagram below (Figure 2.1) reminds us that they only make complete sense when the teacher's contributions are taken into account.

Figure 2.1 *The chain of responsiveness*

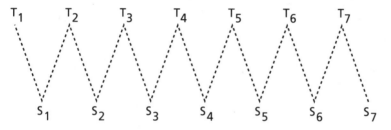

To treat the student's statements $S_1 - S_7$ as an insulated entity is palpable nonsense. Helper and student influence each other: if the tutor's response is appropriate, friendly and accepting, the student's response will be different than if the tutor had been distant and critical. At case and pastoral conferences, student's statements are treated as evidence of problems independently of what produced them, and the context in which they were made. When these are included, the student's statements then assume somewhat different meanings.

In 1981, in looking at learning about learning I stressed the need for students to think about their thinking and problem-solving styles and raise questions about them. Counselling requires that of them. Counselling can become a situation of near desperate questioning by the helper. The tutor can be launched into a fruitless search for questions which will produce meaningful answers. The student, harassed by a barrage of questions, nods agreement, whether or not he or she has even understood them. Escape through compliance is an interesting reflection of coping with classroom demands, but it is an impediment to counselling. A way out of the quagmire is realisation that it is the student who also should be raising questions: asking them about herself or himself; asking them of tutor or pastoral head; adult and adolescent then considering the answers critically. (This will be taken up again in Chapter Four where the RoA interview will be considered.)

Signals of acceptance

As concerned teachers we accept our students, trying to do our best for them: but do they see us that way? In brief counselling interventions, sending an initial signal of acceptance is essential. If a student unexpectedly did badly in an examination, it would be inept to begin exploring without this, eg 'Jane: you probably feel confused and upset, or even angry. You expected to do well; we expected you to do well. I'm so sorry.' It does not deny the reality, yet without it, guilt, displaced aggression, blame-pinning or other defensive reactions would hamper analysis of the problem by obscuring the facts. Acceptance of emotions, such as anger and anxiety which are often kept below the threshold of expression, is essential if they are to be mastered. The statement, 'In this situation you have the right to be angry.', is neither omnipotence in the helper nor an invitation to unbridled expression of emotion. It is instigation for calm, impartial analysis of the situation; impartial in the sense of stepping back, and examining it from relevant perspectives.

Signals of acceptance are necessary at points where tension and self-doubt arise. Experience shows they usually carry the student forward in exploring the problem. Given spontaneously – which does not mean in an undisciplined way – appropriate signals of acceptance lubricate the exploratory process, creating a climate of honesty and safety.

Avoiding contradictory communication

Kindly teachers have been known to reassure anxious students by saying, 'I know you will do well in your A-Level, but don't worry, if by any mischance you should fail, there is another chance in January.' The student may be anything but reassured. She or he may go away feeling, 'He's only trying to encourage me; he doesn't really think I'll succeed.' so they worry more. The helping attempt has been counter-productive. Worse, when the student's anxiety is noted, the teacher labels the student as an anxious person. All therapeutic processses contain the danger of an unnoticed shift from verbs to nouns: from actions to identity. The statement, 'He or she does not cope well in this and that situation.' turns into 'He or she is an immature or inadequate person.' This labelling operates in many areas, causing us to react to the label, and not to the student as he or she actually is. Contradictions in messages and labelling processes go together. We send, on the basis of the labels we have given the student, messages which incorporate our expectations of her or him. These are sometimes recognised – and worse – accepted by the student. In extreme cases, we may be counselling our own invention rather than the reality. This is often cloaked in plausible language and accompanied by laudable intent.

Bateson *et al* identified the 'double-bind' inherent in such situations. Reduced to its bare bones, it is the situation where two messages about something important come together, the second immediately following the first. The second message, however, contradicts or negates the first in some important way. For illustration, take a mother, a 15-year-old boy and doctor, all standing in the surgery. The doctor has been treating the boy for bed-wetting. The mother breezily exclaims, 'Well doctor, he's stopped wetting the bed. He hasn't wet it for six weeks, but of course I keep a rubber sheet in his bed just in case.' That is double-bind. Note the 'of course' which is an example of the kind of phrase which prefaces the negatory statement. The boy's tenuous confidence in an area where complex emotions abound, will almost certainly be weakened. It could be called scorpion communication: there is a sting in the tail. The fact that the sting is unintentional makes it no less painful, indeed the lack of intent may increase its potency for the recipient.

Double-bind may occur with messages coming through channels other than the verbal. A look or gesture may be more powerful than words. Non-verbal and situational messages contradict the verbal. The simplest form of double-bind in counselling is, 'Yes, but ...'. It destroys rapport. This statement may be seen by the student as contradiction of the claimed acceptance and understanding; indeed as arguing with him or her. One learns in exploring and clarifying the problem to tie one's tongue into a knot when tempted to say, 'Yes, but ...'. Usually this is profitable. Later information from the student often reveals that the content of the 'Yes, but ...' would have been irrelevant, perhaps fatuous, and certainly based in partial understanding. It would have introduced a red herring with consequent waste of time.

Other techniques

Using confrontation helpfully

Confrontation as a counselling skill may seem a little surprising, indeed at variance with the earlier part of the chapter. Acceptance, however, does not mean blind endorsement of all the student says or does. For all of us, what we say we do is not always what we do. Ego-defensive attitudes foster unrecognised discrepancies between the two. Counselling alerts us to our capacity for self-deception. Confrontation is a form of clarification in which we call the student's attention to discrepancies between statements, between words and actions, between feelings and behaviour, or any combination of them. Judgement is suspended: the tone and form of the enquiry are neutral, eg 'Just now you said .... Last time we talked you said .... . I'm not sure how they go together. Can you tell me a little more?'.

These challenges are not aggressive: the intent is to increase effectiveness by directing attention to self-defeating inconsistencies. Standpont-taking can be stimulated by asking the student to imagine how someone who matters to him or her would view the apparent contradictions.

Being concrete and specific

Brief interventions are as liable as long interviews to vagueness and failure to be down to earth. Discussion and analysis need to be tied to a specific and recent incident. 'Let's look at the last time you lost your temper.' or 'Shall we find out exactly what happened when you were bullied yesterday?' Once the situation is pinpointed, the student is actively involved in examining it. The most productive arrangement is for the tutor or pastoral head and student to work diagonally across a table. Sitting opposite hints of formality, even interrogation. Side by side may be too close, resulting in the feeling that personal space is being invaded. Familar learning materials are employed: coloured paper, felt pens and lined paper. Drawing and diagrams are used: many pupils' preferred way of learning is visual and active. In several instances I have met excellent use of counselling with computers, *not* as set programmes but with students 'telling' their story to the computer, and then discussing it with the tutor. Graphics are employed in working out courses of action or solutions to the problem. Verbal techniques alone do not always involve the student sufficiently.

One simple approach is systematically to explore:

1. The *situations* in which the student feels and acts in similar ways. What is there in common between them? Differences are equally important. Pupils can be difficult with some teachers, and not with others. The principle of studying the problem in its context prevents one jumping to the conclusion that the teacher *must* be responsible. The cause may lie in threat in the learning material or the composition of the peer group.

2. We ask about what *triggers off* the feelings and behaviours. There is a danger of paying too much attention to the consequences of behaviour and of underplaying the antecedents which lead to the initiation of feelings and behaviours. It is useful to instigate a search for cues which trigger off problematical behaviours, helping students react more maturely to their appearance.

3. A very practical question is 'What is the *payoff* for a behaviour?' For example, most aggression in the secondary school is instrumental: its

purpose is to achieve something, eg maintain or promote a reputation as tough, avoid school work, compensate for inferiority feelings or negotiate a bargain with teachers, 'If you don't bother me too much, I won't bother you too much.' Even anxiety, *albeit rarely*, can have a payoff of this type. It may function to bring a student badly-needed attention from adults, or allow him or her to evade challenging tasks.

4. The *form* the response takes merits deep consideration. Is it direct or indirect, passive or active, physical or psychological? The costs to the student should be discussed.

5. Examination of the *context* includes assessing the impact of friends and others on the student's attempts at change. Adolescents are very vulnerable to emotional blackmail and kindred pressures from peers. The importance of affiliation with peers creates a helplessness which prevents them from seeing, and acting on, fairly obvious ways of coping.

Simple drawings and diagrams help this analysis become a starting point for generating coping strategies. It is not to be followed blindly: the tutor or pastoral head will take the aspects germane to a particular situation. For some situations the simple diagnosis given below may be more useful.

1. *What happened?* The description is made as precise as possible. Ambiguities and contradictions are highlighted and discussed.

2. *With or between whom?* Some investigation of the perceptions and standpoints of others may be necessary. Again, it is simple, 'What would Jane say about the situation if I asked her?'

3. *When did it happen?* Pinpointing this is often illuminating. Bullying and other problems recur in a fairly regular pattern.

4. *Where did it happen?* Bullies often take care to conduct their operations outside the scope of the school. Simple as it is, this question may reveal quite important things, eg the fact that a teacher is habitually late for a class because of other duties has allowed a small group to cohere and intimidate chosen victims.

5. *How did it happen?* Cycles of behaviour exist, but those caught up in them fail to note this regularity. Intervention in the chain of events can be discussed. A 13-year-old quickly identified a series of events which always ended up by him 'getting mad' and fighting. He was then able to formulate a plan for change.

Tutors and pastoral heads will have a sharp eye for the processes touched on earlier; predictions, the approach and avoidance tendencies associated with attitudes to school work, negative comparisons with others and sources of loss of self-esteem. In this chapter, discussion is confined to ways of helping students understand their circumstances and behaviours, eradicating blindspots. Beliefs about the prospects of successful change have to be explored, eg 'It's too hard for me.', 'I'll only get into more trouble.' or 'They won't let me do it'. These are typical of the predictions which, if left unchallenged, render counselling useless.

Other techniques

Where the third level of counselling is operating, pastoral heads will find simple techniques such as open-ended or incomplete sentences useful. If they are to deal with matters other than learning or careers these should be used with caution and respect for the individual's privacy. A version of the open-ended sentence instrument is shown in Figure 2.2. It has led to productive counselling for over 20 years.

Using the open-ended sentence instrument

1. *Let the pupil discuss it at once.* You may need to start this off by asking:

   - Which one did you find most difficult?
   - Which one seemed the easiest?
   - Which sentences seem to go together?

2. *Keep the pupil active.* Avoid obvious questioning and probing. For example, invite him or her to write out the numbers of sentences which:

   - are concerned with pleasant feelings
   - mention worries and unpleasant feelings
   - tell you what other people think of you
   - say something about your desires and aspirations.

   Note that this should not be presented as a test. If the pupil has difficulty with writing, then this could distract them from spontaneous production of responses. In that case, the pastoral head calls out the initial words and writes in the student's response. Even better, the responses can be tape recorded. The student plays them back, and decides what she or he would like to discuss. In every activity, however simple, there must be choice for the student.

Sorting techniques

Sorting techniques are used to involve the student in the clarification process. When working with a single student, master cards are made as follows: *I like this*; *I don't like this*; *I'm not sure about this*.

Figure 2.2 *The open-ended sentence instrument*

THE SORT OF PERSON I AM

Your first name: _____ Date: _____

To help you:

(a)   This is not a test. There are no right or wrong answers. The aim is to help you discover more about yourself.

(b)   WORK AS FAST AS YOU CAN. Spelling and very neat writing are of little importance in this situation. PUT DOWN THE FIRST THING THAT COMES INTO YOUR HEAD.

Finish these sentences:

1   I like _____
2   I'm good _____
3   I am the kind of person _____
4   People always say I _____
5   Boys in my class seem to think _____
6   I want _____
7   My mother _____
8   Girls say I _____
9   It always seems to happen that _____
10   I don't like _____
11   _____ makes me angry.
12   I think fathers_____
13   It seems difficult _____
14   I enjoy _____
15   People sometimes say _____
16   _____ in class.
17   I would like to be _____
18   I worry_____
19   If only_____
20   I can't wait _____

In such individual work the pastoral head will construct a list which he or she believes to be relevant to the student's particular problems or needs.

Tutors working with a form can modify the technique. They ask their tutor group to supply them with situations for sorting. Examples of such situations could include:

Using a computer
Answering questions in class
Going to a party where I don't know many people
Going to the swimming baths
Watching late night television
Asking for a date
Talking to a supervisor on work experience
Being late for school
Visiting a sick friend in hospital

Students write the headings (*I like this, I don't like this, I'm not sure about this*) on a sheet of paper, placing each situation under the heading they feel is right for them. Discussion, which includes explanation and consideration of the consequences, follows in small groups (usually formed on the basis of friendship). In both group and individual work it is important to recall the frequence of 'identity through opposition' and use it constructively. As adolescents work to achieve independence they become clear about what they will not do and what they are not. Identity is initially strongly tied to opposition. Many young people talk more freely and with greater conviction about their dislikes and what they oppose. The effective counsellor accepts this trend, at the same time encouraging them to move to the positive. Students therefore begin with discussion of what they dislike, move on to explaining their likes, finally considering their uncertainties.

Checklists

Simple checklists are motivating. The LIKE ME, NOT LIKE ME format has proved a simple starting point for self-assessment, as shown in Figure 2.3.

The endorsements could be discussed in individual counselling. In the form situation, discussion could occur in self-selected – probably friendship-based – groups. Tutors might well encourage students to develop their own checklists of the conditions necessary for achievement or self-assessment in cooperative activities. In such simple ways counselling becomes that joint enterprise between students and teachers. In the last four years I have seen excellent examples of effective self-assessment and guidance instruments produced in this way. The climate of pastoral care and the readiness of students to accept counselling has improved greatly, according

Figure 2.3

	LIKE ME	NOT LIKE ME
strong		
miserable		
happy		
small		
serious		
friendly		
argumentative		
tough		

to those initating these activities. It seems to be an effective way of developing understanding of the purposes of Records of Achivement.

Assessment

Clarification leads to assessment and mutual agreement on what should be done to achieve mastery of the problem. We have already seen the need for sensitivity towards the world of unique meanings which shape adolescents' interpretation of events. It is tempting to dismiss them as self-indulgent or unnecessary complication. Yet they are remarkably practical. Ravenette (1967) showed that the failure of remedial teaching could be traced to failure to comprehend the eccentric meaning of reading for the pupil, eg 'an activity which no real man should be bothered with' or 'something at which all our family are useless'. Sensitive appreciation of individual perceptions, judgements and interpretations of learning tasks distinguishes the teacher as a professional from a mere instructor. The argument may be clearer if we turn to underfunctioning. Gaudry and Spielberger (1971) and Banks and Finlayson (1973) show it to be a complex phenomenon. There is a tendency for high ability to be matched by high attainment, but a number of other factors determine performance. Family pressures, supports and values; the expectations of teachers; previous learning history; all interact to influence achievement. We may ask two students of similar age and background to undertake a learning task well within their ability. One approaches it eagerly, seeing it as opportunity for displaying competence and as intrinsically satisfying. The other approaches it reluctantly, even with aversion, perceiving it as something to be avoided if possible, unworthy of attention, or irrelevant to his or her purposes. Therefore personal meanings attributed to the task determine performance. Until they are modified, exhortation and encouragement achieve little.

There is risk of distortion and inaccuracy when shaping recommendations and setting targets. Condensing a number of complex and unique factors into a precise statement of purposes carries the risk of simplification in which crucial qualifications are omitted. The assessment appears rational but whose viewpoint is dominant? We, too, are engaged in a search for meaning, which could trap us into selecting from the data those elements that fit our beliefs about the nature of the particular problem. A student's statements may be capable of several interpretations or contain different possibilities for action: we ignore some; selecting those which fit our implicit ideas about causation and effective action. We must never forget that laudable intent does not prevent early closure on problems and ineffectiveness.

Staff development should raise teachers' awareness of the complexities of perception and judgement. The seminal work of Bartlett (1932) and Allport and Postman (1945) is still relevant. Studies of the psychology of rumour showed a dual process of 'levelling' and 'sharpening' at work. The latter is the focusing of attention on certain details which come to the forefront and gain in significance. Levelling means that some facts are glossed over, quickly disappearing. Bartlett found that the essential mechanisms at work in the recall of information were the need to make the account more coherent; omission of material assumed – often without foundation – to be irrelevant; whilst translation of what was unfamiliar into terms and concepts familiar to the communicator resulted in unsuspected change of meaning.

Caution is essential: temptation to decide what is trivial or important in a particular problem on the basis of habitual assumptions is sternly to be resisted. Cox (1978) makes the point well in discussing levels of self-revelation. A young man could discuss an unsavoury murder he had committed with apparent equanimity; that he was the only boy in his class at school not needing to shave produced high anxiety and embarrassment.

A framework for assessment is essential. Three are offered which have to be adapted to the skills of the helper, the maturity of the student and the nature of the problem. The student must be deeply involved, and negotiation of targets and general content is essential.

1. The simplest and most direct is a behavioural one. In agreement with the student the tutor or pastoral head should list:

    ●   the behaviours the student needs to acquire;

- the behaviours already possessed that should be built on;

- the behaviours that have to be discarded;

- the behaviours that have to be reduced in frequency and intensity.

The assessment should specify the contexts in which the behaviour occurs. Clear criteria have to be stated, and the target behaviours made absolutely clear.

2. This framework uses the notion of positive mental health set out in Chapter One.

   - It summarizes the attitudes of the student towards himself and herself. Key areas could be self as a learner, social self, vocational or sexual self. Feelings of incompetency and areas of success might be specified.

   - The interaction between the student, the peer group, local environment and school are specified.

   - There is evaluation of the student's active and realistic attempts to master his or her environment and developmental tasks. The important predictions, areas of learned helplessness and sources of frustration are noted.

   From this overview a more specific assessment is shaped, giving an order of priority for dealing with issues; perhaps learning skills are seen as the first area to be addressed. In another case, coping techniques for dealing with anxiety may be given pride of place.

3. This framework draws on developmental conceptions of counselling and uses the functional approach to attitudes. It is most appropriate for the third level of counselling where the pastoral head can work in greater depth. The student should be a co-equal in drawing up this assessment. A distinction is made for the purpose of assessment between inner and outer factors.

Inner factors include

   - The ideal and actual self. Self-esteem. The impact of lack of self-esteem on relationships and attitudes to others. Is self-esteem justified or exaggerated? Is it used constructively or destructively?

- The pupil's sense of internal or external control: of responsibly believing they are in charge of their destiny, or feeling a pawn and the victim of events. Do they have an excessive sense of responsibility for what happens, although they are not to blame? Conversely, do they fail to see their contribution to events?

- Is there high anxiety and guilt; are they marked by a readiness to respond to new situations and challenges by disproportionate anxiety? Do they deny anxiety when circumstances merit its appearance?

- What is the direction of aggression? Outward and directed at appropriate targets or displaced, perhaps unrealistically directed at the student herself or himself?

Outer factors might well embrace

- Behaviours causing concern for the student and others in his or her life.

- Skills of coping with frustration and challenge; methods of managing tension and stress.

- Areas for improvement in interpersonal relationships: in particular *settings*, eg the family, peer group or with authority; with significant people; more generally, with strangers or intimates.

- Learning skills.

- Skills and problems of communication which appear in a number of contexts.

This framework is most useful with older, articulate students. Let me reiterate, that in every case, whichever framework is used, the student must be a participant in the assessment, and agree its validity. Without this, it is of little worth. The pattern of counselling is logical: exploration leads to assessment; in turn that leads to action, the theme of Chapter Three. We have, however, to be prepared to go back to an earlier stage as more information becomes available.

Activities

1 Listening skills

1.1 The following behaviours (Figure 2.4) are associated with effective listening. Rank them in the order of importance **that is meaningful to you**.

Compare your rank order with a colleague. Justify your choice, remembering there is no single right answer.

Figure 2.4   *Skills linked with effective listening*

Skill	Rank
Sitting/standing still	
Not interrupting	
Giving signs of interest	
Keeping eye contact	
Responding by nodding or making approving sounds	
Looking at the speaker	
Avoiding criticism	
When speaker stops, encouraging them to develop what they have been saying	
Helping when the speaker seems lost for words	

Alternatively, group members can select the three they consider to be most important, explaining reasons for their choice to a colleague.

1.2   The group leader points out

a The different reactions of students to eye contact, using material in this chapter.

b The dangers of making assumptions as a response to faltering or drying up by a student, eg 'What you mean is . . .' or 'What you are really saying is . . .'.

Participants then critically scrutinise the other statements.

1.3   In groups of three, group members discuss the following statements produced by a group of experienced teachers at a training course:

> *She said so many things to me, I couldn't get a word in edgeways – and what I wanted to say is important to me.*

> *He was nice to me and listened but I don't feel any further forward.*

> *He seemed to feel it wasn't really a big problem. I felt silly for mentioning it. But it is a problem to me.*

> *Everything I said was being interpreted in a different way than I meant it.*

> *She made me feel I should have learned enough in tutorials to be able to cope with this – but I haven't.*

> *I know who the proper person is that I'm supposed to go to but I don't want to go to that person.*

The discussion should explore the implications of the statements in as much depth as possible. They summarise much of the content of Chapter Two.

2 Sending signals of acceptance

2.1   Write down an accepting response to the following statements:

> *Everybody is picking on me.*
>
> *I never seem able to say the right thing.*
>
> *I feel like giving up my A-Level courses.*
>
> *I don't want to end up like my father.*

Compare your responses with those of a colleague. Assess their impact on the pupil.

2.2   Now work out replies which encourage honesty and exploration in a speaker who says:

> *I just can't cope with maths. Anyway Mum and Dad say they were never any good at it!*
>
> *Why do they always have to compare me with my brother? We're different people.*
>
> *Teachers keep asking me questions they've no right to ask. They are here to teach, not interfere in what's not their business.*
>
> *Since I came into the sixth form I've learned you can't trust anybody.*
>
> *Why do we have to do that tutor work? I don't see any point in it – we come to school to learn.*
>
> *Adults never understand – they've forgotten what it's like to be young.*

General discussion follows on the best way of coping with such statements without endorsing them if they are unhelpful, or making the pupil feel rejected.

3 Observational skills

3.1   A group of eight or more is needed for this activity. The object is to help group members observe accurately *and* facilitate co-operation between them.

a The group is divided into two. Half the members form a discussion group, and are given a topic associated with counselling.

b Each discussion group member has a coach allocated to him or her, whose task is to observe and when requested give constructive feedback. The coach positions himself or herself so that the partner can fully be observed. They must not intervene in the discussion.

c Coaches make notes on their partner's communication. They may assess the partner's:

- skill at taking up, and extending what is said by others;
- tendency to criticise;
- ability at asking questions constructively;
- clarity and succinctness;
- capacity for showing warmth and acceptance;
- frequency of interrupting others;
- indications of respect for the viewpoints of others;
- tendency to wander from the point.

After 15–20 minutes the discussion is halted. The coaches take their partners to the edge of the room and give them helpful feedback. The discussion resumes with the speakers trying to apply what they have learned. Coaches continue to observe. After 20–25 minutes, coaches again give feedback.

In the next session, the roles are reversed: the coaches become the helped. If the group is uneven in number, one person may observe, and briefly report on general reactions.

3.2 Groups of three are formed. One member of the group discusses a pupil about whom he or she is especially concerned. Another helps her or him clarify the issues and think about strategies for helping. The third will observe and take notes. When requested he or she gives helpful feedback.

4 Clarifying the problem

4.1 Training group members again work in groups of three. One will talk from the standpoint of the pupil. The second helps the 'pupil' clarify his or her perceptions of the problem. The helper will:

a Take the 'pupil' back to a concrete situation, eg 'The last time the group tried to make you do something you did not want to do.' Use the outline of:

- What happened?
- With or between whom?

- When?

- Where?

- How did it occur and end?

b Assist the 'pupil' to look at her or his predictions about the likely outcome of attempts at changing the situation, and also anticipate difficulties.

The third member is an observer who makes notes on the performance of the helper, assessing:

- The warmth and acceptance proffered.

- The tendency to interrupt unnecessarily.

- Assumptive statements – 'What you mean is . . .'.

- Unhelpful statements, eg 'Yes, but . . .'.

- Whether she or he talks too much.

- How she or he directs attention to feelings constructively.

- The way in which he or she encourages the 'pupil' to face the situation.

- Reinforcement of positive statements by the 'pupil'.

When requested she or he should offer a constructive appraisal which is followed by small group discussion. The total development group then explore the implications of dealing with this type of situation.

Three situations are given below. In each one the participants take a different role, allowing each experience of counselling and observation.

Situation one
A year nine pupil is being bullied by a small group of her friends who want her to join in their truanting. Surprisingly, she want to belong to the group and values their friendship, but does not want to absent herself from school, not solely from fear of parental reactions. She has asked you as her tutor for help, but does not want to 'grass' on the others.

Situation two
A year ten pupil is conscientious, but his parents hold unrealistic expectations of achievement for him. Comparisons with an older

brother at Cambridge and threats of deprivation of privileges add to a sense of devaluation. You, the tutor, have been approached for help on the clear understanding that you will not contact the parents because of the pupil's fear of the repercussions from anti-teacher parents.

Situation three
A year 11 pupil wants help in deciding on a course of action. She enjoys school, feeling grateful to her teachers, and would like to stay on for a one-year course in the sixth form or FE College. Both parents are unemployed, and the poverty is real. The parents want the pupil to get a job and 'bring in some money'. She understands the pressures on the parents, and is deeply caring. Some advice has been requested, but you properly feel the situation needs careful exploration.

(In all the situations some preliminary discussion of the likely complications will deepen the activity.)

5 Assessment

5.1 The tutor can act as an 'early warning' system by being alert to the appearance of signs of stress, eg nail-biting. Tutors are in a key position to note the changes in behaviour that occur, and their probable significance, eg apathy replacing interest; tension and irritation at the beginning of the school day; fatigue or hyper-activity where it had not previously been present; deterioration in physical appearance. Discuss the way in which the skills of observation could be sharpened.

Apply this simple, yet very useful, diagnostic framework to a pupil who gives you cause for concern.

a In what situation does he or she behave in this way?

b In what situation does he or she *not* behave like this?

c What are the relevant differences between the situations where the behaviour occurs and where it does not occur?

d What seems to 'trigger off' the behaviour?

e Is there a payoff of either a direct or indirect type?

f What part do friends, peers, teachers or other adults play in maintaining the behaviour?

Step 1 Describe his or her behaviour as fully as possible using the questions above.

Step 2 Speculate on the reasons for his or her behaviour using Step 1 as justification.

Step 3 List the behaviours he or she needs to acquire if the problem is to be resolved. List *in concrete terms* the behaviours he or she needs to discard.

Step 4 What supports are available which could be useful?

Step 5 Work out a realistic strategy for helping this pupil modify his or her behaviour. Present it in a step-by-step way showing that the change will be gradual. Anticipate any difficulties – eg reactions of friends to his or her attempts at change.

5.2 Considerable social-psychological research indicates that a different bias exists in the way we judge others and ourselves. When we assess another person we are more likely to focus on personality as the cause of his or her actions. In our own case, we tend to attribute the reason to the situation, ie as being outside our control. Consider the implications of this tendency for assessment of pupils' problems.

5.3 In social interaction we tend to go beyond the individual's behaviour and attribute intent and motives to them. Consider this situation:

Two teachers are preparing materials at opposite ends of a large room. A pupil enters, and tells one the joke of the day circulating among the students. He enjoys it. 20 minutes passes: another pupil enters, and tells him the same story; but this time the reaction is that of anger. The second teacher is curious and approaches the first who angrily says, 'See that little so and so, he is always trying to put one across me.' But the observer has noted no difference in the pupils' behaviour. The teacher has attributed negative intent to the second pupil for which there is no concrete evidence.

a Consider the likely reasons for this behaviour.

b Discuss the ways in which we should validate our assumptions about the intent of pupils. Do we check them carefully enough?

5.4 There are two common reasons advanced for pupils' behaviour – the first emphasises the origins and causes, the second stresses purpose; he or she behaves in a certain manner because the family background is disturbed, supportive or whatever; he or she behaves in a certain way to get attention or a particular payoff from peers.

In small groups discuss:

a The possibility that blaming the family is unhelpful. Could it distract attention from the task of helping the pupil succeed in school?

b What exactly could a pupil learn at home which impinges directly on performance at school? How could the tutor or pastoral head deal with, for example, predictions of failure, 'get them before they get you', over-dependence on adults or outwitting authority?

c What is the payoff for aggressive behaviour in the school setting?

d Why do teachers who strongly subscribe to the view that attention-seeking is the purpose of behaviour sometimes pay more attention in class to the behaviours of which they disapprove than those they hope to induce?

Next, list the behaviours of students that give you cause for concern. With a partner examine your beliefs about their causes and the purposes they serve for the individual. Proceed to assess the effect of your beliefs on your reactions to the behaviour. Is it sometimes unhelpful?

5.6 Appraise the following statement:

They know where they can get away with it, and it's not with me. They mustn't get away with it or the rot will spread.

Discuss:

a How such a view would influence the holder's response to pupils who present problems at school.

b What assumptions underlie the statement, 'or the rot will spread'.

6 Simple action research

6.1 In the training group work out the ways in which a pupil, whose attitude to a subject was positive or neutral, may acquire a negative attitude to it.

Follow this up by some simple investigation of this with your form.

Discussion or brief written reports will provide worthwhile material.

6.2   Through a simple questionnaire or written reports – both anonymous – get your form to describe the problems they feel are important to them, and with which they would like help. Summarise the results and present them to the form. Then ask them to discuss in small groups the ways in which they could help one another with the problems. The message must be, 'We think you are mature enough responsibly to help one another.' Then negotiate the ground rules and structure for this mutual support. Clarify the tutor's role as consultant, organiser or whatever pupils and tutor deem to be appropriate. The tasks should be related to friendship, learning or everyday situations. This activity is a step towards the development of peer counselling described in the 1974 volume. Note that it does not encourage invasion into privacy or illicit pseudo-Freudian interpretations of the underlying reasons for behaviour: it is about practical support.

6.3   Year 11 pupils sometimes view counselling and pastoral activity as evidence of interfering teachers who ask improperly intrusive questions. Explore:

a The ways in which this image of teachers is built up;

b The steps that can be taken to prevent this and create a positive image of both teachers and helping activities.

3 Successful coping with problems

The content of this chapter

Discussion now moves to ways of constructively and sensibly tackling the problem once it had accurately been identified and its nature understood. No global recipes can be offered in this chapter. The task of tutor or pastoral head is best seen as helping the student to carve out the steps that have to be taken to resolve his or her unique problem. Why must the problem be seen as peculiar to the individual, although superficially it appears far from singular? Differences in context, perceptions, predictions, learning history and the resources possessed by the student ensure that the problem has a personal significance that recipes ignore.

A number of techniques are available, but the selection and weight given to them must relate to what the students believe to be helpful. The active model accepts that students are not the passive recipients of the alleged wisdom of the counsellor: their ideas are at least as good as his or hers. Important elements in the student's drive for mastery of the problem will be reinforcement and the fullest possible utilisation of existing strengths, purposeful self-observation, intelligent anticipation of difficulties and effective inoculation against demoralising feelings of frustration and fear of loss of face.

The developmental and therefore necessarily long-term perspective of counselling skills taken in this text should remove the risk of short-sighted concentration on immediate events as the only worthwhile focus of attention in counselling. Decision-making and problem-solving skills obviously have to be brought to bear on existing difficulties, but they have greater value as tools which advance the wider development of the adolescent. Similarly, role play and simulation are not confined to being activities in which students participate: it is even more vital that students should design them; they should be encouraged to innovate. If counselling is seen as a joint enterprise between students and their teachers, then students have to be given credence as resources for the creation of activities. The learning derived from co-operative design and implementation of guidance activities is at least as potent as that gained in traditional forms of counselling

Recapitulation: constraints and possibilities

The 1974 volume showed that open-minded exploration of students' difficulties leads to an emerging sense of purpose and direction. To this we can now add the TRIST/TVEI principle that the student should have a sense of ownership of both the problem and the means of resolution. With Martin (1987) I agree that a large measure of self-determination is at the heart of the counselling endeavour. Bandura (1977) reminds us, however, that 'self actualisation' is not limited to positive virtues: we have potentials for bad as well as good. Counselling emphasises responsibility for the consequences of our behaviour on others. In his exposition of social learning behaviour Bandura shows that individuals have an active role in modifying the effect of the environmental contingencies which impinge on them. This is a two-way process; reciprocal determination exists. Behaviour is not merely a product of the environment; neither does the individual totally create his or her environment; but as Bandura argues, mutual adaptation exists. 'Because of the capacity for reciprocal influence, people are at least partial architects of their own destinies.'

Perhaps counselling in the school setting is best seen as self-enhancing 'purposeful instructional activity' as Martin puts it. To support curriculum movement towards initiative and independent learning, tutors and pastoral heads have to give students the skills to resolve immediate problems and overcome barriers to achievement. By itself, this is insufficient. Contingency planning is not the prerogative of management alone; it should be given as part of guidance to every student, laying the foundation for coping with the disjunctions of a rapidly-changing future.

The fact that our interventions have to be brief is an apparent constraint, but if the tutor moves with his or her form through the school, the continuity over the years compensates for this. The tutor has to have the flexibility to take up many roles in relation to his or her form – helper, consultant, teacher and partner – while many methods are applicable. There is no right way of tutoring which is universally applicable: merely a way which is effective for a particular student or group in a specific setting at a certain stage in development. Each will have an unique combination of personality variables, attitudes, skills and learning history to bring to bear on a problem or challenge. The criterion for the adoption of a role will be considered assessment of the needs of the student. Note that the definition of need will not solely be in terms of deficits, but includes the learning styles, challenges, strengths and opportunities existing in his or her environment.

Developmental approaches to counselling stress reciprocity in relationships, realistic trust, positive responses to demands and criticisms, considered readiness to meet the needs of others and taking up new responsibilities. It should reinforce capacity for control of impulsive behaviours and stimulate the capacity to take judicious risks. Students are therefore seen as capable of making wise choices, and assuming responsibility for their future development. Tutors and students work as partners in the achievement of mutually acceptable goals. Developmental counselling is truly educative: it is a search after effectiveness, increasing mastery of the challenges facing adolescents, and building commitment to the learning enterprise.

In 1974 I pointed out that there was no reason why coping with the problem, once understood, should be confined to individual counselling. It may be more effective to turn to group counselling, which includes small group work of an informal type in classrooms, and tutor work. Isolated effort may prove ineffective. It was also made clear in 1974 that colleagues should be involved in the task-oriented stage of counselling, with the provider of counselling becoming a mobiliser and co-ordinator of these supports. This is still as vital today. Suggestions were also made for the development of peer counselling. Peers were recognised as acceptable sources of support for adolescents experiencing difficulties. The barriers which impede effective counselling are not present between friends. A friend can support attempts at behaviour change and is more readily available than a teacher. Peer counselling is related to the task of helping students affiliate with the school and use its resources for their own development. A brief quotation from the earlier book indicates the thrust of the argument:

> It is a tool by which pupils can serve their fellows and the school, gaining a sense of worth as they do it and accelerating their own rate of personal development. The creation of a system of peer counselling ... introduces a new element of positive co-operation into relationships between staff and pupils. The division into those who do things and those who have things done to them disappears, for this is implicit in many formal teaching and school situations.
>
> *(The Teacher and Counselling,* 1974)

Today, with changed teaching methods and curricular innovations, the school is more ready for this: indeed the most important counselling resource may be interaction and support within a small group of peers.

What roles should be proscribed for the helper? The most obvious are the quasi-parental and the 'fixer'. Adolescents are struggling to revise earlier relationships with parents, giving them more mature content. Achievement of some degree of social and emotional freedom from parents is a preoccupation. Adoption of a quasi-parental role stimulates irritation in the student, and also brings to the helper the danger of seeing the problem in terms of her or his past or current family relationships which are not applicable to the problem. The danger is more acute when the helper did not cope with that problem successfully in his or her own family. The 'fixer' role gives the helper a comfortable feeling that something useful has been done for the student. Perhaps so: but as a frequent response to the student's problems it erodes her or his responsibility for coping. The 'Me, too' game is also to be avoided. In it, the tutor tries to reassure the student by confessing his or her inadequacies, but often fails to stimulate relevant coping behaviours in the student. This profession of similarity is unhelpful. A model of competence is required from the tutor or pastoral head against which students measure themselves, and from which they can deviate after due reflection.

The gist of this section is, that as the coping stage of counselling is approached, tutors should be keenly aware that coping does not occur in a vacuum, but within a context which partially determines what will be effective. This should be related to the remarks made earlier on reciprocal determination. Tutors should never lose sight of the fact that although investigation and reflection are essential, adolescents live life intensely, and want to get on with it, although not necessarily in school. Stagnation is intolerable: if a sense of movement is absent, then they remove themselves psychologically, even physically if they can, from learning and guidance settings.

Reinforcement and self-observation

Behavioural approaches to counselling are neither mechanistic nor manipulative. Choice, decision making and taking responsibility for the outcomes of action are the salient elements of a behavioural stance. It is a 'bespoke' process in which suggestions and interaction are tailored to meet the needs, capacities and situation of the student.

When does talking about a problem make the student's situation worse? The answer is when we concentrate on the negative and ignore the positive elements in the discussion. Helpers should train themselves to ask, 'To what do I pay attention?' or 'What am I strengthening as I interact with this student?' As I counsel, I select what may lead to productive action, calling it to the student's attention by remarks such as, 'Good.', 'That's fine.', 'That could be useful.' or 'Maybe you could use that.' Counselling builds on the good that exists, but there is no guarantee that the student recognises it as such, so it has to be called to his or her attention. Reinforcement, as usually described, is a rewarding response to a statement or action, which increases the likelihood of it being repeated. To be most effective, it should be given immediately, and, especially in the early stages of the interaction, be given consistently. There is some evidence that intermittent schedules of reinforcement are most effective, but this applies to more technical versions of behaviour modification rather than to counselling skills used by the teachers. Reinforcement should come from a liked or credible source for the recipient. The source may well determine the impact of the response. Helpers should recall that adolescents in years nine and ten may dislike public praise from teachers because they are apprehensive about repercussions from friends. Private praise is still valued, whilst small group decision-making and problem-solving activity can be rewarded without the risk of embarrassing the individual members. Positive acknowledgement of strengths is essential, although this should be spontaneous, and where possible couched in gentle humour. By ignoring negative, irrelevant or misguided statements whenever possible, and concentrating on the active and mastery oriented ones we build up the students' sense of efficacy. Expectations of success determine how long students will persist in the face of hazards and frustration.

Self-observation builds a sense of detachment from pressures, on occasions even precipitating behaviour change. Students can be set to observe their behaviour for a day or two days, or over a longer period in a specific setting, eg physical education, lunchtimes, workshops or a subject. They must be given explicit briefings, and the purposes of the observation made clear. Students should understand that it is an essential step in coping with the problem.

When specific behaviours are to be observed, students should be asked to assess the antecedents to and consequences of the behaviours as well as the form of the behaviour. Our evaluation of behaviour may be limited: the focus may be on the behaviour and its consequences, ignoring the factors or cues which trigger off the behaviour. Yet the competent teacher with few disciplinary problems knows the importance of identifying the triggers for aggression, anxiety and misdemeanour, intervening immediately and constructively, rather than allow a sequence of behaviour to run its course. Identification of the cues which trigger off emotional, irrational or self-punishing behaviours in situations such as examinations, being put down by others, leadership and occupying the limelight, assessment, or being falsely accused, increases the students' sense of being in control. If necessary they learn to avoid such situations, or better, to change them by behaving differently, eg refusing to give the sarcastic individual the satisfaction of knowing that he or she has produced humiliation. The sense of potency is increased by realisation that changes in one's own behaviour usually compel changes in others who have to adapt to the new behaviours.

Appraisal of the cues *and* reactions to them is essential. Trower *et al* (1988) make the fundamental point that it is not events which produce bad feelings; it is the way those events are assessed. As the previous chapter showed, the same event is capable of multiple interpretations. Observation is only the first step in the coping process. In groups, or individually with the tutor or pastoral head, students should question their perceptions of the triggering situation, detecting and delineating alternative behaviours within it, assessing in imagination the consequences attached to them, eventually trying them out in reality. The helper's role is to raise questions for the students to explore, and provide suggestions for more productive reactions to the trigger situations. This, however, does not remove responsibility from the students for modifying, extending and implementing the helper's suggestions.

Observation takes several forms. Peers may engage in the observation. It may be a joint effort between friend and friend with frequent consultation and sharing of findings, or undertaken independently, the results being compared and evaluated only when the observation period is over. The decisions as to which approach will be more helpful, the nature of the report back to the helper, and the form of the follow-up are the responsibility of the student. The tutor's task is to detect snags, make recommendations, but the student has to develop his or her own strategy.

Coping should therefore be seen as a self-managed project for change in which the problem is described in terms of desirable behaviours that the student wishes to acquire. Through having concrete goals, and examining the chain of events necessary to reach them, students apply critical thinking to their relationships with others, spotting the links between events, building a sense of responsible control.

Comparisons can be purposefully made the focus of observation. Change and improvement means asking what they will do instead of the unsatisfactory behaviours. Once target behaviours are decided, they study a peer who successfully employs these behaviours. The chosen model is observed in ways which widen the student's knowledge of the conditions for success. After discussion in which the model is involved, the areas and settings for the observational learning are defined. In practice, more than one model may be used. As I write the memory of one first year sixth form student has come to mind. He was having difficulty with one of his subjects which was to be taken at A-Level. He identified a fellow who was good at the subject; assessed his attitudes and behaviour; talked to him about the subject; was allowed to read his essays and assignments; noted the questions the other raised in class; discussed the way essays and assignments were tackled. Then in his own words, 'I worked out what was right for me. I knew there wasn't much point in blindly imitating what . . . did. Now I'm getting on top of my work.' We have neglected the role of such vicarious learning as part of developmental coping. As Bandura (1971; 1976) reveals, such learning is both economical and effective. The model should be attractive to the observer, should be powerful in the relevant area, and above all receive obvious payoffs for his or her behaviour. The attention of the student has to be directed to relevant features of the model, it cannot be left to chance. Observational learning is not restricted to overt behavioural change, there is often some evidence of attitudinal revision.

Tutors and pastoral heads will provide acceptable reinforcements of new behaviour and coping attempts, but some training of students in self-reinforcement is also helpful. The Premack Principle (1959) means that preferred and frequent behaviours can be used to reward less liked infrequent behaviours. Rather engagingly, it has been called 'Granny's Law', i.e 'You can have the television, when you have helped with the washing up.' Self-reinforcement provides a structure, helps with problems of procrastination which are often anxiety-based and gives a sense of competence. Young people will work out their schedules of reinforcement for homework and GCSE projects sensibly, and are usually extremely conscientious in earning their self-set rewards. We should see that self-reinforcement and self-set rewards strengthen rather than weaken perceptions of competence and self-determination. With self-supported study and active methods of learning being increasingly supported in the secondary school there is a strong case for wider use of self-reinforcement. Extrinsic motivation of this sort is welcome: it bolsters the growth of intrinsic motivation.

Decision making

Decision making as part of counselling takes two forms: decisions made as part of problem resolution or of the student's coping with specific difficulties; then provision of the skill as a tool for general development. Both require tutor and pastoral head to have a model which highlights the main elements of decision making. It is a skill which can be taught. As such, it has to be broken down into its components, examining the relationship between then. As students face decisions in counselling, we sharpen their awareness of what is involved, stressing the relevance to other situations.

Decisions may be regarded as either intermediate or terminal. This arbitrary division is mainly useful for exposition, and we must be aware that what is a terminal decision from one standpoint is an intermediate one from another. Adolescents often focus on what they see as the final decision, but are oblivious to the intermediate ones. This failure is costly, because intermediate decisions may well determine whether the final goal is reached, indeed they influence its nature. All of us have a style of decision making of which we are only vaguely aware. Personality, long-term conditioning and cognitive style are involved. It is linked with a constellation of factors: susceptibility to anxiety, achievement motivation, the tendency towards introversion or extroversion, judgemental and attributional beliefs, including a bias towards seeing control as within oneself or as residing in the external world. These factors obviously interact with our perceptions of the nature and importance of the decision. The context in which the decision has to be made cannot be ignored: it may contain threat or reward strong enough to override personal style and considerations. All this is as important for the adolescent as for the adult. The helper, however, has to:

1. Consider whether it is necessary to create awareness of the need to make a decision in the student. Self-protective blind spots exist, whilst some students are willing to become the passive passengers of circumstances.

2. Ask if the student recognises that alternatives exist. Without knowledge of the possibilities there can be no choice; without choice there is no meaningful decision.

3. Help the student assess the probabilities of reaching the goal. If several *paths* to it exist; what costs and potential rewards does each carry?

4. Draw the student's attention to assessment of the desirability of the final goal and the means of reaching it. What values will be confirmed or violated as the student pursues the goal? Decision making does not concentrate on rational maximisation of gratification to the exclusion of other considerations. Altruism, ethics, awareness of the feelings of others are not to be discounted.

Level of risk in both the adolescent's style of decision making and the decision itself will come to the fore. At one extreme, students may habitually take an unduly risky approach. They focus on the goal without thought of the probability of reaching it, the costs involved, and the implications of failure. Students with this style unthinkingly launch themselves on courses of action, run into trouble, proceeding to cover loss of face with superficial bravado. At the other pole is the 'safe better'. The individual avoids harm, but his or her rewards are minimal. Initiative and enterprise are dampened by desire for safety. Such individuals are liable to fear of failure which is, as Birney and Teevan (1969) demonstrate, a negative avoidance mechanism aimed at preservation of self-esteem. They set themselves impossibly high or ridiculously low targets as a defence against the anxiety of achievement. On the one hand, they cannot be blamed for failure to achieve the impossible task: they should be admired for their apparent striving. On the other, they wish to produce the impression that they could do better if they did try. For the 'safe better', who is such because of fear of failure, the world is full of hostile pressures: they work, not actively for success, but to avoid punishment, blame and shame. The most promising position is a balanced mature compromise between costs, probability and desirability. We have long known that the high achiever likes the 50/50 range of risk, finding the approximately equal chances of failure or success stimulating. The inevitable anxiety is used as a spur to activity, and to sharpen their knowledge of themselves as learners.

The helper, having stimulated awareness in the student of the need to make a decision, encourages further exploration of its exact nature, importance, and significance in his or her life. Its dimensions have to be made evident before information can be sought. Questions are:

- What information?

- Where is it to be found?

- How is it to be used?

- Is it credible, and what are its limitations?

Tutors should be alert to signs of authoritarian thinking which involves classification of things into crude dichotomies of good or bad. Authoritarian students tend to make up their minds instantly about the meaning of a decision or problematic situation. Instant imposition of meaning then leads to rejection of contradictory evidence, and its dismissal in an arbitrary manner. They are unable to tolerate the anxiety-arousing doubts and ambiguities inevitable to decision making and problem solution. Delusory certainty is preferred to working through complications in an open-minded way. 'Oughts' rather than reality shape their decisions unrealistically; like the dogmatist they also tend to pay more attention to the source of the messages about the decision than their content. Unwittingly, they misinterpret the intent of the message.

Impulsiveness versus considered decision making is easily discerned in the authoritarian decision maker. Yet we may not recognise how often consideration of an open-minded nature is followed by impulsivity. Year 11 and sixth form students consider crucial vocational and educational decisions carefully, yet in practice, a chance remark by a valued peer, a momentary intolerance of pressure, or the glimpse of an escape route from current anxieties trigger off an impulsive decision. Public commitment to it amongst a group of peers and the danger of loss of face stifle thoughts of withdrawing from it.

This reminds us of the student's susceptibility to influence. Who makes up the student's mind? Is it parents, teachers, peers, the mass media or some less obvious form of influence? The messages emanating from them are not to be dismissed arbitrarily, but given due attention. This, however, does not remove from the student the onus for making his or her decision.

Tutors and pastoral heads know that decision making is a process over time rather than an event. In it, some possible lines of action will be eliminated. We must ensure that sufficient time is given to this before students embark on a course of action from which it would be costly to withdraw. The counselling skills of anticipation and inoculation are brought to bear as the course of action takes shape. Students are encouraged to scan for potential hazards, assess the probability that they will emerge, evaluate their potential for damage, and decide whether it would be wise to work out in advance tactics for dealing with them. As hazards in the proposed course of action become apparent, the counsellor not only works to help the student find practical ways of coping, but through investigation of possible emotional resonances which could lead to exaggerated, impulsive or irrational reactions, increases the probability of successful coping. Inoculation against emotional pressures is essential if the work of both counsellor and student is not to be undone. Some of the failures in the first job or the dropout in further and higher education could be accounted for by failure to anticipate difficulties. Students often set out on a course of action with firm intent, but encounter unanticipated problems which dissolve their sense of purpose. They then feel vulnerable and doubt their capacity to cope, abandon their endeavour, or worse, pursue it half-heartedly. Building these skills of anticipation and inoculation gives young people that sense of efficacy which produces positive reactions to change.

Consistency is a valued attribute. Yet it can take distorted forms.

Students may be victims of false conceptions of consistency possibly associated with withdrawal of approval if they change tack. Put humorously: there is the view that having made one's bed it should be lain on even if uncomfortable. But why? Surely it can be remade? If this does not work, then one has a range of possibilities. Another bed can be bought or borrowed. If all else fails, one can get into the bed of somebody else. Be that as it may, counselling demands that the shibboleths which reduce integrity and creativity be submitted to ruthless scrutiny.

Problem-solving skills

The overlap between decision making and problem solving is evident. Much that has gone before is therefore relevant to this section. Problem solving is almost certainly best developed as a group activity. Risks exist: there is the danger of 'group think' which intensifies opinions irrationally (see Janis, 1972); whilst the desire for conformity may inhibit the need for logical evaluation of proposed solutions. Despite these allied dangers, Shaw (1981) argues that groups often produce more effective solutions than individuals. He argues that groups are more productive when the problem requires a wide perspective and can be solved through the summation of individual contributions. Perhaps: but certainly it is likely that information and the ideas for solutions will be processed more thoroughly, and impediments identified earlier. Rose and Edelson (1987) pinpoint skills germane to group activity in problem solving. They include the ability to generate a number of possible solutions, whilst as means/end thinking, problem solving requires the capacity for planning a sequence of steps essential to reaching a solution. Groups have to be alert to division of labour and effective use of time.

For making counselling a joint enterprise between teachers and students, small group problem-solving activity is ideal. Students could undertake a survey of problems experienced by their year as a prelude to group problem-solving activity. This could be extended by investigation of parents' and teachers' views of the problems of young persons, comparing them with their own perceptions. If, as is likely, they do not entirely coincide, the students have to assess the implications for communication and relationships. Students could offer selected dilemmas to the form or small groups within it for solution. Critical ability can be developed by tutors presenting a problem and the mode of resolution, inviting students to evaluate it, and produce a better way of dealing with it. Valid justifications for criticisms are demanded from the small groups.

Training in thinking discerningly about their definition of the problem must be given. 'Is *that* really the problem?' should become a habitual question. The techniques of the previous chapter may be harnessed in re-defining problems more accurately. It is wasteful to leave rigidities in problem definition untackled, eg students may hold unquestioned assumptions about what the problem *ought* to be, and of what is required of them. The latter may be an artifact of their belief that they have the right to be told exactly what to do, accompanied by the belief that the end product should be regurgitation of what they have been told.

Habitual immediate reactions have to be questioned. Are they, for example, influenced over-strongly by the appearance of the problem, immediately switching off if it takes a certain form? If the problem has a pseudo-mathematical appearance, although in fact not involving mathematical knowledge or skills, this may instigate a sequence of negative predictions – some version of, 'I can never do that sort of thing!' It is alarming that some individuals continue unchecked throughout their school career to concentrate on feelings of inadequacy, frustration and fears of being shown up rather than dealing with their problems more objectively. This applies to learning problems as much as personal ones. They learn to dissemble, therefore their difficulties are not perceived: if they are lucky friends support them, but benefit from experience in school is sparse.

Alertness is required of tutors. Students will seek an easy way out. Problems then degenerate into mechanical activities in which little is invested. The tutor has, however, to maintain a careful balance between challenge and support. Questioning of false assumptions about the nature of problems, and of inflexible approaches to them is proper; clumsily done, it erodes confidence. Too much frustration without the leaven of success may well activate infantile forms of thinking: usually animism, that is treating inanimate objects as if they possessed will and intention. 'This so-and-so door won't open.' is the type of response produced by bafflement. The tutor's skill is to temper challenges to the student's capacity for accepting them. Without this, self-criticism slides unnoticed into self-derogation; self-confidence sets into complacency. Tutors have to watch for these traps. Often the tendency in areas of personal problems is to confront the student with a summary of one, asking him or her 'What would you do if . . .?' When the range of behavioural repertoires possessed by the student is limited, then this, *by itself*, will probably lock him or her more firmly into self-defeating patterns of behaviour. The difficulties are compounded when anxiety or the tendency to identity through opposition are strong.

With these cautions in mind, tutors and pastoral heads should set about encouraging students to generate hypotheses about the best mode of resolving the problem. This involves interpreting the problem that has been formulated. Again this can be highly subjective and illogically determined by beliefs about causation, assumptions about the nature of such problems, and personality factors such as anxiety or suspiciousness. Inferences have to be drawn from the data. Students clinging to simple notions of 'true' or 'false' have to extend them by estimations of probability: 'probably true', 'probably false' or 'insufficient evidence from which to draw a firm inference'. Our conclusions and inferences in problem solving in developmental counselling are most usefully seen as conditional, propositional and relative, rather than absolute or fixed. Note that although it seems impossible to do without the word 'true', these statements are not about truth *per se*, merely about the confidence that students may reasonably have in the inferences they draw.

In reflecting on feelings and approaches to problem solving as part of facilitating mastery, students should be encouraged to review past learning experience and assess its impact on current behaviours. Gender-based influences and areas of learned helplessness are obvious candidates. Not so immediately striking is the role of the hidden audiences whose judgements have shaped learning and problem solving: parents and peers may be more significant than teachers and they may have conveyed negative attitudes towards problem solving, perpetuating anxieties and feelings of inadequacy. The fear of looking foolish if one's hypotheses are questionable has to be dispelled: unfortunately, loss of face is a generally neglected area of adolescent counselling. Insecurity diminishes the ability to tolerate doubt and make constructive use of it. Students without such tolerance often seize on the first apparently relevant idea and explore no further. Miller (1952) classifies problems in a way helpful to personal problem solution. Tutors will find it provides a useful framework for exploring personal problems.

1. *Approach-approach.* Here two incompatible goals are desired. Resources of time, skills, etc are limited, making it impossible to attain both.

2. *Avoidance-avoidance.* A choice has to be made between two undesirable situations or lines of action. The lesser of two evils seems the only way out.

3. *Approach-avoidance.* Reaching the desired goal entails undesired costs or punishing consequences.

In the stage of verablising and gradually clarifying hypotheses and tentative ideas for a solution, small group interaction is important for the provision of corrective and facilitating feedback. The elaborative listener role is central for this. One student propounds and justifies her or his hypothetical solution. The listener is not passive; he or she comments, corrects, extends, raises further questions or adds new ideas. Hypotheses can be processed in parallel if group members work in pairs. The initial expositor becomes the elaborative listener in turn. Through this, followed by whole group discussion, ideas for a solution are processed in a thorough and critical way. Problems related to personal development usually have no single encompassing 'right' answer: the pertinent concept is that of the degree of 'fit' to the circumstances. Indeed, even in other areas of problem-solving, students will have to accept that there may be no completely satisfactory solution; merely one that modifies the state of affairs somewhat for the better.

Next, the principles for selection of a course of action have to be clarified. Discussion will cover the criteria for priorities, exercise of parsimony, ie selecting the line of attack which gives the best results for the least expenditure of effort and other resources. Possible contingencies have to be considered: this form of strategic thinking has been stressed earlier as anticipation and inoculation. Students have an active role in changing the environmental contingencies which impinge on them, but they have to be trained to be alert to them, rather than being taken unaware. Work on failure in innovation reveals reasons that students can be taught to consider in their problem solving. When the intended innovation – often itself a solution to an existing problem – was only partially understood, something different than intended was implemented: and was indeed, foredoomed to failure. Incomplete or cursory scanning of the context in which the proposed solution was to take place, left unrevealed crucial hazards and difficulties for which the implementors had no resources or remedy once the project was under way. Training and discussion must alert students to equivalent difficulties in their own attempts at change. Groups should be provided with case studies of problems and the way they were tackled, and asked to submit them to careful criticism. Awareness of the need for systematic anticipation, and for sensitivity to the relationships between the separate steps in progress to the goal, elude some students. A helpful device is specification of both the problem and the desired end state, asking students to assess the necessary resources and work out the required steps to it. Flow charts can be used to delineate the relationship of each step to its predecessor and successor.

Counselling only differs from other forms of learning in that the subject and object of the learning are identical: the learner is learning about herself or himself. This is applied to problem solving in groups. The processes at work within them and the student's reactions to them must be evaluated. Questions about who was listened to, and whose ideas were disregarded, yield valuable information. Did a student withdraw from the interaction, or did someone become obstructive? If so, why did this happen, and what was the nature of its impact on individuals and on group performance? Was there a tendency to devalue the task? Who seemed to dominate, and with what results? Topics such as status, influence and support available within the group lead to useful self-assessment. Bales' (1970) three-dimensional analysis of group interaction could be applied:

1. Who was dominant and who was passively acquiescent?

2. As each student interacted in the group what effect did they have on others?

3. Did the individual contribute to achievement of the task or did they impede it?

Other questions might be:

4. Did they stay on target or wander into irrelevancy?

5. What criticisms were raised? About what, by whom, and for what purposes?

6. Did the presence of others help each individual tackle the task, or did it distract them unhelpfully?

7. Did a member of the group give the appearance of involvement and working, yet in fact, contribute little? How is this best dealt with?

8. Was there a discernible leader in the group? If so, how did they exercise their leadership?

Discussion of these points may well stimulate better analysis and problem solving. It may be more productive if, after the discussion, small groups develop their own checklists or framework for evaluation, applying them in subsequent activities.

Role play

It is difficult to distinguish between role play and simulation. Both are concerned with the skills of empathy and standpoint-taking, the learning of social behaviours and skills, eg negotiation or leadership. Perhaps simulation can be seen as more inclusive: role play as a technique within it. Both operate to help adolescents remove themselves from the position where unknowingly they are prisoners of an egocentric point of view. Role play potentially enlarges students' pictures of themselves by showing that the repertoire of behaviours available for coping with problematical situations is wider than they realised. It breaks into the stereotypical responses to situations sometimes found in students, especially those liable to anxiety, or whose initiative has been suppressed within the family.

Behind the use of role play as a counselling technique lies a concept of role as a flexible pattern of behaviour which is modifiable by the individual, rather than a firmly prescribed set of behaviours or a static collection of obligations and rights. The problem is that many adolescents see the expectations of others about their behaviour or destiny as immutable, when they are actually capable of negotiation. Turner (1971) argues that 'role-taking shifts emphasis away from the simple process of enacting a prescribed role to devising a performance on the basis of an imputed other-role.' It is therefore an interpretational and inferential activity. Those who counsel have to train themselves to see behaviour in a role as partially the product of the way *we think* that those with whom we live or work see us. Students have, in turn, to be aided to recognise the connexions between their perceptions and their behaviour. We are back to the fundamental fact that how we see things, determines what we do. If someone sees herself or himself as being rejected, devalued or discriminated against, then he or she behaves as if this is the case, even when the impartial observer is clear that this is not so. Persistence in their view of others, almost inevitably produces behaviours which ensure that others treat them in accordance with their beliefs. Their perception of themselves as scapegoat, victim or whatever is then confirmed: a self-fulfilling prophecy has operated.

Counselling helps students appreciate that their perceptions may be distorted, and they are misreading the cues emanating from others. The impressions others have of them may be very different from the views they believed to pertain. Role play stimulates the ability sensitively to construct in imagination the standpoints and role of the other person, appreciating the pressures, constraints and incentives operating in his or her life. It reveals the complexity of situations taken for granted. Continuity of role play experience is a prerequisite, as is careful planning of the experiences made available to students. Well used, over the years, it inhibits habitual resort to immediate judgements about the intent of others, creating awareness of interdependence and mutual expectations as determinants of behaviour.

The egocentrism of adolescence means we have to persuade students of the importance of standpoint-taking and illustrate its benefits. Conflict situations can be used to demonstrate this. Role play has to be shown to be a serious and worthwhile endeavour: presenting it as frivolous or without intellectual content is scarcely likely to arouse enthusiasm. It must be introduced in a planned, graduated way so that skills are built up. Initially, students should practise assessing standpoints of characters without playing the role – confidence is then boosted. Actual role play is probably best introduced as partner work with the participants sitting. Simple situations are effective, eg

> *You have been asked to see the head of year. When you get to his office a parent has arrived, and is talking to him. You sit down on one of the chairs outside his office. You then realise that the student already sitting there is new to the school. She begins asking you questions that obviously are important to her. You answer them as honestly as you can.*

After seven minutes, roles are reversed. When the time elapses, pupils discuss the experience in groups of four. If necessary (and only if) the tutor provides a 'starter' idea. To conclude, the tutor initiates a whole class discussion on what has been learned, and how it could be applied. The tutor structures without dominating the discussion.

Pastoral heads and tutors will be well advised to invoke the support and co-operation of the drama specialist, English department or head of PSE. They (especially the drama specialist) realise the power and complexity of the technique, and will not appreciate slovenly use of it. Ill-considered forays into role play carry the risk of loss of credibility with students and colleagues. To request it of tutors who have anxiety about class control is to threaten them unless support is provided.

Role reversal, as mentioned above, is crucial. In parent-son/daughter negotiations about such matters as choice of friends or time of coming home in the evening, students should play both roles, experiencing vicariously the feelings and motives of both individuals. For example, the parents intend their message to be one of concern, but the son or daughter interprets it as an indication of distrust. Such discrepancies and misunderstanding have to be explored and related to the student's life. Possible resolutions can be critically examined. One function of role play is to develop greater facility in making accurate discriminations between individuals or situations. Some adolescents fail to see the differences that exist, seeming unable to penetrate the smokescreens of their stereotypical assumptions. Some are dominated by prejudiced 'nothing but' perceptions, ie 'He or she is nothing but a teacher, police officer, homosexual or geriatric'. Exclusive focus on the disliked or threatening elements hinders recognition of contrasting characteristics.

The brief discussion of attitudes touched on the reference groups from which individuals draw their standards and values, and derive standpoints about important issues. Reference groups provide social anchorage. Role play may highlight discrepancies between the character studied and the reference group to which the student is attracted. Students then find themselves investigating key questions, eg 'Because I find a group attractive do I have to do everything its members do?' 'What are the limits to membership of a group?' and crucially, 'Has the group the right to impose an identity on me?' There are benefits for teachers and tutors, too. Stress and exhaustion may leave us feeling helpless in the face of group forces operating among students. Yet such feelings may confuse shadow with substance. What we worry about may only be symbolic in the sense that hair styles, dress and mannerism denote superficial adherence to currently popular identities. The majority of students do not take up the behaviours associated with the particular group or movement along with its outward trappings. The educative response is to use role play and other techniques to reinforce maturity by building students' sense of competence. Situations such as having to put a viewpoint persuasively and coherently to a reluctant recipient; relating constructively to the interventions of authority; coping with audience anxiety; are foci for activities where role play fosters socially productive learning. Enhancing through role play the ability to cope competently with self-eroding experiences such as false accusations, a gross social gaffe, or being the victim of an unpleasant hoax, reduces vulnerability to active adherence to the values and behaviour of anti-school groups.

There is no way of structuring role play which covers all circumstances. Tutors should ask themselves what makes them feel comfortably in control. The fear of things getting out of hand may not be justified, but it is all too real for the insecure, inexperienced tutor. Structure comes from asking blunt questions. Are the objectives clear in his or her mind? Do the students understand them? Will the students see the relevance of the topic? What is the intent of the role play: provision of understanding of the situation; promotion of changes in feelings or perceptions; the stimulation of new behaviours? How likely is it that the particular end will be achieved? Should the students be given the objectives in advance to keep them on target?

Gradual introduction has already been endorsed. In addition, it is important not to embark on a role play without adequate preliminary discussion. It is unrealistic to assume that students necessarily have clearly-articulated ideas or sufficient knowledge about a situation. There are situations where there is no substitute for substantive knowledge. In most cases, a preliminary 'warm-up' discussion stimulates sufficient useful ideas, although the tutor must avoid any hint that he or she expects, or will welcome, any specific stance. Ments (1983) in his valuable text suggests that it is useful to use 'prompt' audio-tapes with brief episodes ending with remarks such as, 'So, what are you going to do about it?' 'Do you think there is a way round it?' Further discussion could then follow, providing a sufficiency of ideas for subsequent role play. I have noted that it is most effective when the stimulatory tapes are made, and introduced, by a small group of form members.

The dangers and limitations of the 'nothing but' mentality have been touched on. Role play was seen as a way of tackling this handicap, but we should not neglect the possibility that role play could reinforce this style of thought. Ments shows that stereotypes should be avoided in the scenarios for role play. 'He is a bighead and boaster' is better replaced by, 'He sees his achievements and importance as outstripping ...'. Descriptions of characters therefore should not be in terms of labels but of their standpoints and feelings. Facetious names given to characters are unhelpful: not only do they stimulate caricature and stereotyping, but they devalue the activity, inviting participants to treat it frivolously. It is the equivalent of the rather pointless cartoons and somewhat silly drawings found in some pastoral materials.

Instructions have to be clear: not overlong or unduly complicated. Students should be able to state what they are going to do, for how long, in what imaginary setting, with whom and in what role. Post-play discussion should be the most vital and productive part of the experience. Misunderstandings emerge and can be corrected; tensions which have built up have to be dissipated. Crucially, reinforcement of useful learning takes place, the tutor also drawing attention to ways of applying what has been learned. It cannot be taken for granted that students will use what they have learned without prompting or guidance. Neglect of application allows the links between role play and the reality of everyday life to remain unarticulated; and so valuable learning is lost.

The peer judges mentioned earlier also have a valuable function in role play. They watch the performance closely, contributing their findings in post-play discussion. They might, for example, dissect leadership style, assess the quality and nature of bargaining or co-operation, or comment on actions which impeded or facilitated attainment of goals. Therefore, they must be given careful briefings, out of earshot of the players. They may be asked to assess the interaction, noting who became dominant, who was relegated to a marginal position, who tended to devalue others. On other occasions they may centre on the content of the role play, evaluating the ideas produced.

When role play occurs at the third level of counselling, it need not be confined to group settings. In individual work the pastoral head is actively involved as a player. To clarify situations and draw out coping strategies the student may take the role of the person who bullies her or him, the parent, or whoever is the source of the problem, while the helper puts himself or herself into the shoes of the student. Exploration of the problem reveals facets of the student's behaviour which exacerbate or maintain the problem, but the student has failed fully to apprehend the significance of this. He or she may be triggering off hostility through bragging, threatening others by 'bringing my dad up to school' or providing entertainment through berserk reactions. This is no alibi for the bullies who will have to be dealt with firmly: the victim is being empowered through learning that he or she can do something to change the situation. The pastoral head playing the role of the victim offers new ideas for coping which are later discussed. The student selects the first step to be taken to cope with the situation and works out how, and when, it wil be implemented. It has proved useful to record the brief role play, with helper and student then listening to it together as the groundwork for deciding on action. Role play here aims to provide an approximation to the situation, letting the student decide whether the enacted strategies will be feasible, and allowing him or her to assess the costs and consequences involved in their real life application.

A variation on the work of Kelly (1955) is useful once the areas of change are decided. The helper writes a brief behavioural description of the kind of person the student claims he or she wishes to be. It is read, and then discussed with the student. Questions are raised about the credibility of the sketch: is the person described too good to be true; is the way he or she is purported to behave appropriate for someone of that age; how would her or his friends react? The student then prepares his or her own sketch, using the helper's as a point of departure. It need not be written, tape recording is just as effective. After this preparatory work the experiment with behaviour begins. Using a flow chart or other diagrams, the proposed changes are broken down into steps which have reasonable chances of success: there is no point in facing the student with an unduly intimidating vista of change. After thorough discussion and careful spelling out of the first step so that the student knows exactly what has to be done, an 'as if' approach begins. The student contracts to behave as if he or she were the person in the sketch, experimenting with the first step for three to five days. He or she then reports back, with the helper eliciting as much feedback about feelings and problems as possible. The next step is then explored, necessary modifications of the original plan occurring in the light of the initial experience. Colleagues are informed, giving unobtrusive support. This version of role play allows students to experiment with behaviours in the context of everyday life without premature commitment or over-investment in them, avoiding subsequent despondency if early attempts at change do not work as anticipated. The intensity and vulnerability of the adolescent facilitates defensive foreclosure, the individual saying, 'It's no good; I just can't change!' Learning about one's reactions and developing new modes of interaction with the environment requires experimentation and tentative exploration, bringing together assimilation of new information or concepts of oneself and accommodations to the social environment.

It seems that developmental counselling must be about reciprocal interaction between the adolescent and his or her environment: a long-term process building on strengths rather than primarily concerned with problems. Imaginative interventions from tutors and pastoral heads using role play and the other techniques discussed here, and in later chapters, should help individuals not only formulate adaptive coping behaviours, but also strike out in new directions. Through well-designed activities in which students are deeply involved in planning, doors to new competences can be opened.

In the first chapter identity formation was seen as a submerged process occuring within a constant flow of apparently trivial decisions. This book reflects this by taking the perspective that counselling skills are integral to a long-term educative process in which neatly packaged recipes play little part because they ignore the individual's perceptions and interpretations of the problem. To offer them is to risk the futility of those earnest Victorian matrons who tried to alleviate the conditions of the poor by giving them bowls of diluted, unnourishing gruel. Good for their consciences, but doing little for the recipients, except confirming their current status. Tutors and pastoral heads must be prepared to invest effort in comprehending the process of adolescent development, and understanding the realities faced by students in a period of revision of identity, and of ever-increasing, potentially conflicting, demands. From our vantage point it may be tempting to impose a more urbane version of what is happening. We may offer palliatives which are not to be despised – yet the basic task of counselling is to aid the growth of efficacy.

Why are the experiences offered by role play, problem solving, decision making and simulation so important as part of counselling? Ivey's (1986) work is helpful in applying Piaget's research and theory to counselling, arguing that it is the equivalent of working through Piaget's stages of mental operations, correcting, as this takes place, errors of causation and over-generalisations from limited experience. Counselling helps students adapt to existing and new challenges by understanding them, making necessary adjustments, and then mastering them. Flavell (1963) in his exposition of Piaget's work showed that adaptation, which is a dual process of assimilation and accommodation, is a 'deep and wide ranging' characteristic of development. Any encounter with a new environmental phenomenon necessarily has to be viewed and interpreted through existing mental structures. The new stimuli have to be made to fit the existing structure of beliefs, perceptions and intellectual organisation. We noted that in counselling we only pick up the signals to which we are attuned: this is a specific instance of the pervasive fact that we can only assimilate those things which past experience has prepared us for. Kelly (1955) put it well when he claimed that intelligent adaptation to outer reality is 'to construe that reality, and to construe it in terms of some enduring reality within oneself.' One has, however, to adjust to what is assimilated: assimilation processes set limits to understanding, because the individual can only take in what previous assimilation and accommodation make possible. Yet they are also the means of extending it.

It is easy to lose sight of these fundamentals in the flux and manifold of school life where the urgent pressure is for mopping up a flood of minor crises or coping with breaches of discipline. Identity and achievement, however, are shaped by these latent processes. Tutor periods need to be reshaped to create an environment which, through the methods touched on above, gives many planned opportunities for the extension of perceptions and standpoint-taking capacity. A prerequisite for a sense of 'ownership' of their development is a radical reformulation of the position of students. No longer can they be the passive recipients of our alleged wisdom; they have to shoulder part of the responsibility for devising and planning activities.

Simulation

Simulation is an attempt to replicate reality. Imperfections are inevitable, for a perfect simulation would *be* reality. Simulation is a simplification of reality designed to bring crucial features to the forefront. It may, for example, make salient awareness of the penalties or rewards resulting from certain courses of action. Students are helped to comprehend the complementary nature of roles and their associated behaviours. They develop a sharp eye for the nuances and constraints of social exchanges and bargaining.

In 1974 in the active model of counselling, I argued that if simulation was to be useful in fostering development, then students should be involved in working out the simulation, and not be confined to enacting roles in situations devised by the counsellor. That view has been reinforced by the work I have since seen done by imaginative tutors and pastoral heads. Groups of students have devised simulations of work, peer group or family situations very competently, presenting the simulation for performance by small groups within the form.

Planning a simulation is a stimulating learning experience rooted in the exchange of ideas which are gradually built into a challenging activity. The group will have to construct a scenario which describes the situation and actors, spelling out, amongst other things, the rules of interaction, obligations and expectations, intent and motives. A simple framework such as that given below helps the group shape the simulation

1. The topic

a Students should discuss the general area from which the simulation will be taken, eg work experience, peer group interaction or leadership.

b Next, they will need to narrow it down. If work experience was selected, they might decide to concentrate on problems of immediate supervision. If leadership, the focus could be on the skills of leadership effective in a particular situation.

2. Focus on the situation

a The group then identifies a specific situation which provides the core of the interaction, eg a sudden flare-up of anger between workers on a production line who are on bonus, a dilatory maintenance man who is not, and a foreman who seems to be incapable of decisive action. Another might centre around unpredicted environmental changes, eg a landslip on a mountainside in which a member of a climbing party is severely injured, blizzard conditions occur, and near hysteria develops, therefore the leader not only has to cope with the objective conditions, but with paranoid accusations.
b The setting in which the action will occur is then described accurately and succinctly.

3. Outcomes

a Some ideas about the desired ends of the simulation will have emerged in the preceding discussion. They should now be sharpened and spelt out precisely. Do they wish to have a single solution or end state which participants should achieve, or is the end point one where students are left with a number of possibilities in mind which are to be discussed in a follow-up session? Both are valuable, but the latter generates more learning.

b Other outcomes might be:

- Leading participants to the point where they realise the need for further investigation of the topic.

- Creating awareness of contrasting attitudes and opinions held by sections of the community about the problem or situation.

- Questionnaires often ask for endorsement of opinions or statements when in fact respondents have given it little conscious thought; therefore the questionnaire crystallises what was amorphous or even creates an opinion. Simulations can be used consciously to make implicit attitudes and opinions overt. Postplay discussion must, however, submit these new-found ideas to thoughtful scrutiny. Examination of the ethics and mechanisms of opinion formation of this type is essential if simulation and allied techniques are not to be unwitting agents of conformity.

- Understanding and respecting in a mature way contrasting feelings and values.

Emphasis on respect for individuality is not encouragement of irresponsible self-gratification. Developmental counselling incorporates Allport's (1955) view of the individual as engaged in a purposeful process of 'becoming'. Allport accepts that limits to human development exist: his is no loose or cosily romantic view of human nature. Anxiety has to be experienced as the individual strives to be the best he or she can be. He does, however, accept that 'these limits are movable by virtue of the capacities for reflection, for self-objectification and to a degree by breadth of education and by the effort an individual may put forth'. Considered and wise use of simulation, role play, etc contribute to this moving of the limits. By themselves, they are far from sufficient, but in combination with other aspects of education they will boost development.

Powerful learning will occur if those devising simulations are encouraged to debate crucial questions. Role play can manipulate students to come to the conclusion that certain modes of behaviour and action are more desirable than others without reasoned consideration of the alternatives. Is there a danger that simulation could reinforce stereotypes and prejudice? The trend in research on prejudiced adolescents, eg Frenkel-Brunswik (1954) suggests they admire toughness, powerful and ostensibly strong individuals, rejecting those who are apparently weak or deviant. For the prejudiced adolescent, ambiguity and doubt is not easily tolerated, and choice raises anxiety which is stifled by immediate judgements to which they hold resolutely. They rely on external controls – like Sumner and Warburton's (1972) group of 'allergic' pupils they tend to believe that 'the teachers ought to make you work and if they don't they're soft', and hence fit objects for exploitation. Authority, if strong, is to be obeyed (albeit reluctantly) or outwitted if possible. For them, the world is marked by danger and potential chaos which is controlled through inflexible judgements and external moral injunctions. If prejudice is stereotypical thinking supported by the factors just mentioned then carefully-devised simulations may help students question their assumptions without postulating intolerable threat. Poorly-designed simulations incorporating caricatures and carried out without sufficient post-play discussion may reinforce prejudice.

In counselling we challenge the discrepancies between what people say they do and what they actually do. But equally self-defeating inconsistencies of this type creep into simulations. Ostensibly, the emphasis is on co-operation, but in a subtle way the procedures undermine this. Students must ensure that what participants actually learn from the interaction is what is claimed in the statement of objectives. They have a keen eye for their teachers' inconsistencies; it will be no bad thing if they exercise it in scanning the simulations they devise.

What model of person is built into the proposed simulation? Students usually enjoy debating this. Is it one of carrot and stick; of the individual having to be pushed into action by threat and sanctions, or activated by the lure of rewards? Are elements of determinism present? Do early family and environmental force have the power we attribute to them? Put simply: am I the mess I am in my dotage because I fell in love with my rocking horse at the age of two, and the confounded thing did not requite my passion? Absurd? Yes, but there may be less obvious absurdities in our thinking about the causes for behaviour and the nature of motive and intent. I would hope that adolescents subscribe to realistically tough-minded self-fulfilment models of humanity which include compassion for others. Many forces have conspired in the last decade to present a seductive version of nineteenth century man or woman devoting his or her energies to material gain, whilst calculatingly maximising his or her gratifications. Note that this does not decry enterprise and initiative; indeed counselling facilitates them. What is being questioned is the limited portrayal of the human spirit and the uses to which energy and ambition are put. Is such egocentric hedonism valid: is there no place for altruism? Raising these issues in the practical context of planning role play or a simulation and encouraging students to come to considered conclusions is good counselling.

Let us return to the planning process using the simple schema below. The following aspects need to be established.

1. A full description of the key event.

2. Descriptions of the role-holders who will be included in the simulation.

3. The social relationships which are supposed to exist between them with, if necessary, the general quality of the interaction between them, eg supportive, antagonistic or competitive.

4. The rewards and sanctions which have to be included.

5. The difficulties that have to be faced.

It is sometimes useful for the planning group at this point to construct a flow chart showing the sequence of events, and the impact of critical incidents. For the purpose of simulation building, critical incidents are those which interrupt, modify or even reverse the chain of events. Then rules have to be examined: a practical point is that they should not be so complex that undue time is used up in explaining them. Students learn much from examining:

1. The clarity of, and the need for, each rule.

2. The function of the rule:

   ● Does it make procedures clear?

   ● Does it come into operation when conflict or stalemate occurs?

   ● Is it about the penalty for a certain action?

   ● Is its function to define how role-holders respond to each other?

   ● Does it provide guidance about the route to a certain goal?

Students have to make decisions which parallel those of the curriculum developer. A balance has to be achieved between key aspects of the simulation and the likely consequences. Making it very close to life may mean including so many complications that it bewilders participants, or too much has to be kept in mind. Oversimplicity might cause important aspects to be left out; so that the role play becomes invalid. It is tempting to devise simulations that generate strong emotions or excitement but this could distract attention away from what has to be learned. Inserting a great deal of information may destroy interest.

One productive answer to some of these problems is for the group to try out a simple form of the simulation. Feedback is given by those who play it. The planning group use this in conjunction with their own observations to prepare a more demanding version. Post-play discussion is essential: it should include the impact of certain roles on those who are asked to play them, and feelings about role play.

There is no uniform way of facilitating students' mastery of the skills of role play and simulation. What is productive in one school, flounders in another. One way is to build up the skills systematically in the first three years of secondary schooling. Simple forms are provided in the first year which are extended and deepened in the next two years. Students are then well equipped to exploit opportunities for their use in later years. Co-ordination between the years is a prerequisite. Another tactic could be the training of a small cadre of students by the drama department who then assist a form, or train a group within the form. The cadre could consist of older students acting as trainers and/or consultants for younger ones, or they might operate at the same age level. The cardinal rule is that development is graduated, beginning in areas where success is likely and credibility is built up carefully over time.

Other simple behavioural techniques

Howard *et al* (1987) conceive of counselling as a series of tasks which have to be mastered. Adaptive counselling and therapy as they have formulated it is eclectic, rather than being tied to a particular theory. The active model of counselling I put forward in 1974 was 'eclectic in using the contributions of both the non-directive and directive school.' Also 'the essence of the active model is adaptation by the counsellor to both the pupil and the school.' Additionally, 'the school imposes many constraints upon the counsellor, yet the counsellor is also engaged in a delicate process of role-making and role-taking which calls for maximal sensitivity to feedback from colleagues and pupils'. The need for an eclectic approach which alerts one to ask, 'What technique for whom, at which time and under what conditions?' is just as strong today.

A reading of Howard *et al* will be profitable. They show that the principles of situational leadership apply to counselling as much as to commerce. The helper has to ask the question, 'How much support and how much structuring and initiation of action will be productive in this instance?' The answers depend on the clarification and exploration described in the previous chapter, or as Howard *et al* put it, understanding the person's 'maps of the world'.

They provide a useful threefold classification of problems. There are those of *competence* for which the helper has to supply new coping behaviours, and also as Howard *et al* stress, new cognitive competences. This reinforces the relevance of the preceding exposition of decision making, problem solving, role play and simulation. Problems of *confidence* follow in which the person has the capacity but fear of loss of face, uncertainty and anxiety are impediments to action. Then there are the problems of *motivation* touched on in the discussion of underfunctioning. Teachers will readily subscribe to the view that such problems are often more troublesome to others than to their possessor. Howard *et al* shrewdly point out that motivational problems often masquerade as problems of competence, something that often escapes the helper who spends energy tackling the wrong problem.

Coping is, as we have seen, based on realistic appraisal and precise specification of the measures leading to replacement of existing ineffective behaviours. Diagrammatic forms of planning are a businesslike method of tackling problems: reassuring the adolescent who fears that counselling implies invasion of his or her inner life. Lewin's concept of 'life space' is a helpful tool. Tutor or pastoral head help the student map out:

- the goals that he or she desires to reach;
- the barrier(s) or obstacles which have to be overcome or circumvented;
- effective paths to the goals;
- resources and strengths which can be employed in moving towards the goals.

This device allows the student's interpretations of what is happening in his or her life to come into the open. It also takes into account the possibility that environmental dilemmas impinge on behaviours drastically. Figure 3.1 is a very basic diagram to illustrate this process.

Figure 3.1

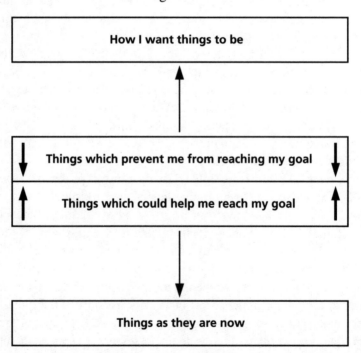

From this a step-by-step plan for action would emerge. In working with teachers over the last 21 years I have learned to respect their imagination and resourcefulness in helping students carry out their plans for change.

The occasional adolescent seems unable to view situations from a different perspective or to be too rigid to contemplate alternative ways of behaving. Some, as we have seen, have learned that resort to endless 'don't knows' allows them to evade responsibility. The simple diagram shown in Figure 3.2 has proved extremely useful on many occasions. The end product contains the following information:

Figure 3.2

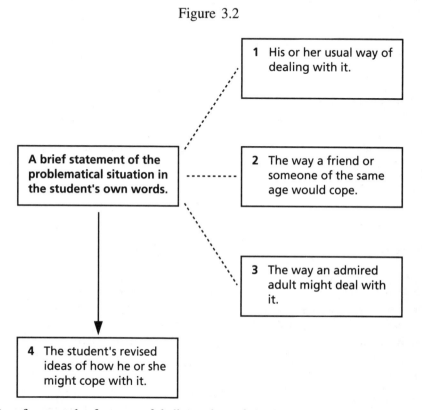

Box four results from careful discussion of the ideas which have emerged during the interaction. Let us remind ourselves of the importance of graduation. The steps have to be arranged in a hierarchy of difficulty: a ladder can be drawn; on the first rung, the easiest thing to put right is detailed; on the second rung, the next easiest, on the third rung, the subsequent step. Fortunately the majority of situations can be tackled in this way, for to change the pattern of behaviour, the task must appear feasible to the student. He or she must also know exactly how to set about it, which means verbalisation and rehearsal of the crucial first step.

Confidence has to bolstered, although the old tag, 'Forewarned is forearmed' is equally applicable. Unless potential difficulties are *anticipated*, and the student *inoculated* against their psychological impact, the change attempt will disintegrate. Failure at the first step – if undertaken without this precaution – activates negative predictions, creating reluctance to invest further effort in the enterprise. Anticipation and inoculation are not pessimistic, but a sensible precaution in establishing mastery. Our responsibility is to strengthen the student's capacity to evaluate possible consequences of action, eg if anxiety or aggression is being tackled, we have to alert them to the need to work out ways of dealing with the emotional repercussions of failing to deal well with a key 'trigger' situation.

Each step has to be scrutinised as it is completed, giving feedback which is used to sharpen plans for tackling the next step. The tutor or pastoral head will still have to challenge constructively. Doubts about their ability to win through tempt some students to retreat to defensive statements such as, 'I'm not motivated to study', which explain nothing, indeed obscure reality. Students tend to rely on such vague utterances when things seem to be slipping through their grasp or as justification for giving up the effort. Here one has to be concrete and specific in one's challenges, asking what behaviours are meant by study, and in what situations those behaviours occur or do not occur. Without this, a state of impasse will be consolidated.

Mobilising resources

From the above, counselling is a process of re-education which involves the student in discarding perceptions, patterns of thinking, habits and reactions which are maladaptive, often because they are rigidly applied to inappropriate situations. New behaviours have to be acquired, and existing strengths extended. For this, support from peers and teachers has to be mobilised. The classroom is the area in which much of the proposed change will be implemented. The pastoral head and tutor will have to inform colleagues, invoking their aid. Even more salient will be the support coming from friends and the peer group.

This takes us back to the immediate level of counselling where the student has the opportunity of acquiring *in context* new responses to others and to situations, understanding the antecedents of behaviour and the relationship of behaviour and consequences. Through reinforcements for new behaviours, especially social approval given unobtrusively by teachers and more overtly by peers, the process of change is facilitated. If there are no immediate rewards for new behaviours they will usually wither away.

Tutor and pastoral head will have to give thought to the need to examine the labelling processes and concomitant expectations which have maintained the student's self-eroding behaviours. They must appreciate the possibility that clumsy or precipitate attempts at involving others may actually reinforce a deviant or inferior identity. Yet the provision of a number of supports and the creation of a climate of positive expectations seems the best prospect for ensuring achievement of counselling goals.

Activities

1 The aims of these activities

a To encourage examination of students' problems from a behavioural standpoint.

b To explore simple applications of life space diagrams.

c To assist you to construct simple role play and simulation activities.

d To evaluate your use of counselling skills

e To examine your decisions and solutions to problems.

f To construct your own model of the counselling process.

2 Behavioural analysis of problems

In examining the situations presented, bear in mind:

- the need to make change appear feasible to the student;

- the advantages or otherwise of a step-by-step approach to dealing with it;

- making the first step in coping one which is likely to yield success;

- graduating the steps to be taken in a sequence of difficulty or risk;

- anticipating stress and difficulty and preparing the student to cope with them.

2.1 Work in pairs on each situation, but when finished, share your plan with another pair or the whole group.

Situation one:
A 12-year-old boy or girl in your form has become the butt of a

somewhat sadistic practical joker in the form who humiliates him or her, causing loss of face and growing isolation from others. The pupil makes it clear that intervention by you with the 'joker' would be unwelcome as it would probably alienate other students. He or she wants help in coping. Work out the steps she or he could take to change the situation, especially preventing the practical joker getting his or her desired payoff.

After working out your plan and presenting it for appraisal, discuss:

a the wisdom of acceding to the student's request not to approach the joker;
b the ways, if any, in which the sex of victim and joker could be a relevant consideration.

Situation two:
A female first year sixth form student is taking physics at A-Level. The evidence is that she is a competent performer in the subject, but she resents the signals emanating from male teachers and peers that she is not taken seriously as a scientist. She wants to discuss ways of coping with this devaluation.

Work out the points she may need to consider, the steps she should take. Direct her attention to the possibility that unwittingly she could contribute to the situation, and the difficulties she may need to anticipate.

Situation three:
A student suffers from audience anxiety if put in the limelight. After taking A-Level the student intends to take a technical training in industry which will include sponsorship. An invitation to attend an interview has been received, but the student dreads 'going to pieces again'. This is no fantasy, as it has happened on previous occasions when they were centre of attention. You want to offer support and counselling. How would you approach it?

Work out your approach with your partner. If it is felt that role play would be useful, explain how you would introduce, use and follow it up.

After discussing your approach with colleages, the whole training group should consider the problem of counselling students with examination anxiety, fear of the limelight or appearing foolish. How does one help a student whose initiative is hampered by undue fear of creating adverse impressions in authority figures?

Situation four:
A 14-year-old boy is approaching six feet tall and is physically strong. He values toughness and cannot endure being laughed at. His problem is that he has the remnants of a stutter from earlier childhood. Normally, it is not noticeable, but it reappears if he is asked a question in class or required to read aloud. He is irritated with himself for what he deems weakness, but more maturely feels he needs help in coping with the situation.

Work out how you would approach the problem in step-by-step way.

3 Anticipation

Anticipate *potential* difficulties that might be met in counselling:

> *An arrogant, superficially sophisticated 16-year-old male from an affluent home.*

> *A recently bereaved 14-year-old student whose surviving parent is not coping well with the additional demands on him or her.*

> *An anxious first-year student with a gift for alienating other pupils by sneaking on them.*

> *A 14-year-old student whose mother has recently obtained a divorce, after she and the mother have suffered violence for several years from the husband.*

Deal with each instance separately. Make individual assessments before the group discuss the situation. Bear in mind that the objective is to alert you to possibilities: nothing is inevitable in such cases. To assume that certain difficulties must be present, is to risk creating a self-fulfilling prophecy.

4 Decision making

4.1 In groups of three or four examine this situation:

> *Jim is 13 and usually pleasant and co-operative. However, he has ended up outside your room almost incoherent with anger. He has had a violent row with Mr Black who pushed him aggressively out of the room, sending him to you to be punished for 'insubordination'. Mr Black is a problem to senior management who seem at a loss in dealing with a teacher whose automatic reaction is, 'Get them before they get you!'. You have mopped up after a number of incidents provoked by this teacher with*

normally well-behaved students of both sexes. Jim claims that Mr Black picks on him, makes sarcastic remarks about his handwriting and spelling, also he constantly refers to Jim's elder sister who tends to truant.

The group have to decide:

a How Jim can be helped to cope with the class situation in which he feels a scapegoat.
b The balance between support of a colleague and professional concern for a student.
c How to defuse the immediate situation.
d The longer-term action that should be taken.

4.2 *As form tutor you have offered support to a student who has had difficulties in relating to fellow students. Now in year nine he or she has indulged in sporadic absenteeism. At a parents' evening you talk to the student's mother who reveals that she conceals the absences from the father. You try to persuade her not to do this, but as the interview progresses, you become certain that she has no intention of changing this behaviour; indeed, it seems likely she will allow the student to stay at home on the flimsiest pretext.*

Working on your own, decide on what you feel is a proper course of action. Explain your decision to a partner. He or she will then examine it, looking for such things as unrecognised risk. You then listen to his or her decision, submitting it to the same close scrutiny.

5 Life space diagrams as a means of organising an attack on problems

5.1 The life space diagram indicates goals, obstacles to reaching those goals, and the supports available to the individual. One form of it can be used as the equivalent of a 'snapshot' in which the major elements of the student's life are revealed. Through it, we freeze, for a moment in time, a dynamic and complex process, allowing the student to survey what is happening, and make decisions about what has to be done.

5.2 In groups of four consider the significance of the life space diagram in Figure 3.3. Is intervention by the tutor necessary? If so, about what? What risks would be associated with intervention? (Note that the boy produced it himself.) The usual format is the individual, school, friends and neighbourhood.

Figure 3.3 *A life space diagram*

PAUL: Aged 14

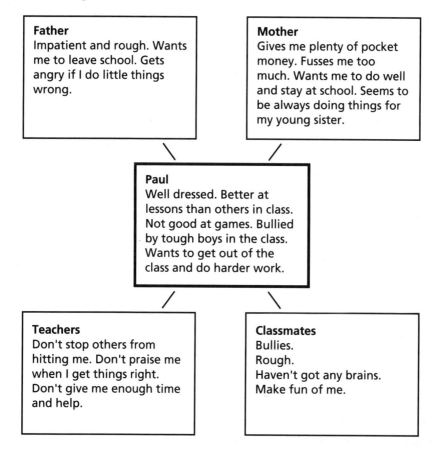

Father
Impatient and rough. Wants me to leave school. Gets angry if I do little things wrong.

Mother
Gives me plenty of pocket money. Fusses me too much. Wants me to do well and stay at school. Seems to be always doing things for my young sister.

Paul
Well dressed. Better at lessons than others in class. Not good at games. Bullied by tough boys in the class. Wants to get out of the class and do harder work.

Teachers
Don't stop others from hitting me. Don't praise me when I get things right. Don't give me enough time and help.

Classmates
Bullies.
Rough.
Haven't got any brains.
Make fun of me.

5.3 Inspect and discuss the following series of life space diagrams which illustrate problems.

a (Figure 3.4) *An individual has deeply offended his peers by crass behaviours and they have 'sent him to Coventry'. He wants to repair the relationships, but they are adamant in their rejection.*

Discussion would focus on the barrier; if it is not surmounted, is there danger of permanent isolation? What are the most effective ways of dealing with the noxious shaded area, surrounding the goal? As discussion proceeds, the plan for action develops.

Figure 3.4

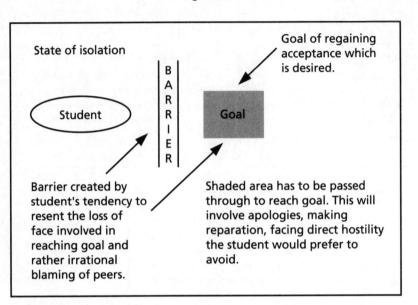

b *A student is trapped by two opposing forces and cannot leave the field because of emotional reactions. She wants to take up a particular post in industry which involves a technical training. An essential qualification is an A-Level in physics, but the individual hates physics.*

Figure 3.5

Barrier created by fear of being unable to find an alternative satisfying job.

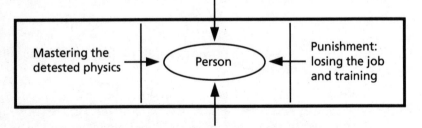

Barrier of shame and loss of face if they give up.

Discussion would centre on the reaction to physics at first. Are there ways of overcoming and coping with the subject? What is the likelihood of success? Are the student's vocational opportunities as limited as she believes? Consideration of the possibility that adherence to the original job choice is a form of avoiding challenge might well come into the counselling.

c This situation relates to past-school experience, but parallels can be found in school.

A tough and energetic 20-year-old male is a non-reader. His attitudes, absenteeism and suspicion of teachers seem to account for the failure. He gets by, but realises that inability to read is handicapping him in gaining promotion at work.

Figure 3.6

Area of 'getting by': rewards stem from his toughness and energy. Worker's present location	Negative area: He will have to admit failure and feel dependent on tutor. Also as a learner he will have to behave in ways he feels inappropriate for his age. Risk of finding out that he cannot succeed in learning to read.	Goal: Reading, and an end to 'covering-up'. Promotion.

Discussion would be practical and wide-ranging. The reality of feelings about dependency would have to be examined. Ways of ensuring a positive response to tuition have to be sorted out. How will he interpret difficulties? The risks and difficulties have to be identified and coping behaviours provided.

d (Figure 3.7) *A 14-year-old girl lives with her mother. Her parents divorced following extreme violence from the father. The girl's mother now sees almost all men as dangerous and bad. The daughter badly wants a boyfriend, but if she begins to form a relationship her mother intervenes and frightens the boy away.*

This life space diagram focuses only on the basic problem brought by the girl. In fact, discussion opened up other complications for which the girl worked out sensible ways of coping.

5.4 Use the simple diagram set out on page 96 and apply it to a pupil or individual you know well. The goal should be specified in down-to-earth terms. Discuss the result with a partner.

Figure 3.7

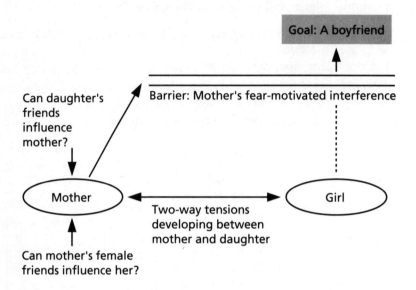

6 Role play and simulation

6.1 **a** Members of the training group gather and list problem situations that members of their form or teaching group feel they would like help with.

b Partners aid each other to develop a simple role play around a situation. It will be useful if the group leader provides a synopsis of the section on role play and the drama specialist is involved. It should not be too long; enough time for adequate post-play discussion should be allowed. If possible, opportunity for role exchange or reversal should be given. The group should try these methods before using them with students.

c Next, a small group should be selected from the form or class to construct a simple role play around another topic from the list. The students selected should have high credibility with their peers and those known to be opinion leaders. The tutor or pastoral head acts as a consultant as the group works out its role play. It is then given to the form.

Students' further participation is normally possible, provided that they feel that they have real responsibility and their initiative is respected.

6.2 Training group members might well co-operate with students to produce simple role play or simulation exercises designed to encourage students to take the standpoints of authority figures, eg parents, police, magistrates, politicians. Counselling skills are not so much concerned with questioning students as with helping them raise questions to which they seek answers. These role play situations should be designed to help students constructively to question the nature of, and need for, authority in an increasingly technological society. Nearer home, they should raise issues necessary for the implementation of the Elton Report on fostering positive discipline.

7 Other activities related to Chapter Three

7.1 Discuss your criteria for:

a Requesting parents to come to the school and involving them in the problem.

b Intervening, or not intervening, in situations such as peer group tensions and relationships.

7.2 Examine your likely response to the situation where a student comes to you and says, 'I would like to talk to you about a problem, but will you promise to keep it as a secret?'

7.3 As coping steps are worked out, students may become alarmed or decide that change is too costly. This results in defensiveness designed to make the helper helpless or cause her or him to retreat to vague moralisms or justifications. How would you deal constructively with these remarks:

> *It's not really a problem. I can stop whenever I like.*
>
> *It's my life. I can do what I like with it.*
>
> *All my friends do it, so I do it.*
>
> *I'm just enjoying myself; so what's wrong with that?*

Such dismissive remarks are frequent when the activity is seen as anti-authority and as offering an attractive alternative to the identities offered by school and family, eg solvent, alcohol and drug abuse. Many other students are wily enough to use them to trap the teacher into producing superficial protestations.

7.4 Select a student to whom you relate well, and who has problems of learning or behaviour which give him or her cause for concern. Attempt to develop a self-modification project which he or she can carry out. It can include:

- self-observation, possibly accompanied by peer observation;
- target-setting and the incorporation of a graduated step-by-step approach to reaching the target;
- the sensible use of anticipation and inoculation as described in this chapter, and dealing with predictions;
- the use of self-reinforcement;
- peer involvement and support.

It will be helpful if members of the training group discuss these projects, alerting one another to techniques and possibilities for action.

8 Self-evaluation

Evaluate yourself on the aspects of counselling set out below. Work with a partner, discussing as closely as possible the complications and reservations that have to be taken into account.

1. Do I tend to tell the student what her or his problem is, or do I let him or her tell it in his or her own way?

2. To what do I pay attention in the student's statements – the negative only? Do I deliberately reinforce the student's strengths, building up her or his belief in her or his capacity to cope?

3. Is my approach one in which I ask many questions, suggesting what the student *ought* to be thinking, or do I help the student formulate her or his own questions?

4. Do I allow the student honestly to reveal their feelings, or do I by words, gestures, and general approach, inhibit this?

5. Am I helping the student think about the problem in ways which suggest the steps she or he can take to resolve it?

6. Can I show warmth and understanding in a way that is reassuring to the student?

The training group leader in leading the discussion should try to ensure that each statement is considered in an analytic way which reveals the limits, necessary qualifications and exceptions. There is little to be gained from their blind endorsement.

9 A counselling model

Construct in small groups a basic model of counselling related not only to your experiences in the training group, but your teaching experience. It will be useful to put your model on large sheets of paper, comparing it when completed with those of other groups.

As you build up your model try to keep the following questions in mind.

a To what values will you give priority?

b What general principles will you emphasise?

c What will be the nature of the relationship between the helped and the helper?

d What do you regard as a desirable output from the counselling process?

4 Counselling skills applied to interviews

Why consider this topic?

Investigation of the time spent in interviewing in a school over an academic year would reveal the importance of the interview. Teachers interview students, colleagues interview one another, teachers interview parents, school governors interview staff, teachers interview members of other professions. But are these interviews yielding valid, intended outcomes, or are they producing resentment or frustration? Without increased understanding of the structure and dynamics of the interview, time and energy – both scarce resources for the busy teacher – will be expended without adequate return.

Interview: structure and techniques

Figure 4.1 *Interviewing: input, process and output*

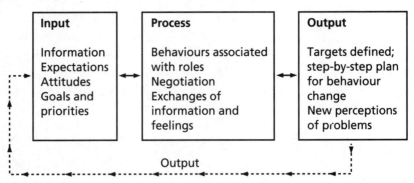

Input	Process	Output
Information Expectations Attitudes Goals and priorities	Behaviours associated with roles Negotiation Exchanges of information and feelings	Targets defined; step-by-step plan for behaviour change New perceptions of problems

Output

The interview, whatever its purpose – counselling, appraisal of teachers or formative assessment of students – is best seen as a three-part activity of input, process and output. Figure 4.1 highlights the mutual dependence of the three elements. Input obviously influences process; whilst that in turn shapes output, determining whether the goals are achieved. Note that these forces are not uni-directional: process may lead to the realisation that the input was inopportune, or to re-interpretation of its significance. The desired output partially determines selection of input and also the techniques brought into play during the process of interaction.

The output will be varied: decisions about a course of action, new and more accurate perceptions of the problem or situation, some small shift in attitude or clarification of the long-run consequences of attitudes and behaviours. But no matter what it is, our professional responsibility is always to assess the consequences and costs of that output for the student. The two are not identical: the consequences could be benevolent; but the costs in achieving them may be unacceptable. These considerations are crucial when the interview is one element only, albeit an important one, in a chain of developmental interactions between student and tutor. Failure to anticipate leaves us disconcerted when students' reactions to previous interview output surface in subsequent contacts.

Sensitivity to feedback is essential for efficiency; it tells us whether we are 'on course', or whether it is imperative that we modify our aims and actions because they are costly and counter-productive. If the output is ill-judged or unrealistic; if, as sometimes happens, it obscures or over-simplifies the nature of the advocated changes; when the difficulties entailed in reaching the target have been underestimated; the result will be a disillusioned student, reacting cynically to future counselling, and conveying his feelings to fellow students in an unvarnished manner. The interviewer's credibility is hardly won, but easily lost!

A facet of insensitivity to feedback having negative repercussions for colleagues is when an inexperienced or fatigued interviewer fails to note soon enough signs of tension. Something disturbing then surfaces in the last few minutes of the interview, but circumstances do not allow one to deal with it. The student therefore returns to the classroom in a state of arousal. Disapproval from the teacher then elicits a stormy response. One's tactics should include discreet alerting of the teacher or spending a few minutes suggesting ways of coping to the student, and making a firm arrangement to see him or her later. Interviewers need to acquire the skills of sensible containment which prevent unnecessary complications.

Input

It is obvious that productive interviewing rests on careful preliminary evaluation of the desired outcomes, the best way of obtaining them, and the detection of potential difficulties. Yet the pace and pressure of school life is such that many interviews occur without even minimal preparation, and therefore malfunction. If the interviewer has a basic structure, as little as seven to ten minutes preparation suffices to orientate her or him, creating vigilance which guards against the worst errors. Longer preparation is desirable; but until tutors and pastoral heads appreciate its significance, they are unlikely to fight to obtain it. I have been struck by the fact that they are more ready to acknowledge the need for follow-up time, than for preparation which enhances the probability of an effective interview.

Input should be assessed on some version of the following:

1. What information is needed? What information does the interviewer already possess about the student and other issues germane to the interview? We may neglect evaluation of it. How credible are the sources? Are we over-influenced by the source? Are there reasonable doubts about the validity of the facts? Hearsay and information for which the source is unknown has to be scrutinised carefully. A neglected feature is the possible impact of emotive information on the interviewer. If one hears that the student is a bully or habitually arrogant in interactions with adults, does this predispose one to misinterpret his or her actions, and assume negative intent where it does not exist? Reputations are allocated to students on flimsy criteria: once given, they attract further unthinking judgements; interviews unfortunately are not exempt from this.

2. This leads one to ask about the existing relationship between the student and interviewer: is it positive, neutral or antagonistic? Each will carry probabilities for distortion. Trust and mutual confidence are the ideal, but the harsh reality is that we have to work with students who are passive, indifferent, perhaps suspicious, and almost pro-grammed to misconstrue the intent of the interviewer. All this calls into play our capacity for taking the student's standpoint *before* the interview begins; accurately employed it allows helpful adaptation, especially in the initial phase of creating rapport.

3. Specification of the information that has to be obtained from the student raises the need to assess the threat to him or her in giving it. If it is likely to be seen as invasion of privacy or as illegitimate exercise of power then we must consider our position. At the very least, students have a right to a reasoned justification. We have ethical obligations as professionals *in loco parentis*. Therefore we must ask if repercussions from the student's friends are likely, or if imparting the information could *lead* to actions and consequences not in the best interests of the student. We must question in certain circumstances whether the grounds for obtaining it are ethically sound and how the student is to be protected.

Attention should be given at the preliminary stage to the setting of the interview. The physical setting evokes associations that influence the interpretations of the purpose of the interviewers. Students are often more sensitive than we realise to apparently peripheral features of the interview. In fact, they are integral because they symbolise authority and status, assuming emotional precedence over the overt purposes of the interview. Television has sharpened students' perceptions of these matters. There is no logical or mandatory obligation to interview in a formal setting which unleashes adverse reactions in the adolescent. Extremely productive interviews occur in relaxed settings which do not evoke unease or resentment by emphasising differential status or reminding students of unpleasant experiences.

Anticipation of passive aggression masked as apparent acquiescence has to be recognised if the interview is not to be a sham, however it must not become a self-fulfilling prophecy. Skill is needed to bring the façade of co-operation into the open, making it part of the interview content without forcing the student into a corner. Many ways of opening such potentially intimidating discussions exist: asking the student what advice they would give to a tutor about the best way of coping with the behaviour; describing it, and then requesting the student to explain what makes someone behave in such a way; or changing the confrontational element by bringing in a co-operative peer who is acceptable to the reluctant participant.

Tricky and threatening topics as the core of the interview require one to take the precaution of assessing the probability of a sudden eruption of anger, even of physical violence. In preparation, one has to identify the cues which have to be registered, and assess the measures which would effectively defuse hostile reactions. As important, and possibly more difficult, is assessment of ways of coping with manipulative students. Students carry distorted interaction learned in the family into their school lives. Emotional blackmail, exaggerated dependency, and attempts to elicit unwarranted sympathy have to be met with pleasant detachment, and the demand that students focus on the pay-offs for such behaviour. Such students are skilled at drawing the unwary interviewer into interaction which has a pathological tinge; eg playing the game of 'Only I understand you' or suborning the principles of counselling by manoeuvring the interviewer into making illicit appeals, eg 'Do it just to please me'.

The process

Much of Chapters Two and Three is relevant to the transactions of the interview and readers are recommended to consult them. The initial skill is that of creating rapport. Unfortunately this can be neglected in the stress and overload with which teachers have currently to cope. Signals of acceptance and respect are a prerequisite for making the interview a good experience for both participants. (We are strangely reluctant to accept that the interviewer has an equal right to satisfaction and the sense of a task well done.) Initial transactions set the direction: failure to establish rapport therefore means the final destination is very different from that intended; often one leaving student and helper feeling frustrated and suspicious. Even in disciplinary interviews the creation of tension is ill-advised; to be fully effective punishment and reprimand must be administered in a context of respect, positive expectation and concern. The interviewer's first remarks should make this evident. We ask, 'What can I say with honesty which will convey my expectation that she or he is capable of responsible action, and that he or she is worthwhile?' Obviously, this will not always yield visible results, largely because the student interprets even positive statements in the light of fairly long-standing beliefs about the motives and values of authority figures. Yet there is no point in confirming those beliefs through unthinking remarks and clumsy behaviours.

A rewarding skill is the capacity to detect low-level signals of anxiety or resentment and bring them into the open in a neutral way for examination. 'Perhaps you are feeling that this interview is yet another way of getting at you, Jim?' is an example of the type of statement, which, if adjusted accurately to the individual, is sufficient to initiate a dialogue which prepares the ground for co-operation. Let us remind ourselves that rapid apprehension of the student's perceptions of the hidden purposes of the interview is essential if it is to be productive. Student's reservations are nicely encapsulated in the typical remark, 'What you are *really* trying to do is . . . '. Much is conveyed by the stressed word. Staff development should assist tutors to gain basic knowledge of attributional tendencies and the associated stereotypical labelling. Students' labels of adults, eg 'She's only a middle-class snob' or 'He's one of them!', operate strongly at the outset of an interview, especially when the experience is new to the student. The second statement savours of the implication 'against us'. Only minimal confirmation is needed to trigger off a sequence of hostile interactions. Be clear that most attributions are positive and students trust their teachers, but it would be folly to ignore these problems. Clear statements of purpose open to discussion by the student are a safeguard against the worst effects of prejudiced perceptions.

Structure contributes to effective interview process: timing being one major structural element, facilitating or hampering effectiveness. Three facets of timing demand thought. First, the balance between interviewer interventions and input and the time available for student activity needs to be examined. It is salutary to tape record an interview and check who talked, for what time, about what, and with what results. Did the interviewer's contribution outstrip that of the student, leaving the latter possibly muttering about not being able to get a word in edgeways?

Next, we assess the proportion of available time devoted to the introductory rapport and orientation-creating phase, the main working section and the final summarisation. The needs of students obviously determine this. A highly anxious student may need more time in the initial section to overcome the inhibiting anxiety; another may require a lengthier final phase to ensure she or he verbalises clearly what has to be done. Timing as pacing is often neglected. Experience enhances the ability to intermesh one's responses with those of the student to create optimal conditions for communication. Time is involved in the length of the interviewer's utterances. For example, some – probably anxious – students welcome longer comments by the interviewer in the early stage of the interview. This allows them to get their bearings and assimilate the ideas put forward. As they gain confidence and begin to make purposeful contributions, the interviewer reduces his or her contributions. This is not a blanket recommendation. Some welcome this: others interpret the initial longer statements as evidence of an attempt to indoctrinate or as yet another instance of 'being talked at'; psychological withdrawal then occurs. Reading bodily signs of tension or facial expressions which indicate the pace is too slow or that a more forceful, quick-moving approach is creating a sense of harassment should coexist with other interview skills.

Timing is essential to ending an interview constructively and reducing subsequent problems. A clock placed unobtrusively behind the student allows unnoticed checks on time. The effective interviewer uses the last stage to structure and encourage the student to accept ownership of content and target. Despite such precautions, certain individuals have well-developed ability at producing last-minute disclosures. The time structure must hold: one acknowledges frustration and expresses regret that the interview must end; making another appointment if merited. Experienced counsellors know and dread the student with a gift for wrong-footing them in this way by giving peers the impression that expressed concerns were dismissed arbitrarily. One does not accept this passively. This behaviour is grist for the counsellor's mill because it appears in various guises elsewhere: its exploration is as useful as is the formal purpose of the interview.

Complications in interview process

Interviews contain conflicting pressures towards co-operation and resistance. Why? The adolescent is trying to maintain self-esteem, but interviews contain elements which make the individual feel vulnerable, even inferior. To understand this we have to acknowledge that messages in an interview are at two levels: that of *overt content* and then the *relational* level. The latter has to be carefully examined if counselling interviews are not to be fraudulent in schools. For the purposes of this discussion 'relational' implies consideration of status, and also of the framework within which communication is conducted between the participants outside the interview. It would be denial of reality to pretend that, despite attempts at negotiation and applying the principles of counselling, a power element is not at work in the interview relationship.

This can be seen very clearly in doctor-patient interviews. Pendleton and Hasler (1983) show that in a situation where the need is for diagnosis that gets to the heart of the problem, doctors almost automatically control the conversation, creating severe imbalance in communication. They initiate an overwhelming majority of questions and statements; interrupt the patient frequently; in effect, they lead and the patient follows. This form of control – which prevents the interviewer getting to the bottom of the problem because the individual cannot tell the story in her or his own way – occurs all too frequently in guidance and counselling in school. We should recognise that Records of Achievement interviews, although surrounded by a rhetoric of co-operation and negotiation, contain issues of control and interaction shaped by the need to produce outcomes acceptable to colleagues. Control in interviews can be established by the use of ironic statements which reduce the interviewee to impotence. The problem of dual meanings has to be tackled. We smiled at the trivial example of 'trying' in the end of term report in past decades. 'Reading between the lines' is yet another phrase which shows that dual meanings exist. We talk of openness of information, but schools are not free from the power techniques used in medical, social work and other professions through the use of language that holds one meaning for participants with privileged access to it, and another meaning for the person to whom it is addressed. Recent advances – and they are advances – may, however, be especially vulnerable to this.

The issue of power in its indirect forms has to be taken seriously. A single whiff of patronage is enough to alienate the older adolescent girl from a disadvantaged background where she has had to fight to escape from exploitation and to achieve status and significance equal to that of boys. It is beyond the purpose of this book to explore these issues in depth. Yet we should be aware that destructive elements at the relational level are sustained when interviewer and student hold markedly discrepant images of the nature and purpose of education which remain unacknowledged, and consequently, unexplored.

What happens when this occurs? Students have quietly effective mechanisms for coping. In an earlier chapter we saw that clumsy probing and intrusive questioning stimulates the use of superficially acquiescent and desirable responses as a form of passive aggression which insulates the student against the influence of the interviewer. When the relational level produces tensions of which the adolescent is uneasily aware, but unlikely to be able to verbalise with precision, an interesting variant appears as a response to the psychological discomfort. Just as some mental hospital patients in the past learned to take up the 'good patient' role to escape from the institution, so do some students distance themselves by playing the part of the co-operative interviewee to gain early release. They strike back at a self-diminishing experience by inciting friends to approach their interviews reluctantly with defensive mechanisms at the ready.

I have emphasised the need to adapt to the student: that is one thing; over-accommodation to what we see as students' needs is another. TRIST and TVEI properly brought to the fore the importance in evaluation of the questions, 'Where are we now?' and 'Where do we want to be?'. When applied to students we can question if they are where we believe them to be, or have they gone beyond it? Over-accommodation underestimates the capacity of the adolescent to cope, failing to credit them with resources they possess. Once again, we have a form of negative control which devalues them, encouraging them to be dependent, if not actually reducing them to dependency. It is a form of stereotypical thinking about the nature and needs of the psychologically and physically handicapped, and of those from disadvantaged backgrounds or whose condition carries stigma. Over-accommodation functions to reduce all within that classification to the lowest common denominator, acting as a social control which keeps them in a well-defined place in society. Counselling must play no part in this derogatory business, it must convey the positive expectations central to recent curriculum development and records of achievement.

Negotiation and the context of the interview

Fact-finding, exploratory interviews flounder through unintended reinforcements. In our anxiety to play our role well, we forget how closely students observe us. Signs of more than usual interest are registered, often misinterpreted. Let me make the point with tongue in cheek. As teachers we make excellent scapegoats for parents; it is therefore only human to perk up when the student discloses irritation with those parents. Nothing need be said: it is sufficient to lean forward attentively, or through a combination of body language and quality of voice convey greater alertness, investing the student's remarks with unmerited significance. Reducing it to the absurd: we can imagine the situation where the student feels the only way to get the attention of the interviewer is by being negative about herself or others.

The 1974 book saw the counselling interview as embodying an underlying process of bargaining and exchange. Today, in interviews about learning and achievement the word would be negotiation; and the activity both visible and prominent. Provided that it is accepted that the decision is knowingly and responsibly made with full involvement of the student, Pruitt's (1981) definition of negotiation illuminates our task. It is 'a process through which a joint decision is made by two or more parties'. The process incorporates 'feeling out' procedures through which those concerned apprehend sensitivities and limits to tolerance, accommodating to each other. This pinpoints the danger that our unjustified assumptions of similarity of purpose of student and teacher may turn the interview into a bland process with insubstantial outcomes. Tensions are not to be created artificially, but neither should they be stifled. Pruitt's point that negotiation requires those concerned to 'first verabalize contradictory demands and then move towards agreement by a process of concession-making or search for new alternatives' should be at the heart of the interview centred on change or target setting.

This aspect of negotiation reminds us that over-reliance on warmth and approval as lubricants for the interview may be debilitating. We earlier saw that counselling itself includes constructive confrontation which draws attention to the discrepancy between what is said and what is done, or between statements. These confrontations carry the counselling forward. May not the minor conflicts and contradictions revealed in negotiation be the core dynamic of the interview?

Potential conflict of another type exists. In the earlier book I used Talcott Parsons' (1957) concept of transactions across the boundary of systems as the basis for the Chinese Box concept of counselling (Figure 4.2). At the heart of the 'nesting box system' is the interview. The output from it feeds into the 'boxes' surrounding it. How far the interaction and output of the interview matches the style of communication and interaction deemed legitimate within the larger systems of classroom, subject department, peer group or home is something the wise interviewer keeps in mind. To ignore the reception that is likely to be given to the targets and methods of coping is risky, and is also violation of the basic principle that counselling treats developmental and learning problems in the light of the meaning they have in a particular context. Students leave the interview to attempt to implement agreed decisions in a school which has its unique culture. This culture or climate breeds expectations and establishes patterns of transactions which acquire an almost coercive character. A certain degree of elasticity exists: but to stretch the limits too far, is to risk stimulating

Figure 4.2 *The 'Chinese box' concept of counselling*

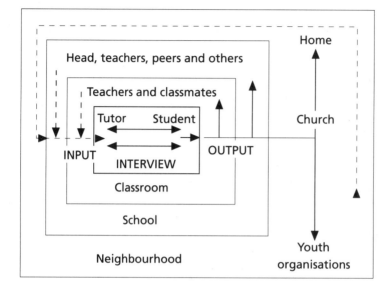

confusion and conflict for the student, and loss of credibility for the interviewer. Evaluation of the nature of both inward and outward transactions across the boundary of the interview and of the reaction they produce should be second nature for the interviewer.

Feedback which keeps the counselling on course does not solely derive from the student. A wider audience of parents, subject teachers, friends and others assess the utility of what was done – or more accurately, what they believe or assume was done. The student interprets their reactions, relaying them to the interviewers and her or his peers. Experienced interviewers are vigilant for situations in which it is imperative that they include this kind of potential aftermath as a factor determining the output of the interview. Sensible anticipation of the reactions of others in the student's life space and the provision of coping tactics for her or him become second nature for the interviewer who does not wish to waste time in dealing with avoidable complications. One learns to assess whether it is too limited in a particular instance to concentrate on student-interviewer transactions and the student's subsequent reactions only.

Most interviews do not present these problems. Experience teaches one to be cautious when a powerful figure in the student's background holds rigid views about the proper course of action or whose biased views lead to misinterpretations. Take, for example, the case where rather staid and elderly parents have firm vocational aspirations for the adolescent which are conventional, academic and safe. The outcome of the interview is a considered decision, based on evaluation of other possible actions, to strike out on an independent and somewhat risky career path the student feels to be right for her or him. The parents' expectations and plans obviously receive a severe jolt. Despite the careful evaluation, and the interviewer's professional stance, the parents cling determinedly to their belief that the interviewer has acted irresponsibly. The argument is not that the student's best interests should be neglected for convenience and an easier life, but that these possibilities should be anticipated and incorporated into the interview.

It is almost inevitable that interviewers will occasionally find themselves baffled by confused and contradictory reactions to their attempt at helping adolescents, or at the centre of an apparently inexplicable emotional storm. The urgent need is for analysis of the network of reactions. Sitting down with a large sheet of paper and constructing a map of the sources and forms of reactions provides helpful clarification. Methodical comparison and understanding of the different perspectives often allows one to perceive ways of commencing to resolve the difficulties; above all, it helps one shed the paralysing sense of helplessness produced by the situation. The interviewer:

● re-examines the student's apparent interpretation of the general intent, precise objectives and output of the interview;

● considers parental interpretations and consequent actions;

● if necessary, considers colleagues' views and reactions;

● assesses the contribution of peers who may have a slant on what is required of the student, influencing his or her perceptions of the goal.

Insights emerge from this first step. They may be sufficient to launch one into effective action. It may be necessary, however, to proceed to inspection of communication and interaction *between* the interested parties. Evidence then emerges of subsidiary problems, the gravity of which had not been appreciated, eg near collusion between a colleague and the parents to create a shared, but inaccurate view of the intent of the interviewer. As this simple analysis of the interpretations and perspectives held by the wider audience proceeds, the ambivalences and tensions evidenced by the student fall into place and lines of action reveal themselves. I have been concerned over the years by the way good individuals become trapped in almost primitive situations of anxiety and blame-pinning. Equally, I have been impressed by how, when they step back from the emotional tangle and apply this simple-minded technique, they successfully set about its resolution.

There are developmental gains in using this approach in counselling sessions in which the student teases out the complications and contradictions. He or she will have to identify his or her contribution to them, often making that the point of departure in changing the situation. The message is straightforward: any interviewer who disregards the principle that the interview output has to be scanned and studied in relation to its context puts herself or himself at risk. He or she is asking to be used as a scapegoat by those who dislike the interview outcomes.

The Record of Achievement interview

Counselling skills should be employed intensively in the formative interview if it is to be a focal point in students' responsible evaluation and planning of their educational progress. In no way is what follows intended to be an exposition of the theory and practice of Records of Achievement. This can be found, for example, in the excellent work of Ashforth (1990), Broadfoot *et al* (1988), Garforth and McIntosh (1988), Hitchcock (1986) and Munby *et al* (1989)!

From the counselling perspective, Records of Achievement are both protest and action against passive and inert forms of learning. Indeed, as Glasser (1969) put it – before they had been broached – action against schools designed for failure. In such schools the students who succeeded were those who responded to academic tasks in ways prescribed by their teachers, and who had learned that memorisation followed by regurgitation was more likely to bring success than independent thinking. The change produced by wise use of Records of Achievement can be encapsulated in this simple, yet far-reaching, statement. *In the past, students learned to expect, and how to cope with, questions from the teacher; now they have to acquire the skills of asking teachers searching questions about learning and success.* This will facilitate the end of the situation where, for some students, learning is amorphous – something that just happens or does not happen – rather than something analysable and modifiable, and within the control of the learner.

Records of Achievement encourage students to build on their strengths and tackle their limitations optimistically, as does counselling. This positive orientation is realistic. We do not delude ourselves about the limits to this: a statement of what someone can do is also, by implication, a statement about what they cannot do. The motivating feature is focus on the positive, obviously not to build complacency, but as a springboard for further achievement. Counselling belongs to the formative activities which contribute to the summative final document. Broadfoot *et al* suggest, however, that the distinction between the two is becoming blurred. Summation probably occurs at each year level, and in turn acts as impetus for the formative endeavours of the succeeding year. Be this as it may, the thrust is to increase students' effectiveness as learners, going beyond weaknesses to identify reasons for them and find remedies, whilst simultaneously boosting existing strengths. Acceptance in counselling is not bland, unthinking approval: it incorporates understanding which leads to self-analysis and a sense of constructive challenge. This is true also of Records of Achievement. Both recognise that even appropriate and realistic approbation which lacks the diagnostic elements providing the means for further development is of little service to the student.

A sensible ploy is for pastoral heads and tutors to explore the possibility that unintended, and obviously unrecognised, forces are undermining the positive effects of Records of Achievement. Broadfoot *et al* (1988) and the DES/Welsh Office (1989) suggest that girls value the one-to-one contact of the interview, appreciating the potential benefits of evaluatory discussion. (Perhaps their differential rate of development allows them to operate more maturely with adults.) Greater sensitivity to questions of responsibility and respect for value-loaded issues might well ally them with the purposes of the formative interview. That is the positive aspect: against it must be set disturbing possibilities that cancel out these benefits. Pastoral heads and their tutors as a team should work to detect and remove them. Are Records of Achievement powerful enough to compensate for the differential reinforcements debilitating to girls that were touched on in Chapter One? Despite noble intent, some of us are aware that work experience as provided in a minority of schools functions to reinforce gender stereotypes about the place and role of women in work. It is possible that Records of Achievement similarly could unintentionally strengthen gender stereotypes about achievement. Will girls who have been conditioned into accepting classroom communication which enfeebles them as learners, foisting a constricted view of their ability on them, be able to withstand these tendencies when some teachers unwittingly transfer them to the formative interview?

Tutors have to assess whether girls are being praised for personal qualities such as persistence, co-operation and conscientiousness, rather than being given constructively tough-minded analyses of their performance. Is there virtue in trying if you get nowhere? The academic equivalent of running on the spot *may* have some benefits, but it is more useful to move towards a relatively unambiguous goal with precision. Overtly, the dialogue between tutor and girl may concentrate on performance, but could there be an unnoticed weighting given to neatness, effort rather than achievement, down-grading elements that are more salient for success? Pastoral heads should recall that early work on profiling indicated – not surprisingly – that long-held frameworks of judgement are not easily discarded. Indeed, individuals believed they were undertaking criterion-referenced assessment, when in fact they were comparing students with an intuitive concept of the norm. Actions therefore subverted intentions: formative interviews are equally vulnerable.

Assessments by both male and female students of the purposes and credibility of teachers' comments will be carried into the Record of Achievement interview. Vigilance is essential if the interview is not to be an extension of the hidden agenda of the classroom or perpetuate labelling processes.

Counselling alerts us to our capacity to gloss over unpalatable facts, and that what we say we do, is not what actually occurs. Records of Achievement are designed to foster motivation and progress in all students: but is there a possibility that the procedures and requirements of the formative interview might favour, or be more accessible to, students from homes with a well-developed verbal culture? Students from such homes may be more accustomed to target-setting and appraisal of achievement; they may already possess the framework of reasoning inherent in modern curricular developments. The work of Broadfoot *et al* touches on the possibility of a disjunction between the emphasis on negotiation in the literature and the reality of what happens in the interview.

This is where the counselling stance can be seen to be crucial. The 1974 active model of counselling saw the interview as composed of status-equal interaction: the views of the student having the same importance as those of the teacher-counsellor. Those who counselled were required, for the purposes of helping and facilitating development, temporarily to abandon their superior status and its ascribed 'wisdom', engaging in open, adaptive communication. This does not always happen in the formative interview as reported by Broadfoot *et al*: teachers were disturbed when they discovered how they dominated the discussion; whilst students correspondingly contributed little, taking a passive role. Both partners therefore contributed to this sterility. Teachers' anxiety for students' progress and their sense of responsibility interact with the students' beliefs that this is the one area where teachers know best, and that they are paid to tell students exactly what to do, obliterating the intended purposes of the interview. If the school has not been alert to students' deficiencies in using the concepts and language of assessment, and has not systematically set about rectifying them, the formative interview is in grave danger of being a barren experience. Only prolonged training will allow students to move, from uninvolved responding to teachers' questions to raising their own which the teacher answers as a prelude to the student making informed decisions about his or her learning strategies.

Training should begin in year seven with a closely monitored sequence of self-appraisal activities aimed at tackling learned helplessness, inaccurate perceptions of the nature of learning, and the impact of gender on performance. The skills of setting realistic, and therefore attainable, short-term targets have to be inculcated without destroying enthusiasm and initiative by dreary repetitions of the same activity. There is evidence that the over-use of learning diaries in pilot approaches to Records of Achievement led to boredom. Target-setting and self-appraisal must be given many forms – individual, group, verbal, diagrammatic – giving students a rewarding sense of self-initiated movement and mastery; the majority of adolescents abhor the feeling of stagnation. In the early years of the secondary school, students retain the enthusiasm of their primary years, but are prone to expressing it ineffectively in global terms of 'working harder' or 'doing better at geography'. Analysis and the consequent step-by-step improvement are neglected. The consequence is that a sizeable proportion of students arrive at year ten feeling that learning is an ill-defined, even chaotic, activity over which they have little control, and from which they derive little pleasure.

Parental attitudes have to be taken into account. The mentality gap has preoccupied industrialists. It means that many people have not realised that yesterday's approaches and solutions are no longer relevant to today's problems. Parents retain outdated perceptions of learning; their children assimilate them; both seeing learning as the collection of scraps of knowledge, and its end as replication of the text, or of what they have been told. In an age of LMS we cannot afford to forget that many parents have little understanding of the purposes and methods of modern secondary education, hankering after the limited aims of earlier years. Even those who endorse change or subscribe to: 'The teachers know best: they are the experts', are often not sufficiently aware to provide the support and opportunities for extension of experience that allow their children to make the best use of GCSE assignments and projects. It is folly to ignore the possibility that Record of Achievement interviews demand a style of discourse underpinned by experiences of which some students have been deprived at home. If the familial regime has been one of compliance to rules without consideration of the underlying reasons or logic for them, we have an unpromising climate for meeting the demands for greater self-responsibility and autonomy in learning. If the justifications for obedience have diminished personal responsibility and stressed adult superiority, then students are ill-at-ease, perhaps confused, in a situation where their statements are valued, and, within its boundaries, status–equal communication is a necessary condition for formative and developmental assessment. The family regimes described condition students towards dependency or provoke habitual unthinking opposition. Counselling, with its stress on the total life context, reminds us that we cannot automatically assume similarity of experience. So that students may benefit from an excellent innovation, we have to attempt to compensate for such far-reaching background factors.

To attribute to the formative interview sufficient power alone to overcome these forces is somewhat optimistic. It is essential that tutors take into account parents' sub-cultural assumptions about schooling and their role in it. Contradictions are easily found: education may be seen in limited terms as a service with an end product – a job. Yet those parents may include some who view work negatively as a situation of exploitation against which the individual must protect herself or himself by any available means. Students may have accepted the validity of these viewpoints, interpreting our attempts at any form of guidance cynically. Such attitudinal learning impinges on our attempts at improving assessment. To recognise these viewpoints is threatening: ignoring them brings the risk of earnestly labouring to little avail. To illustrate: about a quarter to a third of year eight students are in a state of disenchantment or psychological truancy – present in the flesh but absent in the spirit – which is not manifested behaviourally in most until they are in year nine. In discussion with them I have realised that they are aware of the discrepancies between parental views of education and work and those promulgated by the school. Resolution of their quandary is achieved by superficial commitment to school values.

With older pupils in affluent areas a related problem occurs. Parents vigorously support teaching, albeit in the light of their perceptions of its purposes which differ from those of the teacher at times; but they urge their children to achievement. Yet there is a powerful parallel message which says 'Although you must heed teachers' academic advice, be chary of their advice on other matters: they may be well-intentioned, but not worldly wise, therefore cannot be taken seriously. They are losers because if they had any sense they would be earning the real money!' I cannot believe that the formative interview will be immune to such influences. Heads of year or house and their tutors might gain much from sensitive vigilance to those and allied factors.

Increased parental power in the era of LMS may be a complication. The ethos of Records of Achievement properly stresses the responsibility of students, and their ownership of the final summative document. But is it possible or desirable for students to control the feedback going to the parent from the formative interviews? (Broadfoot *et al* show that the distinction between the two is becoming blurred by annual summation based on formative interviews.) A guarded, suspicious approach may be present in both student and tutor if they are apprehensive of repercussions from parents. Schools are extremely sensitive to the impact of feedback to parents, and its consequences for the image of the school in an age of 'marketing'. It seems legitimate to ask how these factors will influence the student's perceptions of the integrity of the process.

Preparation for the interview

Lack of time compels us to prepare the student as thoroughly as possible through group activities in tutor periods. The objectives include anticipating the possibilities touched on above, preventing them from undermining the purposes of the formative interview. Pastoral heads have to accept the primacy of the tutor's role, helping them clarify their approach. Domination or restriction of the student's analytic activity and target-setting obviously has to be avoided, but neither can students be allowed to flounder. What, therefore, do students need from the tutor in both group work and interview? They need a model of competence against which to measure themselves, and then use as a basis for developing their own line of attack. Let me illustrate. If the skills of listening have emerged as a topic to be tackled, the competent tutor does not allow vague discussion. He or she ties it to concrete situations, helping the student see the importance of the question, 'Listening for what purposes?' The discussion could cover:

- distinguishing between fact and opinion;
- recognition of cause and effect;
- detection of the steps in an argument;
- discriminating between what is salient and what is peripheral.

The student then explores his or her level of skill in the facets, perhaps proceeding to clarify ideas of *when* a particular skill is relevant.

Similarly, a competent approach to self-assessment of reading may require the tutor to lead the student to concentrate on relevant areas of skill:

1. Skills of surveying a reading assignment in order to orientate oneself purposefully to the task;

2. Raising meaningful questions as a preliminary, eg 'What do I know about this already?', 'What part does it play in what I am learning this term?', 'What ideas do I have about it?' or 'Why is it important?';

3. The need to select and economically record the key facts;

4. Ways of immediately organising and processing what has been read so that it is not forgotten.

Without the last point being considered there would be little possibility of applying what was read, let alone generating new ideas from it. The competent tutor helps the student assemble ideas and select what she or he finds attractive.

Part of the preparation will be general; part will be specific. The general element will be a module of activities for each year intended to alert students to self-defeating attitudes and behaviours, eg adopting a façade of indifference as a form of self-protection, failure to make the link between anxiety and procrastination with compounding of difficulties, or initiation of a sterile comparison process which depresses achievement still further.

This general approach aims at tackling the broad forces which inhibit success: forces of which we are at least partially aware, yet do not highlight through decision-making exercises, or encourage students to confront in small group discussions and problem solving. Realistic formative assessment examines reactions to frustration in learning and develops ways of coping with it. When and where does it occur? What are students' beliefs about its causes? How can it be dealt with? Systematic and persistent measures which identify self-defeating behaviours which are the equivalent of cutting off one's nose to spite one's face are essential in formative assessment preparation.

It is not discussion *by* the tutor: this turns into muted harangues or ineffective appeals. The need is for vigorous small group exploration anchored to concrete learning situations in the classroom. An outgrowth would be self-help groups in which friend contracts to help friend master learned helplessness in certain tasks or subjects. As with all counselling, fears and evasions will have to be faced in the context of supportive peer interaction. Students may be over-sensitive to criticism or because they lack confidence in themselves, or indulge in self-eroding comparisons, they feel increasingly inadequate. School or college is then viewed as a hostile environment holding omnipresent danger of loss of face. Formative assessment gives us the opportunity to defeat such forces which undo what we are striving to accomplish.

Mechanisms of blame-pinning must be challenged: despite their desire for autonomy, adolescents are all too ready to shed responsibility by blaming parents or friends for their failures in learning – 'I would work if only my parents didn't ...' Alongside them are the real problems of coping with parental inconsistency. Certain parents fluctuate between the claim that all they desire is the happiness of the student, apparently seen as a tension-free, nirvana type condition, and the cry 'You've got to get those GCSEs or else!'

This general programme should be worked out by tutors and pastoral heads in each year group. Pastoral heads as a team must monitor their work to avoid unnecessary repetition and other hostages to boredom. Disenchantment is less likely when the programme and activities are partially based on consumer research. Students, especially after year eight, are less likely to 'switch off' when they see their expressed interests and needs are taken seriously through inclusion in the modules of tutorial activity. There is a strong case for elected representatives in each year working with staff to decide on content and method. This gives tutor activity greater credibility. Versions of year councils may provide a fund of useful ideas, also acting as a source of feedback to which tutors should attend closely.

Records of Achievement do not eliminate gender-based problems. James and Young (1989) found that even enthusiastic attempts to overcome gender-based inhibitions about subjects vulnerable to them were ineffective. Influences stemming from parents, peers, teachers and broader social forces maintained traditional expectations of the sexes and swamped sound guidance given with good intent. Student awareness of *these forces* and their coercive power is a necessary prerequisite for change. If a sense of urgency causes tutors to ignore them for ostensibly more practical and immediate issues, we end up wasting precious time.

Specific preparation begins with discussion of the formative assessment interview. We must not repeat the errors of pastoral care. Students and parents were never given clear explanations of its purposes and, equally important, its limits. Vague descriptions couched in terms of caring invited, and led to, misinterpretation of pastoral work as maternalism or paternalism embodying unjustifiable intrusions into privacy. With this lamentable ambiguity, responsible teachers feared a loss of professional boundaries and felt put at risk. Students have a right to clear explanations of the theory and practice of Records of Achievement. Face-to-face interaction also does not imply interviewing behind a closed door. Two or three tutors with students who are being interviewed could work in the library or hall in the equivalent of the 'open office' setting. Each pair is separate but can be seen to be engaged in a common task. This will relieve the apprehensions of student and teacher.

Students' behaviour is shaped by their perceptions of the kind of assessment acceptable to the tutor. Modesty, or more crudely, fear of being labelled by the teacher as a 'bighead' lead to less than honest self-assessment. Concern for the audience's reactions – primarily tutor and parents – restricts the accuracy of self-reporting. Unthinkingly, one feels that girls are more likely to underestimate their performance, whilst boys will overestimate it. The evidence to support this assumption is very fragile. Tutors should be alert to both tendencies in either sex. We should also note that although Records of Achievement and profiles are descriptive and criterion-based, students are prone to compare themselves with the average performance of their class. Preparation will include discussion of this and related propensities: hopefully, a more mature image of the interview will result.

Guided observation is essential preparation for formative interviews; it also contributes to the development of an individual learning style which is rewarding. Students are trained to observe and report on specific aspects of their performance in class or at home. It need not be a solo effort: friend may work with friend, contracting to check on each other's self-observation; observation undertaken by a small group may be part of a self-help project. The tutor may pinpoint the contributions made in shared decision making or problem solving: again deepening students' analysis of their strengths and weaknesses when they come to the interview.

A number of preparatory activities are productive provided students know how they will be used by the tutor. Writing a self-report in the third person, eg 'Jane is the kind of learner who . . .' forms the background for an introductory general assessment. More precise checklists form frameworks for discussion of specific difficulties. Raising questions to which the student hopes to find answers in the interview not only is a spur to involvement but reduces any sense of vulnerability.

More demanding, but potentially more rewarding, is partner role play of the assessment interview. Preliminary discussion raises awareness in the tutor group of the concordance and oppositions in the standpoints of tutor and student. Then the tutor provides a careful briefing. It has been useful to structure the activity by providing 'tutor' and 'interviewee' with a list of questions and suggestions as starting points for the interview. Alternatively, the tutor prepares those about to play the tutor role, whilst those who are to be interviewees discuss the issues they would like to investigate about their learning. Yet another useful form of preparation if, and only if, it is followed up by discussion of criteria for evaluation, is providing practice in assessing another student's work.

Tutors will have many anxieties about the one-to-one interview. They may feel vulnerable to challenges and deviant behaviours from the student because they are bereft of the protective aura of class teaching. Discomfort exists: they know they should guard against instant evaluations, yet fear not reaching a tangible conclusion. Pastoral heads must create a climate in which tutors feel it is safe to raise such doubts and receive support.

The formative interview process

We are aware of the danger that counselling could be a process of concealed persuasion which leaves adolescents believing they have made choices when nothing of the sort has occurred. Students may have been led to conclusions through unrecognisedly biased presentation of facts by well-meaning individuals who believe that they are working for the best interests of the adolescent. Responsibility must be the watchword of the counsellor. Counselling urges the adolescent to marshal the facts; examine the meaning he or she gives to them; weigh up the costs and consequences of potential lines of action; finally making a considered decision in the light of all these factors. Words obscure unless scrutinised; practitioners should question what is meant by 'guided choice' in their daily practice. What is the balance between guidance and choice, and what choices are actually available to the individual if, as Holly (1987) argues, he or she is 'experiencing a failure of interaction brought about by a breakdown in cultural and linguistic communication between themselves and the school'? Negotiation is essential for resolving this hiatus. But what do we mean in practice by 'negotiation' in formative assessment? Atkinson (1975) suggested that negotiation is about bargaining intended to resolve conflict through compromise. But what are the opportunities for, and limits to, compromise in the classroom and formative interview? There is urgent need for tutors to thrash out where, and on what issues, they can be flexible and allow the student leeway, and on what they must be resolute.

Any negotiation which does occur in the formative interview should be based on what Atkinson describes as a 'mutual benefit orientation' which is integrative. But to what benefits has the tutor a legitimate right? The answers must come from practitioners, but they might be hard pressed to supply them in the current situation of doubt and stress. Pastoral heads urgently need to set in motion a clarification process with their tutors. Most teachers would disclaim the 'gladiatorial approach' mentioned by Atkinson where one sets out to undermine the arguments and credibility of one's opponent. Current confusions might push teachers into it: students who are uncertain about the process, gaining identity through opposition, will relish the opportunity for this type of combat.

In any case, the formative interview is far from immune to the difficulties discussed earlier. Kearns (1985) illustrates gender-based discrimination at work in the RoA interview. Comments directed to girls were more likely to touch on social interaction, but boys received more task-oriented comments. Similar trends exist in self-assessments. Hamblin (1986) also detects tacit collusion between the sexes in the willingness of some year 11 girls to see women as ineffective in work roles and as poor decision makers. Kearns' argument that self-assessment may well function to reinforce traditional role conceptions, paving the way for discussions in which stereotypical self-images are strengthened, has to be taken seriously. Self-assessment can be problematical and counter-productive.

The skills of anticipation of difficulties and inoculation against their effects, the skills of graduation of tasks, beginning with those where success is most likely and the production of a clearly verbalised step-by-step action plan are obviously key components of the formative interview. But formative assessment is not confined to facilitating efficient meeting of school demands: it has a developmental function; stimulating intrinsic motivation – going beyond demanded performance to meeting self-set standards. Self-initiated rewards replace external ones. The price of creating this is constant vigilance by the tutor accompanied by constructive, firm confrontation which challenges discrepancies between appearances and reality. Students are adept at creating and maintaining images they know produce favourable reactions in others. They may recognise that the formative interview is about the lively interchange of views, but sometimes enter into impressive dialogue without any intention of translating ideas into action.

Students assess the anxieties of teachers and use them. Tutors feeling that an unstructured outcome holds alarming connotations of incompetence are liable to abandon negotiation and impose targets arbitrarily. Students wishing to save mental energy welcome and exploit this. A list of the mechanisms used by students to subvert the formative process would make an interesting basis for an INSET day. Tutors wryly comment on a sense of near helplessness when a student manipulates by adopting a posture of modesty to disarm the assessor. The counselling response is to ask the student why he or she feels the need to do this; what response is supposed to be given by the tutor?

A sense of humour is necessary in correcting similar countervailing tendencies. Some pupils over-rely on teachers' assessments of their work, yet also have many ways of dismissing them: 'Old Smith's in one of his moods again!', or 'She's always had it in for me, hasn't she?'. Coping with the avoidance techniques with which many students seem richly endowed requires the counsellor to be concrete and specific, avoiding loose generalisations. Students are pinned down to a relevant incident, 'Let us look at the last time when ...'. Context, feeling, trigger behaviours, consequences and interpretations of the motives of others are closely examined. A plan for action is spelt out precisely so that the student is clear about what has to be done. This is application of Ausubel's (1978) argument that the ability to verbalise the solution to a learning problem refines insights, and will encourage transfer of the principles to other learning situations.

Recipes are not ladled out in formative interviews: the aim should be to build skills of self-management and develop a style of learning that best suits the individual. Self-management involves, among other things, the student discovering the pattern of learning which suits her or him best. We are aware of rhythms in biological fields, but insufficiently appreciate their existence in study. Discussion of them and giving them legitimacy may well reduce the sense of alienation, especially at the end of year ten and in year 11. Alienation is the feeling that learning is an irrelevant, even noxious, imposed task of little personal significance rather than an opportunity to extend one's sense of self. Simple inroads into the theme have proved most profitable. An initial discussion topic would be, 'What is the best time of day for me to read and assimilate facts, write essays or engage in problem solving?' Another point of departure is, 'If I have a block of time for study or revision, what for me would be the best way of using it?' Tutors may need to point out possibilities. Is it more productive if used as an unbroken period? Some students tell me that for them an interruption is grossly disruptive; they cannot pick up the threads again. Others find it better to break study down in shorter intensive bursts of activity with a brief rest between them. They sometimes need to switch topics. Yet another finds she or he benefits most by a relatively long initial period followed by two shorter ones. They often give themselves the reward of listening to a record or CD and having a coffee. The topic or subject may influence the pattern, but awareness of this opens opportunities for further development. Tutors must resist the temptation blindly to supply rigid formulae for learning: recognising that what works for one is ineffective, even destructive, for another. Superficially plausible dicta, eg 'You should *always* study in a quiet room reducing any noise to a minimum' have gained a spurious respectability. But there is some evidence that a small percentage of adolescents may need background noise as a prerequisite for coping with the learning task. Formative assessment requires the student to take responsibility for evaluating and refining her or his learning style: the tutor's task is not to prescribe but to facilitate.

When Records of Achievement allow students to develop an individual style of learning the concept of ownership becomes a reality. The tutor has the dual task of sharpening students' awareness of their learning styles, and, as this occurs adapting to it within the interviews. Hence with one student visual techniques will be the medium for analysis and target-setting; with another the emphasis will be verbal. Without the adaptations assessment is unlikely to be formative: it will deny the realities of individuality and be a sham.

Output

Primarily this consists of a planned, phased sequence of tasks to be achieved. Almost paradoxically from the counselling perspective a major element of output is feedback. Time, although well spent in the interview, in the longer term may be wasted if post-interview feedback and corrective procedures are not instituted, and acted upon. Again, small group work in tutor period provides the best vehicle for student follow-up to the interview. Confusions and misunderstandings become evident in the discussions: the tutor who 'listens in' unobtrusively will gain a shrewd impression of the reception accorded to the formative interview. Self-help groups should be promoted in the tutor periods allocated for reflection on learning generally, and formative assessment specifically. The tutor's role is that of consultant to the self-help groups and a provider of activities which structure the group work. This does not deny the need for students to take responsibility for what happens in the small groups. For many years primary school pupils have made sensible decisions about learning in topic work or the integrated day: formative assessment must give secondary students the same opportunity. Consultation with the form will provide topics related to formative assessment: the small groups then decide what is relevant to them and the order in which they will be tackled, adding whatever they feel is necessary.

Year 11 brings work on the summary statement to the forefront. The counselling emphasis on standpoint-taking is useful: perhaps the most urgent need is to help students anticipate its impact on the reader. Ashforth (1990) draws attention to the desirability for greater awareness of employer's requirements and of what they value. This cannot be dismissed lightly: I have been struck by the fact that PGCE students almost at the end of their initial training are unaware of what their first school will expect of them. They are even more uncertain about what will be valued. Ashforth shows that employers value enthusiasm, the ability and willingness to learn, a smart appearance, punctuality, developed powers of communication and the capacity for team work. Even if they possess these qualities, students have to learn how to convey them without falling into platitudes or unconvincing piety.

The courageous tutor will gain much from encouraging her or his form to explore the following evaluatory questions about the formative interviews:

1. Did I have the oppportunity to say what I felt was important?
2. Were my views listened to with respect?
3. What help would I have liked which I did not receive?
4. At the end of the interview was I clear about what I needed to do?
5. Could I ask questions or did I feel that I was there to answer the tutor's questions?
6. What did I learn?
7. Was it useful?

8. What advice would I give the tutor to make the interview more helpful?

9. Did I know what my first task should be, and did I leave feeling I could tackle it successfully?

Activities

1 Objectives

1.1 To stimulate discussion about the three elements of the RoA interview:

a preparation by student and tutor;

b the diagnostic and target-setting process;

c feedback.

1.2 To develop simple checklists and activities to be used by students to prepare themselves for the formative interview.

1.3 To create awareness of distorting and self-defeating tendencies which make the interview unproductive.

2 Preparation for the interview

2.1 In groups of three or four work out what you would ask students to do as preparation for the formative assessment interview. What preliminary self-appraisal should they undertake? How would they do this? How would you ensure they were likely to approach the interview positively and without pretence?

2.2 Discuss as a group the anxieties that might be held by tutors about the formative interview. What threats does the formative interview hold for the tutor? How would you set about overcoming them?

2.3 Two activities which stimulate discussion about tackling learning difficulties:

a Quickly outline the salient details of the attitudes and behaviour of a student presenting difficulties in learning and achievement. He or she should be well known to you. Then pose three or four questions to which you would like an answer. Pass your 'case history' to another member of the group for him or her to work on. In return, you attempt to answer the questions set out in his or her summary. When ready, share ideas about the proposed lines of action and consider how they could be developed further.

b In groups of four consider the criteria on which students assess a teacher. How does this relate to our criteria for assessing them? Does this illuminate potential difficulties in the formative interview? What inaccurate perceptions and expectations may need to be corrected?

2.4 Construct in groups of four an outline framework for guided observation by students of themselves as learners. Decide:

a whether you would begin by observation in particular subjects or examination of cross-curricular skills such as learning;

b the use to be made of friends or paired observation;

c the form that feedback to the tutor would take;

d whether you would prefer a pre-planned step-by-step schedule or one that is negotiable with students.

Once each group has produced a reasonably practicable framework they should explain and justify it to other groups.

2.5 Using the ideas put forward in Chapter Four in groups construct a checklist, balance sheet, questionnaire or any other device that would stimulate the student to raise questions about her or his performance. Explain how it would be used in the formative interview.

2.6 In the training group work out how the tutor should prepare for the interview. Keep the limitations of time and energy in mind. Look closely at the need to be aware of the desired output from the interview at this preparatory stage.

3 The interview process

3.1 Small group discussion on the nature of decision-making in adolescence is followed by individual work on the exercise below:

a Students are now expected to take greater responsibility for decisions about learning, career plans, further education and other important matters. Ideally, these decisions should be made in a considered way after assessment of the:

- alternative courses of action available;
- costs and consequences to the student;
- impact of the decision on others who are properly involved;

- ethics of the rejected and selected courses of action.

b Describe a fairly significant decision made by a student or other adolescent. Examine:

- *Information*: specify its nature, location and the use made of it. Explain how the young person assessed its validity.

- *Risk*: what risks were present in the situation *and* in the decision made? Were they understood in advance or only appreciated in retrospect?

- *Impulsivity or consideration*: are you satisfied that the decision was a considered, rational one? Is there a possibility that some chance or threatening factor triggered an impulsive decision?

- *Subsequent decisions*: did the decision entail further decisions about the most effective way of implementing it?

Partners then discuss the implications of such decisions, relating them to achievement and career development.

3.2 Tutors undertake a simple investigation with their form of the decisions they believe they should make about learning, and those they believe their teachers or parents should make on their behalf. The training group then discusses the relevance of the views of the students to productive interaction in the formative interview.

3.3 Members of the group collect examples of problems and difficulties in learning that may have to be dealt with in the formative interview, eg in a small group project one student consistently does not do a fair share of work. Through group discussion tutors decide whether the problems they have identified should be raised in the formative interview or excluded. The criteria for either action should be made clear and scrutinised closely.

3.4 Standpoint-taking, ie the ability to see how the other person views a situation or event and the consequent impact on behaviour, is a counselling skill crucial to the formative process. Tutors should therefore sharpen their ability to see things from the students' perspectives. A productive exercise in training has been:

a Tutors work in groups of four, each describing the formative interview from a different perspective, eg an anxious, high-achieving student; an evasive student who does the minimum necessary to keep parents and teachers 'off my back'; a student who predicts failure, indeed has learned to be almost helpless in mathematics and science; a student of average ability who approaches things in a phlegmatic but not antagonistic way.

b Tutors then assess the impact that such a character might have on them in the interview.

c This is then elaborated by work in pairs. One takes the perspective of the character, whilst the other takes that of a tutor. As the 'student' puts her or his points across, the 'tutor' indicates his or her feelings and likely actions. The 'tutor' then becomes a 'student' using as a partner the person in the other pair who took the perspective of a student. Note that this is not role play, but a careful examination of perspective and reactions to it.

d Detailed discussion then occurs of the experience involving all participants.

The training group discusses the impact of gender on the formative interview. The issues raised in Chapter Four about reinforcement of stereotypical images, and the possibility of different approaches to the interview by females and males should be raised. 'Are these reactions likely to be reduced or exacerbated if tutor and student are of the opposite or same sex?', is then put forward for debate.

To end the session the group attempts to decide whether females would benefit from assertiveness training specifically oriented to the face-to-face assessment interview. This should be balanced by the question, 'What preparation is needed to ensure that males use the experience constructively?'

4 Topics for general discussion

4.1 What activities in the tutor group will stimulate students to ask meaningful questions about themselves as learners? How will students react to the formative situation in which they will be expected to raise their own questions rather than supply answers to the tutor's questions?

4.2 The idea of negotiation is endorsed in RoA interviews but this may be somewhat vague. For example, what are the limits to negotiation; how will students interpret it; could the claim of negotiation cover the fact that the outcome is predetermined by the tutor? Despite the emphasis on negotiation, will not the student see the formative interview as a situation of unequal power?

4.3 Is there a need to anticipate contingencies, eg provision of support and revision of targets after illness?

5 Output

5.1 Through discussion which is carefully structured around questions such as, 'How do we ensure as far as possible that students apply what they learn in the formative interview?' each group of tutors should develop a strategy for monitoring the output from RoA interviews. 'What supports have to be provided in the classroom?', and 'What happens if agreed changes are not implemented?', provide obvious examples.

5.2 Students' personal summary statements require sensitivities and skills that are often lacking. Tutors can acquire awareness of the dilemmas by taking the perspective of a student about to write her or his personal statement. They ask:

- What questions will be in his or her mind?

- How will students be assisted to look at their statements from the viewpoint of a future teacher or potential employer?

- What images of themselves do they want the statement to reflect?

Group discussion fastens on ways of helping students accurately to anticipate the reactions of readers. Can they do this without adopting the 'insurance policy' tactic of false modesty as a safeguard against being accused of brashness or indulging in gross over-estimates? These tendencies invite interventions by tutors which, thoughtlessly undertaken, leave students feeling the final product does not belong to them, with consequent resentment reducing its value in their eyes. This may be communicated unwittingly in discussion with employers, creating doubt about the credibility of the document.

5.3 Monitoring the use of feedback should preoccupy the training group. Feedback should be used to modify tutors' methods and alert them to counter-productive elements in the interview. Student assessments given in terms of 'helpful or unhelpful' will be too imprecise to be helpful. Anonymity is necessary to inhibit defensive production of socially-desirable, approving endorse-ments which may lull tutors into complacency. Training groups might experiment with the production of a questionnaire which is tied to concrete situations. If feelings and attitudes are to be gauged, they should be separated from specific behaviours. Care should be taken to avoid bias towards either the negative or positive: balance is essential. Construction of such a 'feedback questionnaire' should be an on-going project over several years, involving a gradual homing-in on the needs of a particular age group in a specific school with its own problems and strengths. Regular modifications allow adaptation to circumstances without abandoning what has been successful.

Other ploys will be useful: students in the tutor group may be asked to produce recommendations for the improvement of formative interviews. They must be given evidence that their ideas will be treated seriously and used whenever possible. Essays could be written describing the interview: a random sample is analysed by tutors for content and discussed at a training session. Anonymity will ensure to some degree that tutors' judgements are not contaminated by their knowledge of students. A telling exercise is to present a group with an audio-tape or drawing (but not a cartoon which could evoke responses unrelated to the situation) of a student about to begin a formative interview. Students are asked to write down what student and tutor would be thinking as they begin the interview. Then the end of the interview is heard or seen and students are asked, 'What was in their minds as they left the room?' and 'What did the student say to her or his friends about it?' Form discussion then follows; tutors will also find it enlightening to read the gamut of responses: more or less identical experiences are interpreted very differently.

5 Applications of group counselling

Group counselling as the potential spearhead for the development of the school as a caring community

Widespread failure in integrating the pastoral and curricular has condemned the pastoral to the status of an inferior welfare system merely reacting to alleged crises and at best offering 'emotional first aid'. Little systematic preventative work is present, and there is only sparse evidence of vigorous attempts at providing students with coping behaviours and a sense of mastery of their learning. Energy has been invested in punishment which, even when effective, merely inhibits rather than teaching new behaviours. Currently, there is a need to bring into being the positive discipline described by Watkins and Wagner (1987). Counselling and pastoral work have little perceived relevance to the achievement of educational objectives in many schools. Pastoral heads are enthusiastic, possess skills backed by experience, yet they deny or undervalue their potential as innovators within the organisation. They seem unable to escape from the futility and stagnation imposed by the flood of trivial tasks which overwhelm them. Energy is invested in holding things at bay rather than in educational leadership, therefore job satisfaction is tenuous or eludes them.

What can be done? The imaginative use of group counselling could break into this abortive state. Counselling groups run by year or house heads could develop and test materials and methods meaningful to the school at its particular stage of development and to available resources. Intervention profitably begins by pastoral heads turning themselves into a counselling group supporting one another in tackling the forces which block development and in devising measures for resolving problems. (For a fuller exposition see Hamblin, 1989.) They will need critically to examine their beliefs about what will work and what will not work in the school. Predictions about the outcomes of courses of action will have to be assessed, and challenged or discarded. Part of the essential groundwork will be casting a suspicious look at attributions of intent to others, and exploring the reality of self-perceptions as competent or inadequate.

The need for this approach to innovation and pastoral heads' self-development will not be laboured here. It is enough to realise that the works of Bandura mentioned earlier, Rotter *et al* (1972), Phares (1976) and Bandura *et al* (1988) all suggest in their various ways that a sense of personal control is fundamental for motivation and high performance. It is equally vital for the courage to change and innovate rather than remaining passive victims of current frustrations.

Pastoral heads share the burden with other teachers of assimilating a never-ending flood of documents. In common with others, they are worn out by administration which at best seems to have only marginal relationship with classroom interaction and the task of educating. Suggestions for innovation then evoke the response, 'Yes, I suppose so, but where do we find the time?' Certainly, there is a limit to what can be asked of a profession, and time is in inelastic supply. But that does not destroy the utility of asking, 'Are we using such time as we do possess to the fullest advantage?' Group counselling will be rewarding use of time when used in a meticulously planned way as a springboard for innovation within the year or house. From the group counselling sessions should come ideas, methods and materials that can be employed in tutor groups *and* the classroom. Possibilities include:

1. Planned involvement of students in action research projects on learning and social skills in which they take a major responsibility.

2. Crystallising ideas, translating them into activities, allowing tutors to see them being used in the counselling group, and discussing possible adaptations.

3. Constructing modules of activities centred around themes of developmental significance, eg assertiveness, communication skills or attitudes towards learning or success.

4. Experimentation with the use of students as mentors and the development of activities involving students of different ages.

5. Planning, initiating and supporting co-operative activities between different forms in the year or house.

6. Investigating problems associated with work experience, career choice and using RoAs.

These groups embody the idea that people will work harder to implement decisions they have freely made. Goals are pursued more vigorously when they are self-set. Group counselling should act as a powerhouse for facilitating the skills mentioned above, and also generate means for educating the emotions in conjunction with appropriate curriculum areas, stimulating the skills of standpoint-taking essential for interaction rooted in mutual respect. There is the possibility that counselling groups could merely be the equivalent of withdrawal groups in which students were given remedial help. The intention was good and concern evident, yet students, particularly those not belonging to them, saw them in terms of deviance. The groups discussed here have to be seen as opportunity groups conferring prestige on their members: participation in them is seen as a privilege for which individuals strive. The identity offered by membership should be one of vitality, enterprise and initiative. Belonging involves mature contribution to school or college, exercising responsibly the skills necessary for success in life. It requires a deeper and more insightful form of the entrepreneurial skills and initiatives fostered by TVEI.

In years 11 to 13, group counselling should be forward-looking, giving young people the skills of creative man or woman management essential for professional success. This is not about manipulation of others, but learning to understand one's judgements and create the conditions for colleagues to be the best they can be. No recipes exist for this challenging approach: each group of pastoral heads has to work out strategies appropriate to the context in which they have to function. Implementation will be gradual; whilst the operation will have steadily to be refined and deepened over a number of years. Continuous dialogue between teachers and students about purposes and methods provides continuity and the dynamic for development. Every effective teacher knows development cannot be imposed: it can, however, be facilitated through clarification of issues and encouragement of experimental action undertaken without unnecessary inhibiting anxiety about the responses of others.

Nature and purposes of group counselling

Let me now give a basic framework. Group counselling as undertaken by pastoral heads and their deputies is usefully seen as a carefully structured and controlled learning process providing knowledge and skills about interpersonal relationships, learning, and the behaviours effective in a particular context for a specific purpose. It induces maturity of the type described by Hersey and Blanchard (1977). This encompasses self-confidence, willingness to take responsibility, exercising it sensibly, the possession of high but realistic levels of aspiration and the capacity to use experience provided within the group. Participants are offered a number of viewpoints about themselves from their fellows, and given productive encounters with problems and issues. Feedback from the group should highlight useful behaviours and encourage extension of them.

The group leader's orientation is towards what individuals *do* within the group. Students bring in the attitudes, behaviours and preferences they habitually employ in other group situations. As students work on the tasks of the group the leader is alert to these tendencies and at an appropriate point asks members to reflect on them. Examples of the topics examined are:

1. What role does the individual take up as the group does its work? Is this a preference appearing in other groups?

2. In the group tasks do they tend to rely on others or do they prefer to initiate action? If they see themselves as varying in this, what accounts for the changes?

3. Why does an attempt at taking up a leadership position sometimes result in the creation of bad feelings and the alienation of others?

It can be seen that how the task or theme is tackled is at least as important as the task itself. The leader must help the student apprehend the meaning and significance of her or his behaviour. Their attention must be drawn, for example, to the way in which they cope with tension and uncertainty – by clowning, collusion with others in undermining the purposes of the group, attempting to make implicit bargains with the group leader of the type, 'If you don't bother me too much, I won't bother you', or distracting attention away from themselves by derogating or accusing fellow students.

We therefore see that a major purpose of group counselling is to draw participants' attention to self-defeating behaviours, eg reactions to embarrassment and frustration which make matters worse or leave the student feeling more vulnerable. 16 to 19-year-olds frequently comment on their inability to put themselves across as they really are in group situations, or more passively ask, 'Why do things go sour on me in this group?' The fundamental principle is that the bias of communication is towards the reinforcement of responsibility and self-understanding, employing the general counselling orientation of building on strengths realistically whilst coping with self-defeating behaviours. Fellow participants are employed as agents for development by:

●   acting as evaluators of planned decisions and of the reasons for success and failure in implementing them;

●   taking a helping role with a friend;

●   engaging in setting targets with a partner or small group, contributing to specifying the steps necessary to its attainment, and making an agreed, clearly defined contribution to reaching it.

The structure of group counselling

This description of the type of interaction which is typical of purposeful group counselling must be supplemented by a broad structure. Obviously it will have to be modified for particular purposes in specific settings, but it should provide a sense of progression and purpose. Four stages can be detected:

1. Creating a climate of safety by clarifying the ground rules that will operate, thereby encouraging honest communication.

2. Making clear the goals of the group counselling through negotiation with students.

3. The major work phase.

4. Ending the group in a way which ensures as far as possible that students continue to apply and extend the activities or skills. This may include follow-up meetings for structuring this – say four weeks later, and then six to eight weeks after the first follow-up.

The first stage is about giving the group a sense of identity and establishing trust. This is not easy if members are gaining identity through opposition, tend to distrust adults and are vulnerable to fears of being treated as deviants. The latter will be stimulated if the group leader initially emphasises problems and deficits, and not opportunity for achievement and success. Adolescents struggle to preserve face with their peers and activities which bring this into question will be rejected. It is easy to talk about establishing trust, but it is something that has to be won through the group counsellor's demonstration of competence, and evidence that the initial activities are beneficial. Trust depends on delivering the goods.

In the main stages the group should function to produce ideas for achieving the agreed goals. They can be then tried out indirectly through role play, simulation, standpoint-taking and problem-solving exercises. Direct action occurs by applying what has been learned in classroom, peer group or home. In 1974 I argued that the counselling group should be a base from which students venture to experiment with new styles of coping and mastery, returning to assess the results, and develop the next steps. *Adventures in coping* is no bad name for this process of formulating strategies, working on analysis of successes and failures, learning from mistakes and rectifying errors of judgement. Leadership will be discussed in a later section, but here we should note that leadership and counselling roles are diffused among peers, tutors and others who come into the group as helpers. This is stimulated by small group work and the emphasis on developing helping relationships between group members. It is not haphazard, however, for the pastoral head retains oversight, devoting considerable energy to planning and co-ordinating the efforts.

There will be a flow of activity and communication both outwards and inward across the boundary of the counselling group. The outward flow will be an integral part of the major task of the group when action research projects form its core. In other instances it will consist of small group activities planned within the group but implemented outside it. Feedback about the degree of success is a key element in input. Even more useful will be ideas for new developments and enhancing the efficiency of group participants. The counselling group is not, and should not be, a closed group. It should be dynamically responding to information and support coming from outside it as tasks are undertaken.

Ending the group

The first session is especially crucial because it creates the climate which facilitates achievement of goals. The sense of purpose and shared endeavour provides the foundation for later action. But the last one or two sessions are equally important for preparing participants to maintain or pursue extensions of what has been done in the absence of the group. Bolstering of the sense that much has been learned and achieved is essential for continued progress. Small group discussion is harnessed to allow the working out of future steps. Reporting back of these plans to the whole group follows, in which ideas are subjected to critical, yet sympathetic, scrutiny. It will be necessary to specify exactly what is to be done in the next four to six weeks, after which the group will be reinstated to consider further developments. This final stage holds its own challenges. Difficulties must be anticipated and coping measures verbalised. The theme is, 'How will you react if . . .', or 'What will you do when . . .?'. Avoidance of this could undermine the good achieved. Intelligent and honest anticipation of difficulties is the best safeguard against regression to earlier ways of behaving.

Leadership style in group counselling

The question must be, 'Which aspects of leadership style contribute to effective group counselling?' We have to be clear that it is impossible to give a recipe for success. The personality of the leader, the needs of group members, the purposes of the group and the skills and methods available to the leader all contribute to what will be a productive style. This is far from unique. Reddin's (1970) warning to management about the normative fallacy has to be kept in mind. This unhelpfully assumes that there is one 'right' leadership style which will cover all situations. Flexibility of style is essential to meet the differences of objectives and goals between groups. As with individual counselling, one may have to change style as the group progresses, moving from initial acceptance to overt challenge as the group coheres, and becomes involved in the task. These adaptations are based on the skills of reading signals given by members and responding with precision, for example, judging when to concentrate on the task or when to use the social-emotional leadership skills of conveying appreciation of feelings, reducing tensions between members of sub-groups. The leader's skills of standpoint-taking will be called into play, but this is not unique to group counselling. A teacher who has the ability to create a positive climate for learning constantly intervenes in this way in the classroom.

The group leader's role certainly is not passive. He or she will maintain vigilance for role-sending and other potentially destructive mechanisms. The essential of role-sending lies in signalling expectations to a group member that she or he is expected to behave in a particular kind of way: it is pressure to occupy a particular role which holds the individual in it. A group may create a scapegoat who is the recipient of blame for what is at least partly the fault of those who blame him or her. A more positive (at least ostensibly) form of role-sending occurs when an articulate member of the group is persuaded that she or he can provide solutions to others' problems. This allows group members to avoid shouldering responsibility for their own development. Attention is drawn to what is happening; recipient and senders being encouraged to look critically at their behaviours. They are then asked to consider the costs of such actions and replace them.

Traditional defences against maturely facing the facts of one's self-deception and reluctance to discard self-defeating behaviours operate as strongly in counselling groups as in real life. Leaders help individuals become more alert to them. Actions and statements are justified in retrospect, acquiring logical status or respectable motivation, allowing one to present a comfortable façade to the world. We may attribute to others qualities of temperament or motivation that we cannot accept in ourselves. Denial of our own aggression, or inhibition about expression of it, makes us over-sensitive to it in others, perhaps convincing us that they harbour hostility towards us, although there is no evidence to support these perceptions. 'Kicking the cat' or diversion of anger from the cause of it to someone who is weaker or less threatening also appears in work with adolescent groups. The leader, however, does not wander into illicit interpretations of personality, instead the emphasis is on the consequences for the individual displaying the behaviours, and on behaving more constructively. Note too, that members assess their own behaviours, and do not attribute motives and causes to others. Such pseudo-therapeutic tendencies may either come dangerously near to reinforcing omnipotent adolescent fantasies, or reduce the counselling situation to triviality.

The task therefore is to aid students to make sense of group interaction. Provided that the cautions outlined in the preceding paragraphs are taken seriously, it is possible to accept the conclusion arrived at by Lieberman *et al* (1973) that attribution of meaning and the expression of caring are indispensable conditions for successful group caring. Attribution of meaning does not mean indulging in loose speculation on the motives of other group members and thereby boosting one's sense of superiority. It means that individuals consider their own behaviour and assess its impact on others. Meaning is attached to the less tangible. The development of an implicit agreement, and the expectations of others held by the individual, or her or his predictions about the outcome of activities provide examples.

Bearing in mind adolescents' healthy detestation of even benevolent paternalism or maternalism which undermines their freedom for initiative, caring is best expressed through evidence of the pastoral head's careful preparation for each session. Caring is shown when the group leader structures sessions, providing appropriate materials and activities. It is also conveyed through anticipation of difficulties or anxiety-provoking reactions from others. This is balanced by positive, yet carefully judged appreciation of students' attempts at mastery; indiscriminate praise undermines confidence. This is no more than applying the skills of good classroom teaching to personal development.

A straightforward way of looking at leadership in group counselling is to ask whether the group is meeting members' needs for recognition, achievement and responsibility, producing a sense of progress. This does not do away with the need to evaluate the conflicting expectations of different groups within the school about the purposes of the counselling group. Other students, tutors or subject teachers will have different, possibly conflicting, perceptions of what the group is about. The leader will have to evaluate them, negotiating or correcting them, whilst maintaining credibility with students. Explanation of the problem to group members normally produces a mature response.

Group dynamics

Students in years ten to 13 feel self-consciously aware that adults and peers are judging them, and as a consequence, become preoccupied with the impression they make in group settings. There is a strong case for group counselling which encourages students critically to examine the mechanisms and dynamics of group functioning. This is not an argument for self-indulgent exploration of feelings, or for such activities as trust walks which cause embarrassment and arouse scepticism in this age group. The latter are inappropriate because they obscure the importance and complexity of trust. Not only is trust *partially* specific to situations and individuals – a feature held in common with honesty and leadership – but there are developmental factors which call for caution. Struggles for autonomy are liable to be accompanied by guilt or anxiety. The 16- to 18-year-old has some of the characteristics of the hedgehog; a prickly back and a soft under-belly. They are vulnerable and defensive. There is deep-seated anxiety about whom to trust, coupled with suspicion of the intent of others. Some may still be relying on opposition as a means of gaining identity. This should steer us away from forays into emotions, but also remind us that counselling is about thoughtful exploration of issues.

A first step could be for the group members to assess the role they prefer to take up in a particular group to which they belong. Note the assumption that although there may be similarities between behaviours in different groups, there may also be variations. Skills, confidence or status lead individuals to take up different roles in different groups. We explore the satisfactions offered by the role or the stresses emanating from it, assessing the reasons for its occupancy. A simple activity such as listing the roles that could either be allocated or taken up in a group provokes searching questions. Students become absorbed in finding answers meaningful to them to 'Why does the "resident cynic" take that role?', or 'What are the functions of the clown? Are they as obvious as they seem?' Sensitive standpoint-taking is often displayed in answering, 'How does a scapegoat acquire this position in a group, and what part does this type of blame-pinning play in group interaction?'

Students may not have acquired the skill of 'reading' their position in a group. They rely on vague impressions and self-deceptive assumptions, and are defensive in their conceptions of the reasons for it. Simple adaptations of Bales' (1970) 3D analysis of group interaction have stimulated important learning. First, the power dimension in the particular group is scanned, students assessing whether, and in what ways, they veer towards dominance and submission. (Later, they may well turn their attention to the value connotations of these terms. Is it 'good' to be dominant and 'bad' to be submissive? Discussion often moves on to the nature of power in a group.) Attention then focuses on the general tenor of others' reactions to them. As they interact, do they evoke hostility, indifference or positive feelings? Can trigger situations associated with strong feelings be identified? It is helpful to ask participants to contrast two groups; the second being one where they experience different reactions from their fellows. Third, the contribution they make to achieving the goals and tasks of that group is examined. Their adherence to, or rejection of, the values of the group both overtly or at a hidden level are discussed. Students are usually alert to the interactions between power, attraction and allegiance.

Positions can be plotted on a diagram which has three axes. (The third axis is shown as a diagonal line.) Deepening of understanding occurs through speculation about the implications of occupying a particular position, eg someone who is dominant, arouses negative responses in others, and strongly adheres to the norms of that group. He or she faces certain problems, but they also create difficulty for others. Useful insights are gained, and interactional problems are made amenable to analysis. Individuals learn about themselves without risky self-revelations.

Students over-concentrate on personality and underplay the skills demanded by the situation in their views of leadership. Yet the nature of the leadership tasks and the possession of requisite skills is at least as important as personality. Hersey and Blanchard (1977) and Reddin (1970) are amongst those who in management studies stress the inter-relation of the followers' characteristics, the nature and demands of the situation, and the qualities and skills of the leader. Followers are not the hapless creatures of an immutable social matrix: bargaining and exchange are at work. Hollander (1964) takes a social influence approach. As a group leader successfully fulfils the expectations of her or his followers a stock of 'idiosyncratic credits' is gained. The leader has achieved the credibility necessary for innovation and deviation from existing expectations. Successful innovation enhances credibility, increasing the stock of credits. Continuous failure would lead to exhaustion of the credits, and eventual replacement of the leader.

Students in the later years are fascinated by their growing alertness to such processes. Awareness of the existence of task orientation and social-emotional aspects of leadership arouses debate; sometimes creating new recognition of pervasive stereotypes or crude dichotomies in their judgements. A simple question, 'Do men and women have different styles of leadership?' reveals gender stereotyping. This could be followed by investigation of the possibility that females have more developed interpersonal skills and the maturity to be less defensive and aggressive in leadership roles. 'Is there any evidence that females are less concerned with high performance and achievement than males?' is a question which stimulates intense consideration.

The counsellor will raise the distinction by suggesting that task leadership consists of consideration, the desire for integration of the work group or whatever, and the ability to pour oil on troubled waters. The task leader may not be abrasive through personality or intent, but still creates friction by having to over-ride objections and push for task completion. Integrity requires the counsellor to point out that the sharp separation of the two orientations is for expository purposes only. Both are needed. The question is, 'How do we determine which mix of the two is productive in a particular situation?'. Members of the group sometimes wryly admit that they are more inclined to pour petrol on stormy waters and set fire to it.

A simple activity for use in group counselling is given below. In the post-activity discussion participants should be encouraged to relate discussion to their future careers or education.

Leadership and the situation

1 Why should we think about leadership?

a In our careers and even our hobbies we will be asked to demonstrate the skills of leadership. Leadership is not just a matter of personality: people are leaders in some situations and not in others. It is sensible to think about our skills of leadership as we prepare for our futures.

b There is *Task leadership* and *Social-emotional leadership*. Task leaders are good at organising and planning, getting the job done. But they can be abrasive, upsetting other people, and insensitive to the feelings of others. The social-emotional leader restores good feelings, keeps the group together, and pours oil on troubled waters. We need both skills of leadership, but certain situations demand very different skills from leaders.

2 Activity one:

a List the groups and situations in which you seem to act as a leader and those in which you tend to be a follower.

b Then discuss with a friend the reasons for the differences. This will act as a 'warm-up' for the next activity.

3 Activity two:

a Leaders have to meet the expectations of those who follow them: they have to deliver the goods. We should see leadership as a bargaining process in which the leader receives benefits such as admiration and deference in return for meeting the wishes and needs of his or her followers.

b In each of the situations below list, as shown, the skills of the leader and the expectations of those he or she leads. Work in groups of four.

Situation one
An Outward Bound mountain expedition. Fog has fallen suddenly – in this locality the leader knows it is slow to disperse. One member of the party has had a serious, although not fatal, accident, whilst another has become hysterical. There are eight members of the party.

The skills of leadership needed in this situation	The expectations held by members of the party about the leader

Situation two
A manager of a large factory faces the prospect of an imminent strike due to the introduction of new conditions of work. It is imperative that the strike and consequent 'shut down' are avoided as this would be very costly. The workers are extremely angry and will not wait for official union action.

The skills of leadership needed in this situation	The expectations held by the workers in this situation about the manager

Situation three
A surgeon is leading a team of fellow doctors and nurses in a new and previously untried dangerous operation. The surgeon is committed to the operation and sure it is a medical advance. The team has been involved in considerable research, but there has been a great deal of cricitism of the operation which much medical opinion considers to be premature and based on inadequate findings. The team are therefore uncertain and extremely anxious. These feelings are heightened by the fact that the availability of future funds will depend on the result of the operation.

The skills of leadership needed in this situation	The expectations held by The team about the surgeon

4 Activity three:

Now look at your future career or intended sphere of work and discuss:

a what decisions you are likely to make;

b when and where the skills of leadership will be demanded of you.

Another structured assessment activity which is very productive if the group leader raises questions is now given. Students are asked to assess two people who are members of a group to which the student belongs or with whom she or he works. *The names are not to be revealed.* They are asked to select one person who is positive and well integrated into the group, and another who seems negative and marginal. They then:

1. List each individual's relevant characteristics using as a stimulus the points below which are somewhat loosely related to Bales' (1950) Interaction Process Analysis.

   - supports or raises the confidence of others;
   - deals with tensions and/or demands constructively;
   - shows understanding of others' standpoints;
   - asks for others' ideas;
   - withdraws frequently from interaction;
   - evaluates ideas fairly;
   - initiates new activities;
   - deflates others;
   - raises objections habitually.

2. Then they are asked to imagine that the positive person has left the group. They discuss the changes in interaction that would occur with a partner.

3. Next, they remove in imagination the negative person. (The positive individual is restored to the group.) How would interaction change? Again, this is done with a partner.

4. The session ends with the whole group sharing their findings and working out their implications. The skill of the counsellor is to formulate an initial question which orientates without being directive.

Schools have become acutely sensitive to transactions across their boundaries with the larger audience of parents and neighbourhood. Such transactions, inwards and outwards, are equally crucial in shaping the identity of members of adolescent groups, contributing to the stability and success of the group. Investigation and comparison of the boundary transactions of friendship, sporting and learning groups provides a framework for the understanding of image creation, conflict and co-operation. To compare what happens when membership of the group is voluntary or compulsory adds further enlightenment.

Sub-groups within a larger group can be both powerful and constraining. If, in the coeducational setting, there were indications that girls were being pushed into marginal positions in learning and leadership situations, an essential early step would be specification of the content and significance of the transactions between sub-groups of boys and girls. If there is evidence that the sense of membership of such sub-groups is accompanied by behaviours detrimental to learning and equality of opportunity, there is a very real and immediate problem to be tackled. The counselling group then should form the base for guided observation of verbal behaviours and sub-group interaction which maintain or justify the situation. Then in Lewin's (1947) terms, the group works out a step-by-step plan for unfreezing habitual, probably unthinking, exchanges between the sub-groups. The group members act as models for the new patterns of behaviour, finding support and sharpening their tactics within the counselling sessions. Part of the task of the counselling group is to describe what is happening clearly enough to reveal possibilities for change.

There is much more to be discovered in considering boundary transactions. What motive and intent is attributed to those whose actions impinge on the group? How valid are the judgements of this? It is good preparation for the future for students to tease out the course of events that occurs when a group comes into conflict with another. They may be less likely to be carried along unprotestingly by the course of events. Among the possibilities they discover could be a sharper reaction to deviations from the group norms, closer surveillance of boundary transactions, and more stringent definition of the nature and requirements of membership. Participants may recognise that threat, when severe and prolonged, leads to dependence upon directive leadership. Awareness of such possibilities seems a useful life skill.

Group counselling profitably encourages individuals to study the groups to which they belong. What do they know of a particular group's origin and history? Even the simple question, 'What makes you stay in the group?' initiates a series of questions. How did the sense of cohesion develop, and is it likely to be maintained in the future? Cohesion seems to be a product of the prestige of belonging to the group, its history of success, and the presence of rewards for its members.

Expectations operate within a group and should be scrutinised critically. We have already seen that leadership is concerned with the management of conflicting demands expressed as expectations. They are beliefs about what are proper attitudes and behaviours for the occupant of a certain position in a group. Students are in danger of becoming victims of group expectations when they view them as immutable and incapable of challenge. Close examination of the source, nature and legitimacy of the expectations operating in a group facilitates mature relationships within it.

Cohesion within a group carries dangers. It can place blinkers on students by encouraging unthinking endorsement of the group's reaction to individuals and situations. Such swamping of individual differences and reservations by the group view may lead to habitual prejudgements of experience to which individuals resolutely cling, rejecting criticism and alternative viewpoints. Students are well served when the counsellor brings such possibilities to the forefront. Why? The process of mutual persuasion and reinforcement also means that an initially strong position becomes more extreme, reducing individuals' responsibility for their actions. Consensus becomes so strong that contradictory information is ignored and reality over-simplified, perhaps grossly distorted. Apparently admirable consensus then interferes with effective decision making and problem solving. Myers (1982) provides an excellent account of this process.

Students can be asked to work out methods of preventing 'group think' trapping individuals in limited or risky ways of behaving. It may also inhibit action and lead to undue caution. Remedies include:

- ensuring that group members' values, attitudes, abilities and knowledge are sufficiently diverse to stimulate debate and provoke challenge of the leader's viewpoints;

- inclusion of partner and small group work where members can process issues more independently;

- including the role of devil's advocate as part of decision making;

- allowing individuals to write down their personal viewpoints on large sheets of paper, pinning them up for consideration;

- the use of 'brainstorming' to encourage questioning;

- after a decision is made, giving individuals time to evaluate it before implementation.

Associated with this consideration of mutual influence would be analysis of social anxieties, especially audience anxiety as described by Buss

(1980). From the standpoint of developmental counselling, fear of the limelight, loss of face, anxiety about creating adverse impressions in authority figures, reactions to praise or negative judgements from others provide topics for group work provided that the counsellor avoids giving patronising or superficial recipes for action. She or he must be able to accept that the adolescent may oscillate between cynical rejection of ideas and equally impetuous endorsement of them.

Problem solving in group counselling

Group counselling is a series of productive encounters with problems of adjustment and development; institutional as much as individual. The former will be concerned with the contributions that students make to the creation and maintenance of positive discipline and to the school as a caring community. The individual itself falls into two parts. First, increasing students' understanding of the principles and forces involved in productive group counselling where it is part of providing the 16–19 age group with the skills of creative man or woman management as a foundation for later professional development. (Much has been covered relevant to this earlier in this chapter. Examining judgements, perceptions, attribution of intent and methods of managing tension and anxiety are part of preparation for the future.) Second, the group can provide a setting for the clarification and resolution of personal problems.

A sense of balance has to be maintained about problem solving in group counselling. There is always the possibility that students are working within a group setting, but not working as a group. Enthusiasts give the impression that group problem solving is necessarily more effective than individual problem solving. That is an over-statement. It is not difficult to conceive the possibility that one individual solves the problem, whilst the others have done and learned little. The question therefore is with what type of task, and under what conditions is group problem solving superior? I have found this question has made a good theme for an initial meeting, creating the climate for effective co-operation.

Group problem solving requires a climate where individuals feel their contribution will be respected, and that evaluation of ideas although rigorous, will be free from bias. If, however, as Janis (1972) argues in his discussion of group pressures towards uniformity, the individual feels that forwarding an opinion or advancing a proposal for action, serves no useful purpose, then group problem solving is more illusion than reality. Students may pay more attention to the source of the message than its content: in group counselling and problem-solving the counsellor has to intervene when the validity of information and ideas is being assessed largely on the credibility of the source.

One condition is that group members should have produced the problem because it is relevant to them currently or seen as significant in their future work. Parents provide very useful material from their professions as a basis for problem solving. The researcher in industry, bankers, doctors and nurses, lawyers, and supervisors are amongt those who can present the counselling group with meaningful problems which not only sharpen skills but deepen personal awareness. One group had to face bluntly their previously unacknowledged prejudice against the aged when deciding what should be done for or with an 80-year-old with pneumonia who could be treated, but was likely to be sent out of hospital confused and incontinent. Commitment to group problem solving is increased if the group sessions are preceded by a period where potential members research the problems they wish to consider, and then negotiate with the leader the content of the sessions.

In negotiating the content the points made by Shaw (1981) are illuminating. He suggests that group problem solving is more efficient than individual when the task demands the application of complex knowledge and needs to be viewed from a number of perspectives. It is more productive when the solution entails a number of steps that have to be undertaken in a precise order. Group members then call attention to deviation from the path which might go unrecognised by the person working alone. Certainly, the probability of recognising less obvious complications is increased, and difficulties are anticipated. Against this can be set the time needed for orientation of the group to the task – not so important if the procedures outlined at the end of the previous paragraph had been adopted – and the likelihood that minor conflicts and misperceptions have to be dealt with before abilities and energies are harnessed in search of a solution.

The leader must not lose sight of the fact that alongside the overt problem solving runs the task of increasing participants' insight into their attitudes and behaviour. A sharp eye is needed for the tendency to withhold useful information or only part with it reluctantly. Acting as a passenger carried by others' efforts, or the tendency to wait until the task is well advanced and then make destructive comments, provide obvious examples. Public confrontation is not necessarily the best way of dealing with difficulties. Group counselling may provide material for individual counselling; the interchange between the two settings being mutually reinforcing.

Observation of the forms co-operation and competition take in group interaction cannot be neglected. Related to this is consideration of the ways in which the presence of others influenced the individual's performance. Was it, for example, a spur to achievement or did it have a deadening impact, creating an inhibiting self-consciousness? Vulnerability to observation is yet another factor leading to increased adherence to the majority viewpoint and refusal to consider minority ideas.

In discussion of what happens in groups in the world outside school or college the phenomenon of diffusion of responsibility in highly emotive group situations is a worthwhile topic. If responsibility can be placed on others, actions can be committed which would be rejected by the person alone. Examination of the mechanisms which contribute to this loss of personal responsibility is a worthwhile pursuit. Rhythmic chanting and movement – a marked feature of such group activities – seems to function temporarily to suspend individual identity, submerging the individual in the group's purposes. Understanding of this *may* help the student to withdraw in the early stages of the process. Creating alertness to it, and helping adolescents to work out tactics for interruption of the pattern of behaviour by withdrawal without loss of face is good developmental work. Even better is exploration of why, despite acquiring awareness of such group dynamics, people still succumb to group pressures in the real situation.

Risk is a key value in some groups. The characteristics of those attracted to such a group, the situations in which high risk is seen as legitimate, and where risky behaviour is seen as appropriate, provide a starting point for group discussion. Subsidiary topics include speculation on how a self-picture is developed in which high risk is significant. What makes people admire the risk taker, and what are the distinctions between psychological and physical risks? Small group discussion on what attracts someone to be a paratrooper, the risks inherent in different audience and interpersonal situations can be summarised on large sheets of paper, displayed and debated by the whole group. Those producing the ideas will be committed to them, and more ready to defend them.

Personal guidance in groups

The form of group counselling advocated has utility for experimentation and innovation within the pastoral system. The theme that counselling is a joint enterprise between teachers and their students is given reality in this approach. We have also seen that it can be a tool for deepening students' understanding of group interaction and dynamics, giving them the confidence and skill to function competently in group situations, also preparing them for later education and careers. It can also be a means of economically helping a carefully selected group of students overcome attitudinal, behavioural and relationship problems. Aggressive behaviours; lack of, or self-defeating forms of assertiveness; absenteeism; bullying; problems of isolation; and inadequacies of learning and study skills respond to structured group counselling. The energy and commitment so admirably displayed in supporting individuals would yield greater results if invested in group counselling.

As a team, pastoral heads should stand back and assess the problems that face them. The group counselling planned in response to the findings should be conceived in positive terms as opportunities to acquire skills. Any tinge of inferiority or deviance would alienate students and foredoom the effort to futility. Building helping relations between groups of members will be a priority, thus ensuring that support is available outside the group.

No prolonged discussion is necessary, as essential techniques have been laid out in preceding chapters. The structure is that outlined in this chapter, making the objectives and the number of sessions clear. Behavioural techniques can be drawn on from Chapter Three. In applying them the group should be broken down into small groups of three or four, who after working on activities engage in discussion with the other members. Special emphasis should be given to Bandura's (1969) observational learning, the carefully introduced use of role play and problem solving. Initially, in these activities the structure must direct interaction towards new ways of behaving. Even a very simple tape recording illustrating someone coping successfully with teasing, or rejecting without loss of face the invitation to undertake an illicit activity, triggers off intense discussion and willingness to consider revision of current behaviours. The group leader, of course, stimulates this by well-timed remarks and questions. Passive imitation is not being advocated: students are encouraged to criticise and evaluate the suggested actions and produce their own version of mastery behaviours. The need for training in anticipation of difficulties, inoculation against letting them force the individual into retreatism, and for taking a 'one-step-at-a-time' approach with explicit description of what is to be done at each step should not be neglected.

Pastoral heads may feel that shortage of time makes production of bespoke materials for these counselling groups an intolerable burden. That is to handicap themselves by taking the somewhat omnipotent position that they are the only people in the school capable of it. It may be an example of the secondary school tendency to squash the initiative shown by pupils in the primary school. Students interested in drama in years ten and 11 have the ability, and often the willingness, to produce short audiotapes and plan useful simulations. If the school ethos is one which both stresses, and actually respects, students' manifestations of responsibility, they will come into the groups and act as role models and operate as aides to the group leader.

The next issue is that of building meaningful transactions across the boundary of the counselling group with the realities of classroom and peer group. The methods are similar to those I employed in a very recent two-term course of training in counselling skills for school nurses and youth workers. A weekly package of work-based activities ensured that theory and techniques were applied. Not only did this maintain continuity, preventing the group experience from being divorced from everyday work, providing material for further processing and development in the group, but it built a sense of ownership and pride in people who were uncertain of their capacity to counsel. This is also the case with adolescents. When students are encouraged to take in a planned way – with appreciation of potential hazards – the ideas and skills promoted within the counselling group into the reality of everyday life, commitment is fostered. They should be trained to set and prepare assignments to be undertaken between group sessions. Also who better than older students, who have a lively appreciation of the difficulties that will be met, to help in that preparation? Considered 'pairing up' of group participants to set self-observation tasks, or applying what has been learned in a relationship of mutual support allows students to coach one another. If deemed helpful, this can be structured into explicit contracts to provide reciprocal help.

It is very easy to underestimate the efficacy of simple activities which function as compensation for inadequacies in social learning. Students benefit from pondering on the relative merits of two proposed reactions to a situation. Presentation of tape-recorded situations involving anxiety, threat or challenge can be devised which, at certain points raise questions, eg 'What would be the best thing to do now this has happened?' or 'What shouldn't he or she do?'. Adequate time for discussion has to be allowed if the session is not to founder. Activities where students choose one course of action from three or four possibilities are useful if provision is made for evaluation. Another student may act as a peer judge or devil's advocate. Group counselling recognises the importance of responsible peer evaluation as a safeguard against blind reliance on peer group pressure. As always, the group leader will be watchful for signs of students giving what they believe to be the expected or desired answers, rather than expressing a genuine opinion.

Ideas for activities can be found in *A Pastoral Programme* (1986) or in Rose and Edelson's (1987) multi-method approach. The latter book offers the practitioner interested in developing personal guidance in groups an impressive array of techniques.

Activities for year and house heads

1 Raising awareness of group interaction

1.1   Take a group to which you belong and discuss with a partner:

a Its main task or the reason for its existence.

b Who seems to do the work within the group, and who seems to avoid it, or whose membership seems to be nominal.

c The pattern of communication within it. Look at the qualities of those who seem to receive or give high amounts of communication. What are the characteristics of those who seem to be ignored?

d The relationship, if any, between communication and status in that group.

e The expectations that other members have of you. How do they influence your behaviours and perceptions? What would inhibit you from changing them?

f What elements of competition and co-operation exist within the group? Are there particular circumstances which bring them into play?

g What decisions are made by group members? What values and/ or assumptions seem to underlie them? How are they made – eg through consultation, without any general discussion, by a sub-group, etc?

h The nature of threat and sources of tension within the group, and the ways individuals cope with them.

(Obviously this exercise is somewhat superficial, but it serves to stimulate thought and awareness of processes.)

1.2   **a** With a partner list the characteristics you would observe if asked to appraise an individual in a group setting.

b Then, after sharing ideas with other pairs, assess what additional evidence you would need to check that your judgements were valid. What precautions against bias might be needed?

1.3   Awareness of the complexities of assessment is stimulated by this standpoint-taking exercise.

a *Step one*
Take the position of students and describe significant features of

classroom interaction from their point of view. Summarise them on the left-hand side of a sheet of paper.

b *Step two*
Now describe salient aspects of classroom interaction from the teacher's standpoint. Summarise on the right-hand side of the paper.

c *Step three*
Examine similarities and differences, evaluating their consequences.

1.4 In small groups make a list of the roles that could be taken up in a group, eg the clown, the earnest seeker after knowledge or the 'resident cynic'. Then with a partner select the two you would find most difficult to cope with. Discuss the reasons for this.

1.5 Work out with a partner the conditions in which group problem solving is more likely to be effective than individual problem solving. Also consider what might hamper it. Submit your ideas for evaluation by the group.

1.6 As a whole group discuss the criteria for *not* including a student in group counselling. Conversely, assess what would make it a good experience.

2 Developmental activities for the use of group counselling by year or house heads

2.1 Undertake as a team effort action research exploring ways of using group counselling as a means for stimulating innovation, and for developing and testing materials for use in tutor periods. It is best seen as a feasibility study over two or three terms involving individual experiments and research which are elements in a carefully co-ordinated plan. Regular monitoring would be essential. Students should be consulted, and their suggestions incorporated into the developmental work. This approach probably offers the best chance of breaking into sterile approaches to counselling, and making counselling a joint enterprise between students and staff.

2.2 As a team explore the skills of learning required for success in GCSE projects and assignments. Then divide into pairs to develop the content of six to eight group counselling sessions to be undertaken and applied in the first term of year ten. Possible topics include self-management and ways in which students work effectively or unproductively, locating information and efficient use of libraries, developing productive reading skills, recording and presenting information. You will need to keep in mind Kolb's cycle of:

- actual learning experience;
- examination of it;
- developing ideas and techniques for improving it;
- applying the ideas as soon as possible.

Your structure for the sessions could usefully be:

- statement of purpose;
- training and practice in the skills;
- arrangements for application and reporting back.

2.3 As a middle-management team isolate the elements of group behaviour you believe it would be useful for years 12 and 13 to consider as part of preparation for their future careers. Then set up a joint working party with students to extend and refine your findings, and also work out mutually acceptable forms of group counselling. As a joint venture, plan a unit of six sessions. After it has been carried out, decisions can be made about future developments. This approach is essential to reinforce students' responsible sense of control of their futures.

2.4 As a middle-management group explore the barriers to mature involvement of students in a group guidance. Then sketch out a plan for encouraging this, concentrating on the initial steps, ensuring their success.

2.5 Let students undertake the group decision-making exercise set out below. They are then asked to invent in groups of three or four a detailed decision-making exercise on a theme they consider relevant to their future careers and purposes. Then give it to their fellows, requesting suggestions for its improvement and for further activities.

The earthquake: a decision making exercise

The problem

1. *Instructions:*

a The objective of the exercise is to make you more aware of your decision making and the way you tackle problems in small groups.

b Work in groups of four sharing ideas and coming to a group decision about the course of action you would take.

c If there are disagreements you cannot resolve, record them.

d To get the same urgency as there would be in real life you are allowed 15 minutes only to cover this complex situation. You have no time to waste and cannot afford to make poor decisions.

2. *The situation:*

    You are a committee of four respected citizens who have been put in charge of rescue operations in a small town with a population of about 80,000, high in a mountainous region in South America. It is early winter: the severe cold has not yet occurred at nights. The town is about 50 miles from the coast.

    The town has been devastated by an earthquake: bridges, roads and the railway have been destroyed. The most optimistic estimate is that it will be 48 hours before help from outside will reach this isolated town. Air drops are very unlikely as this poor country lacks resources. The airstrip and its buildings are now rubble. Electricity is not available: there was no gas. Telephone communication is impossible, either inside or outside the town. Sewage has contaminated the water supply, whilst the hospital is scarcely able to cope with the injured already there and more arrive each hour. To add to the general misery, sporadic outbursts of looting are occurring in which tinned food and other necessities are being taken.

    Your fellow citizens rely on you for leadership. All but the small criminal minority who are exploiting the situation will follow your directions.

3. *Your task:*

    a Describe the way you would tackle the situation. Set out the steps you would take clearly.

    b It is important that you give reasons for what you do.

4. *Post-decision work:*

    a Now discuss your decision-making style, asking yourselves about the following:

    - Did you look at the implications of the information, eg the possibility of cold nights in this altitude?
    - Which aspects did you give immediate priority to and why?

- What other information would have been helpful?
- Was there a high level of risk in any of your decisions? Could you justify this?
- Were you influenced by your beliefs about how other people would view your decisions, ie your fellow citizens.
- Did you begin to rely on one member of the group to provide the answers – letting him or her take over so the others stopped trying?
- Did one of you raise objections as a blind habit, rather than as helpful evaluation of other people's ideas?
- Did you support and build on the good ideas of others?
- Did one member of the group seem to have their ideas dismissed without much consideration? Why was this?

b Now two of you will join with another pair from a different group and compare the courses of action you decided on. Look closely at both similarities and differences in your plans. Justify what you did by careful argument, but also be prepared to admit that the others may have thought more clearly about some points. Be prepared to learn from each other.

6 Counselling skills related to work with parents

The increasing power of parents

Recent legislation, coupled with the fact that schools are being forced into competition for students, has enhanced the power of parents. Wolfendale (1989) (Ed.) argues that increased parental influence may also bring greater vulnerability to political pressure. Fidler and Bowles (1989) (Eds) also call attention to the wide-ranging implications of parental choice of school coupled with the consequences of consumer orientation. This is a healthy corrective to their exclusion from school policy making. Parents have been seen as regrettable necessities who must be prevented from interfering with the proper conduct of the school. In their turn, parents responded with suspicion, which readily could be transformed into active hostility. Current emphases, however, carry potential dangers. Musgrove (1971) claimed that the authority of the specialist acted as a check on the power of the autocratic head. It provided a base from which arguments against doubtful innovation could be raised. If the expert authority of the teacher is unduly weakened by excessive adaptation to what parents and students claim are their needs, loss of direction and aimless drift could result. It is difficult to see how the conflicting statements of need from different sub-populations could be reconciled. Adaptation to the lowest common denominator or 'marketing' education as a superficially attractive product are liable to stifle imagination and creativity, contradicting the declaration that initiative and enterprise should be at the forefront of education.

Why then should we consider interaction with parents to be an essential part of counselling? Essential because, despite the reservations voiced above, understanding family roles and interaction and working with parents makes us more effective as educators. It allows us to act with greater precision in the classroom. The view of counselling offered in this book as a joint enterprise between students and staff increases the demands for responsibility by students, but also makes visible the professional skills and authority of the teacher.

In a situation where role confusion all too easily arises the boundaries to the teacher's task must be clear. There are ill-defined overlaps between parental roles and those of teachers; not least being the fact that both have to use a relationship to achieve their particular goals. Other demarcations must be clear. Employment of counselling skills does not require the teacher to conceive of himself or herself as a diluted social worker – a somewhat damp concept! It asks the teacher to work developmentally and creatively to liberate students from attitudes and behaviours that handicap them. There is no suggestion that the teacher can, or ought to, change families. The most that can be done is to help students react to adverse family situations in less costly ways to themselves and others, and encourage parents to co-operate with the school. The teacher can empathise with the student enmeshed in unhelpful family networks of communication and habitual patterns of interaction, facilitating the student's understanding, and judicially supporting her or his attempts at coping. More importantly, the main thrust of the endeavour is to help parents use the resources and expertise of the school. As this occurs we should work to deepen their understanding of modern teaching methods, appreciating the demands these make on students. We should sharpen their perceptions of education as the means for acquiring the styles of thought and problem solving that allow students to cope with change in all aspects of life. In an age of disjunctions from the past and increasing unpredictability of the future, we must build with parents the school as a community giving young people self-respect rooted in consideration for others, and the ability to maintain responsible self-direction when faced by doubt and contradiction. We need counselling skills to convey our ideals as a profession for education to those who find difficulty in comprehending our vision.

A framework for assessing family interaction

The exposition which follows falls into two parts. A general discussion alerts the reader to broader elements which have to be kept in mind and help one read the situation accurately. Precise questions are then raised which allow tutor or pastoral head to perceive what *may* be significant in a *particular* situation. Earlier, we saw the importance of questioning the implicit theories of personality which underlie our judgements of others. The framework defends us against the danger of imposing unquestioned assumptions about the causal links between a student's behaviour in school and events within the family. Let us remind ourselves of the importance of standpoint-taking – without it, counselling will be about what we believe the problem ought to be, rather that what it *is*. We have to identify the foci for misunderstanding, and critically, discrepancies between what parent and offspring claim they do, and what actually occurs.

Guilt is uppermost in many parents' reactions to their children's problems or failure in school: their first remark is 'Tell me, where did I go wrong?' This invitation to allocate blame could lead one into a fruitless search for causality, diverting attention away from coping in the here and now. Anything dynamic from the past will be found in current difficulties without searching for it. Earlier, we gave due regard to the adolescent's difficulties, but the tensions experienced by parents are as great. Parents feel trapped in a web of contrary injunctions. They feel damned if they act, and damned if they draw back from action. On the one hand, they may feel urged to respect their child's need for independence and give him or her autonomy, but they are also simultaneously reminded of the real danger of drugs, illicit sex and the consequences of young people's desire for excitement and thrills. Therefore they are expected to control and constrain.

Listening to the clamour of specious advice given to parents, one wonders why they do not retreat to schizophrenia. At least teachers with counselling skills will listen and find out what the problem actually is, rather than abortively address their version of what it ought to be. Let us take seriously the possibility that we underestimate parents' hurt and distress. I meet some who feel diminished or rejected by the 'cognitive conceit' of their son or daughter. They sometimes feel used and disregarded by the son or daughter who views the home as a downtown hotel, adopting a patronising attitude to the proprietors. It would therefore be folly to concentrate on the standpoint of the adolescent alone. The standpoints of all concerned must be understood and seen as valid data in counselling. Somehow, it is easy to see the student as reacting to the family situation, when in fact he or she initiated the problem and actively maintains it. By the time a problem reaches the tutor or pastoral head mutual exasperation may be so high that only careful disentangling of conflicting viewpoints will defuse it.

Communication, both in face to face interaction and in the letters and messages which go from school to home, is easily misunderstood by parents who themselves experienced failure at school. They may hold a sense of resentful inferiority which easily becomes antagonism. I hold the fanciful notion that there exists in certain schools the equivalent of a Dickensian Clerk to the Court of Chancery whose role in life is to produce school communications which seem designed to confuse or alienate defensive parents.

Sensitive recognition of parents' sense of inadequacy – even if masked by aggression – will prevent them leaving meetings in which teachers have invested thought and energy feeling they were denied the opportunity to ask the questions they wished to ask. Worse, they go away feeling they have been given a placebo to quiet them or that words were put in their mouths. Their anger simmers and their spleen is vented with neighbours and friends contributing to hostile mythologies about the school in the neighbourhood. A ploy which raises awareness is to ask a group of teachers to explore their feelings when they go as a parent to a meeting at their child's school.

The task therefore is for both sides to discard suspicion and anxiety, engaging in a long-term enterprise for the well-being of the student. It will be facilitated if the tutor stays with her or his form for at least several years, providing the parent with a stable point of reference. As we interact we should never lose sight of the fact that socialisation within the family creates an orientation through which students view the world. Thankfully, it usually tends to be positive, but at the *negative extreme* students may have been given a constraining view of school; the dichotomy of *us* against *them* (the exploiters) may be shaping the student's interpretation of the motives behind teacher behaviours. At one extreme students' responses may be dominated by threat or the imperative of 'get them before they get you'. At the other, they will be shaped by expectations of support and rewarding interaction. If tutors are not to reinforce negative perceptions, they must be alert to the salient features of the family climate which shapes the student's interpretation of the world. It may be pessimistic, optimistic, paranoid, aggressive or passive. It may be strongly evident or barely discernible, but it will be there and should be taken into account. Only then can they act with precision.

Rigid stereotypes have to be discarded. We have witnessed a startling increase in the number of one parent families – mainly mothers alone. This may be a cause for concern, but a one parent family is not necessarily a more adverse environment for child rearing than a two parent one. The most destructive environment occurs when, over a long period, parents locked in conflict create gross tensions as they manipulate the children as pawns in their battles. Emotional blackmail and guilt are commonplace; damagingly, the children transfer them to extra-familial relationships. Divorce or separation probably bring relief to the children, although the reverberations continue for years in some cases.

One parent families are successful to the degree that the parent is able to carry out the duties traditionally divided between two parents. Issues of control and organisation frequently seem to be the locus of tension in a one parent family. Yet two parent families are not immune from them. The threat 'Wait until your father comes home!' may well be hollow. Inconsistencies in demands and control methods allow students to play off one parent against the other. Fatigue and financial worries plague both, although the parent alone may lack the emotional support given by a partner, and may be especially vulnerable to the impact of unemployment and illness. Two parent families may present frustration for the mother. Women are entitled to a career. There will be no real equality of opportunity until the husband is as prepared to move to foster his wife's career as she has been in the past. Perhaps these brief remarks suffice to show that neither family type has inherent superiority, nor has either a monopoly of problems.

It is difficult to decide if we are moving towards a classless society. Whatever the reality, broad concepts of middle or working class figure prominently in discussion of educational success. Sometimes the distinction is between an underclass of 'roughs' and a virtuous group of 'respectables'. Our judgements and expectations could be distorted by unquestioning reliance on some stereotype of alleged middle class values we assume to be in concord with the school's objectives. Conversely, the label 'working class' may cause us to allocate unwarranted and exaggerated importance to remarks which seem to indicate antipathy towards education, but which in fact have little significance for the parent. Hargreaves *et al* (1975) point out that the teacher who provokes hostility and difficult behaviour in a student blames the family background, casting responsibility for change solely on the student. This then renders him or her powerless, denying the possibility that changed behaviour on her or his part would call out more positive behaviours from the student and parent. Reliance upon unexamined and unchallenged stereotypes of the relationship of family background to school achievement and behaviour impede co-operation.

Neither is neighbourhood a certain guide to attitudes toward authority and performance in school. The range of differences between families in a street condemned as 'delinquent' or 'anti-social' may well be amazing when investigated without pre-categorisation. We are now sensitive about allocation of reputations to individuals, but the reputation of area or street may well lead to immediate imposition of uniform expectations on what in reality is highly varied.

A simple framework which usefully can be held in mind when discussing problems is given below. It is not intended as a checklist, but as a device for raising the awareness of tutors, and a brief discussion which hints at themes to which the helper must be sensitive.

1. *Role* In a two parent family what elements of their respective roles are salient for the parents? Is there evidence that the male sees his role as primarily anchored in the occupational world, and his interaction with the family is then peripheral and seemingly of minor importance? Decision making by the family may be joint or strictly demarcated.

Does the male tend to leave key decisions about school to his partner, absolving himself of responsibility when things go awry? There is an important distinction between socially approved absence such as that of the organisationally committed executive or long distance lorry driver and that carrying social stigma.

2. *Power and decision making* Where does the power lie? This is not always obvious. Mothers make contact with the school, appearing to take responsibility for the student's performance in school. They may gain skill and confidence in putting across their viewpoints. If, however, in an interview with both parents, I note that the mother waits for a scarcely detectable signal from her partner before proceeding – perhaps an almost imperceptible nod of the head or eye contact – then I suspect the near silent one of controlling the interview. Power probably lies with him. Skill will be needed to bring him into the open and encourage him to declare his position. When he does speak, I signal understanding and invite a further comment. It is also useful to look at him immediately at the end of a statement showing that a direct response will be welcome. The counselling skill is that of interrupting habitual patterns of behaviour without making an issue of it.

3. *Discipline and order* The two are related but not identical. It is sensible to ask if the family provides the adolescent with a predictable, orderly environment. This is not restricted to any particular class or 'type'. Some well-off bohemian families exist in a continuous state of confusion and flux leaving the adolescent bereft of bearings. He or she then learns to hedge his or her bets, manipulate, not take adult statements seriously or respond with anxiety. Work with such students aims at enabling them to create their own order.

   Discipline within the family can over-rely on positional controls. Queries about the reasons for carrying out instructions may be met with an imperative, 'Because I say so, I'm your father!'. Sometimes necessary, but parental over-reliance on such injunctions inhibits the growth of moral reasoning. When extreme, compliance is resentful, and rebellion likely. Personal controls call on the student's self-respect and sense of responsibility, requiring standpoint-taking and assessing the consequences of behaviour. Social learning is encouraged, the resulting sensitivity to the feelings of others promoting a climate favourable to the development of altruism.

   The tutor or pastoral head aware of self-defeating practices at home, eg physical punishments or withdrawal of privileges as a reaction to academic difficulties, can alleviate the situation, even if it is only by avoiding replicating parental orientations in disciplinary encounters with the student.

4. *Structure of the family* It is obviously useful to ask if the student is one of a large family or an only child. This does not mean that family size is relevant to the problem: it may or may not be. More important than size may be the density of the family. If five or six children came in quick succession, the later ones may have been deprived of the mother's attention at critical stages without an adequate substitute being available. If problems of poverty and unemployment were also present the mother may have been stressed and exhausted, and the children pushed into undue and premature reliance on their peers outside the home.

It is possible that the child's position in the sibling group may contribute to the difficulties. There is some evidence that the first born – especially boys – may be more liable to anxiety and have a higher need for affiliation than those born later. A commonsense explanation suggests that this, *when* it does occur, is an artefact of parental insecurity and aspirations for the child. Parents are less secure with their first child, lacking a benchmark against which to measure his or her development. They may indulge in frequent comparisons with relatives' offspring, to the disadvantage of the first born. More may be invested emotionally in the first born, and he or she may become the carrier of high expectations for achievement.

Students in the middle of the family have a different experience. They may have felt caught in contradictory pressures. Perhaps attempts at emulating the older brother and sister brought rebuffs if the age gap was marked, or parental injunctions to wait until they were old enough. Reverberations from these experiences extend well into adolescence, influencing the tendency to see younger brothers or sisters as pests and invader of the student's territory – physical and psychological, eg impinging on friendships.

The youngest child is traditionally viewed as 'spoilt'. The parents' age at the birth of the youngest has significance. If the parents were in their forties, fatigue and withdrawal of attention may occur, especially if the parent is coping alone.

A cautionary note

The illustrations given above are just that. It is hoped that they provide tutors and others with insights into family interaction. It would be fallacious to assume that any of the above are automatically germane to the particular situation. A way of looking at the problem has been indicated: to see it as more heightens the risk of perceiving the problem inaccurately or constructing pseudo-causal links – truly a trivial pursuit. The possibility that a new life style for the family is developing which could change the relative importance of the factors discussed in the next section cannot be disregarded. Regional differences are present, probably because affluence and the career demands on adults for enterprise and blurring of traditional separation of work and leisure are major contributors to the new family life style. I note earlier and greater independence of young people from their parents. Parents and children appear to be living increasingly self-contained lives, quite amicably, but with reduced interaction. Physical space is shared; psychological space is increasingly demarcated. Parents and children are both absorbed in their social networks and friends, each detaching herself or himself from the world of the other. Parents often seem to have no option but to succumb to the occupational imperatives.

Aspects of communication

A vital question is, 'Does this family setting encourage the development of empathy?'. It is not only a basic skill for effective counselling, but central to the student's moral development and maintenance of civilised relationships. When family experiences foster self-respect and the parent or parents have demonstrated understanding of the student's feelings and perceptions, she or he will have optimal chances for gaining a clear and positive identity. Commonsense suggests that the child surrounded by contradictory and inconsistent messages, not only from parents to her or him, but between parents, has a shaky foundation for building a clear concept of self. Coping with ambiguity and muddled familial messages creates insecurity and also distrust because the young person is never sure whether the adult means what has been said. Tentativeness is therefore essential as a coping mechanism.

In training counsellors it has been helpful to conceive of the family as a field containing forces which underlie overt behaviours. Action is shaped by the attribution of motive and intent to each other. Part of this is the product of stereotypes and peer culture. Parents are as susceptible as are their children! Let me illustrate, however, from years nine and ten. These students seem convinced they have the worst parents in the world: other parents give their offspring more pocket money; let them stay out longer, and are more trusting. By their reactions to these self-generated beliefs a self-fulfilling prophecy is created. Beliefs are expressed with such vehemence that the parent feels there is no option but to behave in a restrictive way to show they are in control. Counselling creates awareness of the misinterpretations on both sides. Parents believe they are sending messages of concern about friends and use of leisure time, they are unaware that they do it in ways which cause daughter or son to interpret it as distrust or believe that independence is being smothered.

An exaggerated form of ascription of intent which needs sensitivity and expertise is that of the scapegoat. Family therapy probably will be needed; certainly tutors will need to be circumspect, concentrating on building up the student's success in school. One child in the family becomes the recipient for all that the parents fear or cannot accept about themselves. It is as if the child has become a sponge soaking up aggression, blame and guilt that would undo family stability if not kept under control by seeing one individual as the cause. The scapegoat is held in that position by expectations and the mythology surrounding him or her. The situation is beyond the competence of the teacher. Some compensation for the negative treatment meted out to the scapegoat may be possible, but even this has to be given with caution. Expert help is necessary.

'Just what is a good child in this family?' This is not trivial! Bruch (1974), Crisp (1980) and Chernin (1986), in treating anorexia nervosa highlight the contribution of defining goodness in terms of eating. The good child is one who compliantly consumes the food set before her or him. Parents override the child's bodily signals, 'But you must be hungry. Eat it.' Such psychological intrusion fosters complications about autonomy and identity. Just as potentially sinister is the definition of goodness in terms of excessive prudishness or passivity. The teacher who considers it proper to work with families will find it useful to assess what the parent(s) hold as the ideal son or daughter role, comparing it with the views of the student. Reasons for conflict and ways of dealing with it emerge. One sometimes has to ask if the family has the capacity to grow with the adolescent. What was a supportive family at the age of eight may well be a restrictive one at 14.

Closely associated is the meaning of the child in the family. A somewhat extreme but far from infrequent example is where the child is perceived largely in terms of trouble. (This is not scapegoating. The parents are looking for an explanation rather than blaming.) 'We didn't plan to have him. The wife had a bad time carrying him. Do you know – nothing's gone right since he was born!' Here the child is the focal point of a mythology rooted in parental need to make sense of events over time. The facts are accurate: what is questionable is their association with the child.

Anyone interacting with parents in some depth gains an ear for key themes which recur when parents talk freely in an accepting atmosphere. Transactions and messages revolve around them, eg 'things getting out of hand' or 'right or not right for a boy/girl'. Consideration of key themes or symbols often gives meaning to what seems inconsequent, irrational or absurd. This is not an invitation for the tutor to indulge in fantasy, but to listen carefully, and then check the evidence.

Rejection and deprivation are frequently called upon as explanations for behaviours. Whilst this is not a textbook of developmental psychology, we should register the complexity of these terms. If it is a two parent family and the student's relationship with one parent is defective, can the other parent compensate? Many extensions of this question confront those concerned with family interaction. Are relationships substitutable or of equal value? Answers depend on specific situations. The difficulty is heightened by the subjective connotations of acts and messages. A statement may have different meanings for the student according to the source from which it comes. If made by the mother it will have one import and evoke a particular reaction; the identical statement by the father has a different meaning and produces a sharply contrasting response; when made by a sibling both again are different. Such possibilities make analysis of family interaction both fascinating and tantalising.

In counselling we are aware of low level signals which alert us to the fact that what people claim – indeed believe – they do is not what happens in reality. As important is the discrepancy between verbal and non-verbal messages. Bodily signals can be stronger and more salient than verbal statements which may be shaped by parental beliefs about what is right and proper. To illustrate; a 13-year-old girl showed great anxiety for which no explanation could be found. Her parents co-operated; the home was caring, but still the anxiety did not abate. A home visit was made one evening. The girl had bathed and was in her dressing-gown. Her mother was brushing her long, thick, tangled hair. The mother's voice was soothing and her words loving, but she was using a wire brush with ruthless determination. Her posture was tense; indeed the mother was obviously anxious. (Not because of the counsellor with whom she had a good relationship!) Contradictions were obvious and a start could be made on their resolution. Sense could now be made of what seemed inexplicable. Occasionally a parent talks about the son's or daughter's absenteeism, stealing or self-inflicted injury with apparent concern, but tone of voice and a particular kind of smile refutes this. It may be embarrassment, a response to anxiety or even indicate that vicarious gratification is being gained from the disturbed or deviant behaviour. Hasty conclusions are avoided, but the signal that all may not be what is claimed can be registered, and if judged appropriate the matter raised at an opportune moment.

An almost unending range of events may be found to be relevant to problems located within the family. Two examples follow. Redundancy and unemployment will obviously change interaction and not only create financial problems. The sense of loss of significance sometimes causes the male to exert his authority in curious ways. Strict surveillance of activities, early 'locking up' and rigid control of expenditure on food not justified by household income are fairly common. The unemployed girl becomes resentful because she is expected to carry a heavy load of household duties not required of her unemployed brother. Dissatisfaction then spreads to her younger sisters still at school. Parents fearful of unemployment may unhelpfully pressure their child unrealistically to achievement. Stress or rebellion result. The unemployed boy may be indulged by the working mother, creating all-round resentment.

The presence of a handicapped child or one injured in an accident may generate problems, especially if the parents have not dealt with the emotional complications. A sense of stigma may colour relationships and emotions, eg where the child is HIV positive and parent or both parents feel responsible. Self-condemnation distorts the capacity to relate to the child – it does not matter whether it be defensive over-protection or guilty withdrawal. Such parents merit our understanding and support. Sometimes manipulation by the handicapped child of her or his condition, creates a sense of mingled threat or resentment in the other children. Parents may not be able to explain that a child has, for example, leukaemia, causing the brothers and sisters to feel he or she is being unfairly indulged. Compassion dictates that we support parents in such difficult tasks.

The impulse to pin down a cause or find a neat explanation for a family problem is strong. But those who offer counsel have to tolerate ambiguity and uncertainty. Rarely will there be a single cause: a constellation of mutually reinforcing factors is more likely. Even to make precise statements about the relative contribution of each element may be hampered by unquestioned assumptions that something is necessarily of consequence. Nowhere is it more important to realise this, than when adoption figures in the problem. Most adoptions are successful: the chances are that any problems which appear have little, if anything, to do with the adoption as such. The apprehensions of the parents when normal adolescent difficulties arise may inhibit their resolution, especially when after adoption the parents had a natural child. Even then, this is probably more to do with parental personality than the adoption *per se*.

Working with parents professionally

We have known for many years (eg Morton-Williams and Finch 1968) that parents and students have a markedly different view of the role of the teacher, than teachers themselves hold. The teacher's role is seen as instructional in a restricted way – to impart facts and basic skills. The emphasis is on the school as a service in which the end product is readiness for the world of work. There may be little realisation of what readiness for a technological world means.

Some parents cling to memories of the classrooms of their childhood, believing the end of learning to be replication of texts and repetition of teachers' statements. Learning as a process involving the imagination to extend the meaning of the facts; producing hypotheses to be explored thereby giving rise to fresh insights, is lamentably remote from many parents' view of the classroom. They see the praiseworthy learner as passive, maintaining the current state of affairs. Yet, as Ansoff (1984) argues, industry has to cope with discontinuity, disjunction and gross unpredictability; learning to think conditionally and propositionally is important if we are to anticipate possible contingencies. Learning should be preparing students to think in this way – a way which may be foreign to their parents.

There is a mentality gap evident in a few teachers who have not learned that yesterday's solutions do not resolve today's problems. But the lag is greater in parents. Little has changed since the sixties when it was commonplace to dismiss the teacher's task as an easy one. Apparently, impeccably behaved eager learners absorbed wisdom imparted by unstressed teachers! Even more biased were perceptions of teachers as self-indulgent creatures who told others to do what they themselves did not do.

Counselling skills therefore should be profitably employed by tutors in their interaction with parents to consolidate the image of the teacher as a caring professional and gain their co-operation. The core task will be to extend Hamblin's (1981) view of learning as a continuous dialogue to include parents and launch a constructive attack on inert and passive forms of learning. We have to stimulate the sense of enterprise and initiative that will be necessary to cope with new forms of work and the challenges of increasing self employment. Flexibility of thought will be necessary to allow individuals to cope with the retraining and recasting of perceptions that will be demanded of them. Parents also have to appreciate that reliance on external checks and surveillances will be inadequate where enterprise and striving to make an impact on a rapidly changing world is prime. Controls from within based on self-respect are of greater import.

Tutors should be taking a major role in interpreting the implications of change to parents, attacking loose notions that the profession impedes change or is hostile to it. In 1986, I drew attention to the need for the school to be a community based on Curle's (1972) belonging identity and identity through self-awareness. Just as with co-operation and competition both are necessary and there is a creative tension between them. The former provides the security which allows adventures in experimenting with identity. The latter allows the person to anticipate potential hazards and detect lines of development. In that brief discussion I touched on the limits of belonging identity as Curle saw them, but said, 'Identity through self-awareness is concerned with stringent evaluation of our powers and limitations. Perhaps it is best viewed as building the capacity for rational self-vigilance.' Now I would extend this to the need constructively to scrutinise institutions. Counselling as a joint enterprise between students and staff facilitates this. Again in 1986 I argued, 'we have to help pupils shed their attachment to authority based on coercion – no matter whether it be reward or threat – and move towards Kolberg's (1969) self–referring principles of conscience.' There is a paradox: through professional expertise, teachers have to enable parents to challenge limited views of education but also constructively to question the credentials of alleged experts, including the teacher. Leadership skills of a high calibre will be needed if parents are to cope with the anxiety entailed in shifting to a more open vision of the school.

Parents and teachers alike are deeply concerned with discipline, but within and between both groups, views on its nature, and methods of maintaining it are highly discrepant. It is curious that a topic of common concern should also be potentially divisive. Year seven tutors have a unique opportunity to build relationships with parents through allowing parents to discuss their worries in an accepting setting without loss of face. Uniqueness derives from the fact that the transition impinges on parent almost as much as on child. Anxiety and hope are in uneasy tension; parents are conscious of the new demands to be made by the school and of approaching puberty; but it also brings the sense of a fresh start and perhaps a desire to shed the past.

Explanation of school rules with their underlying rationale offers a start. Rules about safety, pupil-pupil interaction and teacher-pupil interaction are explored in ways which show they are as binding on the teacher as on the pupil. If the school is to be a community breeding respect for self and others, the inculcation of courtesy which is more than a sham will be the next step. Parental responsibility will be heavy in this, Sugarman (1973) points out that the socialisation task of the school boils down to control of impulsive behaviour. This is achieved by growth of the capacity to take the viewpoint of others and assess one's own contribution to the chain of events. In working with parents, I have found it useful to give them incidents to analyse in terms of antecedents, circumstances and outcomes. They then cull others from life within the family and work on them with another person.

Schools no longer concentrate so heavily on punishments. Students' active involvement in authority stems from the work of the Elton Report (1989) but many parents still hold to a unilateral view of discipline based on injunctions rather than something to be promulgated within the peer group through support and example. The nature and effect of rewards is a worthy topic for parent-teacher meetings. Parents have to appreciate the impact of their casual, indeed thoughtless, remarks about teachers, discipline and learning activities. 'Tommy-rot' applied to an activity can echo in a student's mind, conveniently appearing as a reason for evasion of the task when frustration is experienced.

There is small chance of making the school a community if we do not face the social and developmental forces which exacerbate students' tendency to dissociate from school. Contact with parents in year eight – the year of disenchantment for about a quarter of students – is beneficial. Stress is the lot of the parent whose son or daughter opts out psychologically from school, and who is aggressively manifesting identity by opposition. Parents compound difficulties by unwittingly reinforcing gender stereotypes and helplessness in learning. The tutor's contribution can be vital. Parental irritation and vaccilation will act to push the adolescent into identity-submerging dependence on a peer group.

Much needs to be done to assist parents to understand the relation of technology to social change. More specifically, they must learn about its application in education. This can usefully be linked with explanation of how parents can support the new emphasis on self-appraisal and students' self-monitoring of progress through realstic target-setting. Without tutor/ parent interaction, school and home could pull in contradictory directions, cancelling each other out.

In later years of the school, tutors and parents should examine reasons for success – not restricting it to the academic. Attitudes to authority and altruism can be looked at afresh. The impact of parental anxiety on students takes less obvious forms in years ten and 11. Certain parents are facing diminishing career prospects and loss of job satisfaction, experiencing anxiety about what the future holds for them. The malaise of their own situation stimulates emotive criticism of what the school offers, owing more to parental insecurity than reality. It also causes them to criticise their children over-zealously. A well-established relationship with a trusted tutor provides the means for a parent to talk through his or her feelings and disentangle the muddled perceptions.

It is naïve to believe that students will necessarily welcome teacher-parent co-operation. Parents are painfully aware that the older adolescent holds a 'conspiracy theory' of the motives for adult action. Perhaps this is inevitable when independence and being one's own man or woman head students' desiderata. Upper secondary school students may see such contacts as denial of their maturity. Life in school is seen as a matter between themselves and their teachers. Parents are intruders. Yet contact with parents is essential in helping them understand the stress of revision for examination, and students' ambivalence which springs from self-doubt. Parents refer back to their own school experiences for guidance, not realising the extent of change. Tutors will have to negotiate with students and parents the type and amount of school contact that is desired *and* desirable.

For some years yet it is likely that students will be handicapped by limited parental notions of learning. Parents may find themselves unable to discuss tactics and strategies for assignments and projects with their children, building approaches to learning suited to a technological age. Tutors now have the additional task of freeing parents from being imprisoned in rigid, simplistic beliefs about the nature of learning.

Divorce and separation

Greater acceptance of divorce does not eliminate problems of adjustment for both parents and children. Social supports are readily available for bereavement, but ugly tensions easily manifest themselves at divorce or separation. Students disturbed by family breakdown may behave in ways which attract bullying. (Bullying will be discussed at the end of this chapter.) Women – and men – involved in divorce may experience frustration, loneliness, insecurity and a sense of stigma accompanying – sometimes hampering – their determination to cope. At the onset of the discussion, let us note that both parents and adolescents legitimately resent any indication from the school that they are viewed as a problem, or worse, as deviant. Teachers' concern is real, but thoughtlessly or clumsily expressed, it can be noxious. A 13-year-old boy refused to attend school after the father left home in an atmosphere of anger and recrimination. When counselled, he expressed bitter resentment at teachers' demonstration of concern. 'The head of house keeps asking questions about home, and other teachers ask me how I am. I know my father has gone, but I'll put up with that. What I can't stand is them treating me as if I am different. They're making me stand out from my friends.' He is aptly showing that care ill-expressed is hurtful and damaging.

Tensions proliferate in separation and divorce, not only among those directly involved. The following situation is not that unusual. A newly-divorced woman accepted her parents' offer to help with looking after the children. The bitter grandparents soon found themselves criticising the father, and were affronted when the resentful children reacted with hostility. When she arrived home from work, mother faced a barrage of complaints from the grandparents – whose insensitivity caused the incident. On the other hand, grandparents may unconsciously try to put right the mistakes they made with their own children. But this attempt at compensation is foredoomed to failure because it is not based on the reality of the grandchildren's needs but on perceptions – probably inaccurate – of the past. In one instance over-indulgent grandparents not only undermined the mother's discipline but began to usurp her place in the children's affections. This came as a double blow to a woman still trying to cope with the aftermath of divorce: 'I'm working my fingers to the bone to keep the home together. And then what do I find? The kids think more of their gran than me. I end up feeling there is nothing in life for me.' Faced with a situation like this, a wise pastoral head or tutor will listen carefully, encouraging the mother to work out tactics for dealing with specific difficulties, but will not be trapped into giving superficial advice or taking sides.

Whilst teachers cannot intervene in any depth, they should have skill sufficient to allow them to assess the severity of problems and recommend sources of help. The history of the family before breakdown will largely determine reactions to separation and divorce. How much did each parent contribute to the marriage, and how committed was each to it? Were elements of instability present? When there is a history of either parent threatening to leave over the years, or it becomes evident that a climate of emotional blackmail and inconsistency has been the norm this signals a need for unobtrusive assessment of the child's reactions. The remaining parent may need counselling from an appropriate agency. However, as teachers our task is limited to providing the conditions in which the student can function competently despite home circumstances, allowing him or her to talk to a trusted person if wished.

All three conditions – the third is bereavement – require the capacity of the partner remaining with the children to organise and manage daily family life alone. That parent may, however, have a pervasive fear that things could get out of hand, even become chaotic. Some women begin the post-separation or divorce experience holding a legacy of complex residual feelings derived from physical violence and/or mental cruelty. (So may men, but it is rarer.) There will be fatigue and financial worries, possibly bolstered by gloomy predictions about the future. This infects the student, increasing anxiety, but more significantly causing her or him to react to career choice and other decisions with indifference or cynicism because they seem remote and trivial in the face of other pressures.

This section has highlighted problems. There is a danger of forgetting that divorce and separation is not inevitably a stormy experience: it can be conducted in an atmosphere of respect and mutual concern. The best response the school can make is to have available to parents tutor meetings concerned with developmental tasks related to friendship, careers, learning and health. Although intended to help parents understand their children's needs, they would find much applicable to their own dilemmas.

Nunnally, Chilman and Cox (1988) provide a sensitive and important analysis of divorce and separation. The time span is longer than many would suspect: two to four years are needed for individuals fully to come to terms with the emotional and social repercussions of divorce. A process occurs in which individuals detach themselves from bad experiences. Such trauma never go completely, but they cease to dominate the individual's life. 'Peace' is made with the ex-partner, and the person understands his or her contribution to marital breakdown. Superficial reconciliation with the course of events is not enough; there must be a self-searching process which increases the capacity for making new relationships. Tutors and pastoral heads must be aware that considerable time is needed, and that the reverberations do not subside quickly.

Support may be most crucial as divorce or separation occurs. We have already seen that it is vital that our intentions do not undermine the student by amplifying emotions or producing a sense of difference. The teacher who helps must avoid being partisan and blaming; resisting the temptation to offer platitudinous advice. Ambivalence and tensions require calm acceptance: at one time the student appears to have accepted the situation; the next minute, protest and blame-pinning dominate his or her behaviour. In this phase, the helper has to give acceptance without reacting directly to fluctuations. A rock-like steadiness is needed to provide the essential reliable point of reference in a shifting scene. This necessarily means stable expectations. As in the post-divorce/separation period, parents tend to lower their expectations of behaviour, indicating indirectly that they will not follow up misdemeanours. This removes the anchorage necessary for the adolescent to cope with the emotional – even irrational – behaviour of key adults. School has to be the source of structure and containment which allows the student to cope with uncertainty.

Conflicts of loyalty are probably inevitable; they will be intensified when one parent is determined to end the partnership and the other is reluctant to see it concluded. Occasionally, the student experiences anxiety because he or she believes he or she made a major contribution to marital breakdown. 'If only I had behaved better, my parents would not be separating.' Guilt and a curious omnipotence are intertwined. The most a tutor or pastoral head can do is to listen with compassion, allowing discharge of tensions. If the feelings are intense and persist unabated, specialist help is essential. Given time, students usually manage to put their contribution to family breakdown into perspective.

Obviously, there is a chance that post-family breakdown circumstances will affect school performance. If the parent having custody shows a diminished capacity for parenting, friendly support from tutors and valued peers may well compensate. Judicious action by the tutor in guiding supportive peers is often invaluable. If schoolwork deteriorates, the same applies. Whatever the problem and form of help, the principles remain the same: sensible reinforcement of self respect through boosting a sense of efficacy and control, whilst reducing any sense of 'difference'. Interestingly, Nunnally *et al* emphasise that boys appear to have a stronger reaction to divorce or separation than girls. If this is a valid difference, it may be due to the mother having control of the boy and using inappropriate forms of discipline or her doubts about the future accentuating insecurity. At times in adolescence the father's role as a model for his son is crucial: when deprived of it, the boy behaves in exaggerated ways. Maybe boys display their feelings more forcibly than do girls. A problem for both sexes, of which tutors should be aware, is when the parent with whom they are in daily contact over-relies on the student for support. The parent should be helped to look at the burden imposed on the student, and work out healthier ways of coping.

For example, if children remain with their mother, but father has access, he may use this to undermine the ex-wife. Dad takes the children out, gives them an enjoyable time, appears as their 'friend'. He may suggest that 'things would have been different if your mother hadn't been the kind of woman she is'. Later, when the mother (who has to take full brunt of the need for discipline) exercises a proper sanction, she meets an angry blast incorporating the ex-partner's statement. Her existing insecurity is compounded.

Worse occurs in situations when father becomes unreliable in contacts and keeping promises made to the children. Children are prepared for the visit or outing, but the father fails to appear. Blame-pinning is inevitable. Too often, adolescents resort to the time-honoured tactic of blaming the person they love most – their mother. For her it is painful and bitter. Compassion demands we provide signs of acceptance for the mother, whilst a sensible explanation for the student will go a long way to maintain equilibrium. But the counsellor must never become embroiled in such emotional tangles. There is a concerned emotional detachment that has to be achieved.

Pastoral workers should anticipate difficulties by working out procedures for coping with the parent who does not have custody but arrives at the school attempting to see their child or children illicitly. Circumstances vary so much that a prescription would be meaningless. Pastoral heads should establish, as far as possible, the likelihood of such problems in initial contacts with the parent having custody, ensuring that the tutor is warned of potential risks and complications. Knowledge held solely by the pastoral head does nothing to protect the tutor from unwitting errors of judgement. The greater the responsibility expected of tutors for the students' well-being, the more essential is it that they have knowledge of home conditions.

Bereavement

Bereavement of those we teach touches us deeply and we desire to be of service. Respect for the student should hold us back from unwarranted intrustions into grief and family tensions. Honest concern and sympathy is essential: indication of availability and willingness to listen is humane; but to meddle is dangerous. This is the area where self-indulgent attempts at uninvited counselling, imposition of our own suppositions about what is happening, and unjustified assumptions of similarity of the bereaved adolescent's experience to our own are even more reprehensible than usual.

It will be a safeguard for tutors and pastoral heads to begin their training by systematically exploring the web of emotional and social forces associated with bereavement. It is unclear as to how far Gorer's (1965) conclusion that death is the final obscenity which we cannot face is still true. The cumulative impact of scenes of violent death on television may have modified this, but only I feel in a superficial way. We talk more freely of death, yet evasive mechanisms still seem rife. We are prone to sentimentality; we prettify, and through petty hypocrisy adopt a palliative approach to the passage out of this world unless we are the sufferers or bereaved. Values are less clear cut, even confused: we see the certainties of earlier ages as delusory. These factors underlie our response to death. Doubts exist about the nature of a good life in an age when conflicting concepts of rights and duties abound, and technology renders much obsolete. These issues are profound as a multi-cultural society properly forces awareness of different perspectives of the fundamentals of life and death on us. Encouragement to view life largely in consumer-based and instrumental terms adds to the poverty of spirit that leave us ill-prepared to deal with death.

Even the rituals of mourning have lost some of their significance. Social anthropologists saw them as placing protective boundaries around the bereaved. They also functioned to activate a psychological process in which the deceased is gradually integrated into a meaningful group of dead which had personal relevance for her or him and for the living. The factors discussed in the preceding paragraph in conjunction with geographical mobility – death reactivates our ties to a village or particular area giving a sense of belonging – and changes in family structure, further erode the anchorage offered by the rituals, leaving the individual destructively vulnerable to grief.

Caution is essential. Even these token indications of the web of influences show that impulsive excursions into counselling risk damaging students. Our concept of the nature of death will be at odds with that held by students from a different culture. The self-aware involved in work with the bereaved know that their maturity is not as substantial as it seems. There are many invitations in bereavement to regress to over-simplified 'black or white' judgements and reactions. The dead person may be invested with the attributes of saintliness, their human failings ignored. Only later, as the bereaved person works through the stages of mourning Bowlby describes, will a balanced appraisal be reached. The implicit injunction, 'Speak no ill of the dead', loses its grip on the mourner. For some, grief may distort their perception of reality; they vehemently blame someone or something for the death, and no amount of reason or evidence can persuade them to change. The counsellor needs to understand and accept these reactions.

A life space approach

Counselling deals with problems in context. This requires us to look closely at the student's life space *if* we can justify intervention through counselling. People do not live in isolation: they are interdependent, engaged in building up networks of relationships and expectations. Bereavement cannot be understood in isolation from this. Students have created idiosyncratic definitions of major life crises which give meaning to the behaviour of those involved. Therefore the helper has to be sensitive to the forces operating in the student's life if acceptable support is to be given.

A practical guide for intervention includes the idea of a threshold for tolerance of stress. The adolescent may be able to meet demands directly related to the bereavement, but in conjunction with the pressures of revising for A-Levels their capacity to cope is destroyed. The safer and economical course of action may well be for tutor or pastoral head to help with revision skills and build a strategy of time management, reducing total stress, restoring the power of coping. Indirect support can be the best form of bereavement counselling, boosting self-respect and the sense of being in control.

Bereavement includes anger as well as grief. Blame-pinning is almost inevitable. A deep need to explain misfortunes and allocate responsibility survives. From it stems confusion, anger and guilt: energy is fruitlessly expended in stifling these feelings, when they are better faced. Spiritual advisers may urge acceptance, but the bereaved blames the hospital, doctors, nurses, drugs, one another, and perhaps most damagingly herself or himself. Such attributions are not random. They reflect long-standing family tensions. When conflicts have been suppressed or unacknowledged, blame-pinning is likely to be intense. Unfaced guilt exacerbates such dissensions.

Consideration of other aspects of life space then follows. Who died? What was the nature of the relationship with the adolescent? To say the student was the daughter of the deceased means little. The relationship 'daughter' may have involved deep love, rebellion, fear, dependency, mature interaction or uncommitted superficial linkage. The helper does not probe: this would be intrusively impertinent. But she or he will apply the skills of reading situations, picking up cues sent by the student. Care is taken not to assume inevitable connexions or stereotype potential reactions. A 'distant' relationship does not necessarily bring indifference to the death. A sharp emotional response embodying regret or anger for what was denied could result. Neither foreclosure on possibilities nor reliance on platitudes will be of use.

Next, the life space approach takes into account the manner of the death and the significance of that to the bereaved. Suicide, for example, is not only traumatic, but may bring a sense of stigma. A parent's reactions of guilt or failure if the spouse committed suicide may create a sense of deviance which is communicated to the children. The family is then separated from support. The death which the spouse has invested with shame, functions to erect barriers of suspicion which lead to misinterpretation of the motives of those offering support. Even a heroic element in the death brings its own problems, for example, a serviceman dying in the attempt to save a friend, a member of a lifeboat crew swept overboard in the cause of duty, or a mother overcome with fumes as she tries to rescue her children in a fire. More complicated forms exist where the heroic element involves a person's attitude to physical deterioration and acceptance of intolerable pain. This element of 'heroism' could inhibit the grieving essential to adjustment, restrictively tying the survivor(s) to the deceased, who is maintained as a dominating influence in family decisions, or even used as a weapon for emotional blackmail!

The life space approach is sensitive to possibilities, alert to the consequences of emotional and other frustrations without assuming their inevitability. Scanning includes:

1. Was death due to a long illness or was it sudden, catching everyone unaware? The former allows anticipatory grieving and preparatory role

changes. The eldest boy may take over some of the duties of the father or the eldest girl begins to substitute for the mother in practical ways with the younger children. However, denial may occur. The medical prognosis is discounted; when death occurs, the bereaved are in an anarchic emotional state because the blindly-held prophecy of recovery has been abruptly disconfirmed. Reverberations from this are far-reaching.

2. Alertness to the tensions emanating from the death of a brother or sister are especially relevant for the school. Parental reactions could vary between subsequent over-protection or rejection of the surviving adolescent. Typical questions to ask are:

   - Was the dead sibling younger or older than the adolescent?

   - Is the gender element important?

   - Was the adolescent negatively compared with the deceased at home or school? (Recall that adolescents are deeply ambivalent about comparisons. Whilst they detest being the focus of comparisons, they constantly resort to them when under pressure.)

3. At what developmental stage was the adolescent when the bereavement occurred? One example suffices to illustrate the reason for the question. The death of a girl's mother just as she reached puberty had a profound impact on her sense of identity. This was compounded by the fact that she was ill-prepared for puberty and found menstruation painful; in addition her mother died from cervical cancer, which the girl linked with her own femininity.

4. Of prime importance is the relationship with the surviving parent. For example, the shock of a mother's death temporarily halted hostility between father and son. But after a few months the tension was reactivated, without the mediating effects of the mother who dampened down the conflict. In another instance, a sixth form girl gave up her studies to take a job, in order to escape from a violent, alcoholic father. Later she entered an unsuitable relationship, with disastrous consequences.

Other questions entailed by the life space approach:

1. Which are likely to be more important, short or long-run issues? Concentration is normally on immediate grief. In fact, the long-term consequences of a failure by the surviving partner to adapt and cope with changed circumstances will be more devastating.

2. Indirect effects of bereavement have to be taken into account. Coping with the direct grief ensuing from the death of a loved brother or sister

may be achieved admirably. The adjustment may be undermined months later by an insidious process in which parents transfer the aspirations held for the dead sibling to the survivor, eg gaining an Oxbridge place and jettisoning her or his own plans. Affection for the parent and reluctance to hurt them leaves the student in a dilemma particularly hard to talk about.

Mourning as a process

A prerequisite for offering support to parent or student is a more precise understanding of the sequence of reactions to death. Kubler-Ross (1970) enlightens us about the reactions of the dying, although her stages are sometimes, I suspect, interpreted more rigidly than she intended. Parkes (eg 1972) offers valuable guidance for counsellors, but nothing surpasses Bowlby's (1961) insightful analysis. I shall rely on this as the basis for what follows.

First, there is initial numbness and failure to comprehend the full significance of the death. There is much to be done, blunting the full force of grief. Once the funeral is over, deep yearning and awareness of loss, mingled with protest and anger is experienced. For many, the deepest need is to talk about the dead one as a way of sustaining her or his presence. This, unfortunately, may be intolerable for others because they are intimidated by the pain of the bereaved's grief. Omnipotence makes one feel that one has to do something to stem the grief. Steadfast helpers wait acceptingly, providing a stable point of reference in a world which, for the bereaved, has lost its familiar shape.

Psychological and physiological reactions to the trauma continue for longer than we think. The adolescent has to maintain equilibrium in a setting where probably the most important adult in her or his life manifests unpredictable irritability, depression and moodiness, including self-punishing 'if only' reminiscences. Stress and insecurity are countered by well-judged enlistment of peer support, sensible structuring of school demands, and friendly recognition of the individual which facilitates communication without intrusiveness. As with divorce, we must avoid putting the adolescent into a special category: resentment would result.

The acute emotions may be followed by a period of disorganisation; almost certainly depression and the feeling that life has lost its purpose. The strain produced by parental distress falls sharply on the adolescent. When performance in schools falls off, tutor support acts as a lifeline. We may also offer simple practical measures for *self*-organisation in the home where the formerly relied on adult has temporarily lost her or his hold on things. A restrained explanation of the dynamics of bereavement will help restore perspective. This does not deny the need to be alert to the student's feelings and grief. We must indicate that we are concerned and available if the student would welcome this. Practical support will afford opportunities for students to bring their feelings into the open and tutor or pastoral head can then respond in ways that are in the best interests of the student.

Disturbances of the mourning process are rare, but pastoral workers should be aware of such possibilities and recognise them. They should not attempt to deal with them: to do so would be outside their competence. The most the school can do is sympathetically to point out the need for help, and suggest that the parent contacts a bereavement service or her or his general practitioner.

If the parent's grief has not abated in intensity after three months he or she *may* be in danger of developing a depressive illness, if treatment is not given. Survivors occasionally report symptoms similar to those experienced by the deceased. There are suggestions that this is most likely where cardiac disease and cancer were the cause of death. No organic reasons for the symptoms are found despite their reality for the patient. In some cases delayed grief may occur. The individual apparently has coped well. Indeed, they seem to be untouched by the death. Feeling has been repressed. When grief breaks through, those around the individual are at a loss and support is difficult to find.

Bereavement involves grief or the emotional reaction to loss, and secondly, coping with role adjustments and the additional tasks entailed. Counselling skills in the school setting are largely mobilised to help the adolescent cope with the second. The task is to increase the student's sense of efficacy in daily living after bereavement. This is achieved by giving just enough support to allow her or him cope with home conditions and function competently in peer group and school. To do more would erode autonomy.

The tutor's watching brief

The life space approach leads one to consider the consequences of bereavement over a fairly long period of time. We have seen that the indirect pressures of the surviving parent's incapacity to adjust constructively may be more stressful than the actual bereavement. Stress may be added to by health problems. There is some evidence that the bereaved family consult their general practitioner more frequently, and have more illnesses than was their norm, in the six months following the death. If the student has shown signs of anxiety during her or his school career, the tutor should act as a steadying force by reminding the student of the association between stress and vulnerability to infection. If both parents were markedly older than usual, anxiety is easily provoked by illness of the survivor.

The first Christmas after bereavement posits threat, especially if it comes within six months of the death, and readjustments are still under way. Even without these emotional pressures, Christmas is as likely to be a time for reinforcing family conflicts as it is for reconciling them. For the recently bereaved, Christmas holds near irreconcilable emotions: gratitude and dissatisfaction, eager anticipation and disappointment. In one case a grieving mother built up an idealised picture of Christmas, but began to highlight the differences between the paucity of the approaching festival and those of the past – providing a constant reminder of family deprivation. Her adolescent child was more pragmatic, accepting the inescapable, but resenting the mother's interminable 'harping on about it'. Counselling skills were needed to help the young person to disentangle and disengage from the emotional complications of this first post-bereavement Christmas.

The first anniversary of the death acts as a 'marker' which aids resolution of trauma – 'It's now a year since Fred died'. As it approaches, the survivor may display signs of tension, or very rarely, irrational symptoms if the mourning process was interrupted or distorted. We may have to put what is happening into perspective, giving the young person understanding and helping her or him to show sympathy and love whilst maintaining a self-preserving distance from parental emotions.

Family reactions seem almost infinitely variable. Much again depends on the emotional health existing before bereavement struck the family. Inability to talk about the dead person and the cause of death is unhelpful to the adult: for the adolescent this parental response is often intolerable. Adolescents wish to talk, but find themselves blocked by the parent. Even talking with the tutor then brings a sense of disloyalty. Recall that the family is no stranger to emotional blackmail! Affectional bonds with the dead can be used to manipulate the adolescent into conformity through guilt, 'Your father worked so hard and would have expected you to ...'. Once again the task is to help the adolescent find ways of providing support for the parent if they desire to, whilst maintaining his or her psychological boundaries.

The death of a student calls for the application of counselling skills to create a climate of safety and acceptance in which feelings can be voiced and questions raised. Trust of the tutor is crucial to help students understand and come to terms with the situation. Students have to interpret the death of a peer in the way helpful to them. Tutors should resolutely avoid imposing their own views of the meaning of death. Younger students will have an imperfect grasp of the reality of death. Confusion and distress will result if they are pushed towards an adult conception for which they are unready. Care has to be taken about phrases soothing to the adult's ear when communicating with younger students. 'Gone to sleep' or 'Taken to be with God' have alarming implications for them. Older students will recognise, and dismiss, their placebo intent.

We must not manufacture problems but we should be watchful for repercussions arising from the deceased's position with peers. Anger may be high if she or he was popular, and death was caused by an untoward accident. Death by solvent abuse or drugs stimulates attempts at blame-pinning. Where bullying has occurred, although there is no direct connexion with the death, guilt and anxiety may appear. This is even more likely if death was through self-inflicted injury. (The term 'suicide' implies intent to destroy oneself and it is difficult to determine such intent.) If judged wise, and confidentiality of *access* can be given, individual counselling can be offered to distressed students.

The form as the most personally important unit of organisation to which pupils belong is the place where students decide what action they should take to express their emotions and to demonstrate to the parents of the dead student their concern and care. Here is an opportunity for standpoint-taking. Students should look at the death from the parents' viewpoint, attempting to decide what would bring a little comfort to them. A planned gesture of concern is truly therapeutic when coupled with a simple act of farewell and remembrance. The form can be sad, but are legitimately free to pursue their own futures.

Bullying

One badly handled case of bullying may well alienate some parents, the suspicion that it occurs, but the school conceals it, will have a deep influence on parental perceptions of the school. All three groups – students, parents and teachers – seem powerless in the face of the problem. Indeed, it is likely that we do not know the extent, frequency and intensity of bullying in school, although Besag (1989) in her valuable work claims that at least ten per cent of students at any one time are involved in bullying either as victim or bully. The figure *may* be larger: victims' fears of retaliation and teachers' fears of inflaming the situation if they intervene may obscure the actual incidence. Also the dividing line between legitimate teasing and the more noxious activity of bullying is not always clear. Practical jokes hide sadistic intent, the payoff for the joker being confusion and humiliation of the victim. This is not trivial. Roland and Munthe (1989) provide some evidence that much bullying is disguised as teasing. I believe that this makes what is harmful appear innocuous. Parents, when they know bullying is occurring, scapegoat teachers. In other cases they become anxious because they sense their child's unhappiness, but find the attempt to discover what is wrong resolutely blocked by the student. The frustrated, anxious parent then is antagonistic to the school which they see as the source of the trouble.

Response to bullying is akin to that of any other problem:

- raising the level of awareness of it;

- giving action against it legitimacy;

- offering focused support for all implicated.

Bullying can be physical or psychological, active or passive, direct or indirect..The last occurs when the bully manipulates others to carry out her or his work. Tutors will need some training in coping with the particularly testing areas of psychological and indirect bullying. Strategies also have to take into account gender which affects the motives behind bullying. It is likely that boys bully mainly to assert their personal power, whilst bullying by and of girls is more often intended to reinforce the identity and solidarity of a friendship group through distasteful treatment of the bullied who is excluded from it.

Counselling looks at the total situation, arguing that both bullied and bully need help. Besag (1989) shows that both bully and victim will have social difficulties. In this valuable and practical investigation she shows that cessation of bullying is not the end of treatment. Victims have characteristics that may attract bullying. Hamblin (1978; 1984) emphasised that this may be so, but the bully cannot be allowed to use this to excuse or justify bullying. It merely underlines the fact that bully and bullied are caught into a destructive relationship in which both are being harmed. Justified indignation should not deny the bully essential help. Humanity and economy of effort demand preventive work from tutors. Early identification of potential victims and bullies should be a priority if staff time is not to be invested unnecessarily in coping with the aftermath of what could have been anticipated. Counselling is alert to the probability that both will acquire a negative identity that holds long-term consequences and that crystallisation of undesirable personality qualities will be facilitated by failure to act.

We have to be alert to where bullying occurs. For example, where students travel by buses hired for the purpose, much unreported bullying occurs. For reasons best known to themselves, some drivers ignore it and do not alert the duty staff, allowing a curious sub-culture to develop on the bus in which small groups form and the roles of victims are allocated. The EWO is an effective resource in establishing what is happening and working with parents.

Self-awareness is essential: there may be a tinge of contradiction in our attitudes towards bullying stemming from childhood experience. Emotive topics – bullying is certainly one – seduce one into reliance on platitudes, eg 'boys will be boys' and 'girls will be girls'. Some may say that bullying is a fact of human nature, therefore students have to learn to cope with it. I do not believe it to be an inevitable part of being human. They must cope but support is required. Tutor periods must provide activities that build the sense of control and show that the victim can do much to free himself or herself. The bully should not get the satisfaction of seeing her or his victim humiliated. In line with the 'counselling as a joint enterprise' thesis of this book, older students and classmates can be enlisted to support and develop ideas for coping. Help should similarly be made available to the bully. A neglected resource is drama: the skilled drama specialist can do a first class job in producing awareness of the many facets of situations and enhance the capacity for coping of students. He or she could work directly with parents stimulating insights into the dilemmas faced by adolescents.

We all know that fears of bullying are strong at transfer from primary to secondary school. Older pupils perpetuate myths about initiation rituals – heads being immersed in lavatory bowls, etc. We should anticipate sources of anxiety in which the vulnerable reveal themselves and invite exploitation. (Having a PE lesson and subsequent shower at the new school in July saves a lot of agonising during the vacation.) Parents and students should know that the tutor will listen and act as a stable point of concern, helping students develop responsible ways of coping. Anxiety and vulnerability to bullying occurs at other transitions, eg from lower to upper school when the school is on a 'split site'.

The total thrust of tutor effort is to build up the ethos that bullying is a weak, immature and contemptible activity. An integral part of this is a straightforward statement of values and intent. Dangers exist that clumsy statements may excite apprehension in parents, yet it must be evident that the school will act firmly about bullying.

Difficulty with buses was mentioned above, but this was a specific instance of the bullies' mechanisms for evading observation. They operate on the way to school or in home or in crowded areas of the playground where observation is difficult. Roland and Munthe make the interesting suggestion that older students could provide information with impunity, and be used to shadow a victim in circumstances where staff are not present. It may pay schools seriously to consider adopting their suggestion that carefully trained peer mediators be used to promote reconciliation between bully and victim.

Narrow focus on the problem will lead to failure to change what is happening. For example, thought has to be given to the possibility that the bully cannot escape from his or her role. Peers expect the individual to occupy it, any attempt at abandoning it would be met by aggression. The bully motivated by anxiety is likely to have a minimum of attractive characteristics, low self-respect and few friends. For change to occur these defects will have to be rectified through planned, carefully phased, peer support.

Parents who suspect their child is a victim of bullying, but cannot persuade him or her to talk about it are in a quandary. They need support to avoid intimidating attempts at questioning, or worse, emotional pleas which accentuate existing insecurity and distress. Parents' attempts at exposing the problem leave the child feeling bludgeoned and with an even greater sense of desolation and isolation. Comparison of information by parents and tutors often provides clues, which if followed up through shrewd discussion with fellow students, reveal the problem. Tutor and parents then work out the most productive way of intervening. The student must be fully involved as well, estimating the snags and potential success of lines of action. Failure to include them would reinforce the sense of helplessness which so often is a salient part of the problem.

Parental unawareness and the flight to denial that their child is a bully present a challenge to the teacher. Parents shattered by revelation of their son or daughter's involvement in bullying may react by aggressive attack on teachers and the school. The best ploy is to wait until they run out of steam, listening with courtesy. Responding angrily would not only be a loss of professional position, but gives their forceful denial legitimacy in the eyes of the parent. Their acceptance of the situation, however, is no guarantee that we will be able to deal with the situation. Family therapy or other psychological help may be necessary. When the bullying could reasonably be taken as a product of gross inconsistencies within the home, or as a reflection of stresses produced by parental emotional disturbance and/or marital frustration, it is imperative that the problem be dealt with by an appropriate agency. Counselling skills are destructive when employed to pre-empt specialist treatment.

Activities

1 Analysing family interaction

1.1 Objectives and general remarks:

a To allow you to stand back and take a wide view of the structure and dynamics of the family.

b To remind you of the complexities of family life for all its members.

c Whilst you cannot investigate a family directly, you will find it helpful to relate what you do to families you know well. The activity therefore lies halfway between observational exercise and theoretical or 'armchair' analysis.

1.2   Instructions:
First tackle the questions on your own. When finished share your findings with a colleague. Lastly, finish with a group discussion.

1.3   Assess the content of parental roles as you conceive them. Assess the major operations in each role, and also indicate overlap between them. Explore:

a How decisions are made about major commitments within the family. Do you think there is some degree of specialisation about decision making between partners?

b The possibility that, despite women working, and men taking a greater share of housework in recent years, the male role is still primarily anchored in the occupational world, and the female role largely focused on what happens within the family. Justify your conclusions.

1.4   Describe and evaluate the impact on children's development of both constructive and unhelpful forms of discipline within the family.

1.5   Is the child's position within the family a factor worthy of consideration? Examine:

a The rewards and hazards of being the eldest child.

b Particular sources of tension and difficulty for those occupying a middle position.

c Influences for good or ill on the younger or youngest child's development, particularly if born late and the birth was unplanned.

1.6   Consider the impact of density on family interaction, ie not merely the number of children, but where the births came in quick succession.

1.7   Generational tensions and rivalries appear within the best of families. Consider:

a Rivalries which occur between mother and daughter, father and son, father and daughter, mother and son.

b Tensions arising between adolescents and younger brothers and sisters.

1.8 What difficulties might be aroused by the presence of a sexually active adolescent in the family? Scan possibilities as widely as possible.

1.9 Describe a family mythology about one child being different from others, eg a child described as 'nervous' without backing evidence, or 'He's brought nothing but trouble since he was born'. Assess the effect of this on the child, relating it to the school situation.

NOTE: Considerable time will be needed for these exercises, eg an INSET day. Or sections could be tackled separately. The result should be a wealth of material for training tutors, or as a basis for discussion groups with parents.

2 Parental involvement

2.1 Assess parental reactions to such school occasions as open days or evening meetings. Work as a group of three or four. Begin by assessing which parents attend which activities.

a In the earlier years of the secondary school is it mainly the mother? If there is a problem who tends to contact the school? Do fathers show more interest in Year 11 and in discussions about A-Level choice and careers?

b Do you attract more articulate and affluent parents but fail to reach others who remain as a passive, yet potentially critical, audience of the school? What could be done to involve them? Are traditional meetings and interviews relevant to their needs? Consider the italicized words in the frequently heard statement 'The parents *we want to get at* don't come to school'.

c Look closely at the nature of communication between parents and teachers. Is there a possibility that teachers talk too much, and in a controlling way? Could parents go away resentful under a mask of politeness because they feel blocked from asking the questions they wished to ask and were put in a subordinate position?

2.2 Identify likely causes of anxiety for students, parents and teachers about meetings. Examine sources of dissatisfaction other than those mentioned above and look for sources of satisfaction which could be built on.

2.3 In what ways, and about what, are your parents likely to support the school and actively help? How could this be harnessed more effectively?

2.4 The small groups combine to work out the implications of their findings for staff development and tutor training.

NOTE: Again, this could be an INSET day exercise for middle management.

3 Written communications

3.1 Copies of letters and documents going from school to home during the preceding three terms are photocopied and carefully scrutinised. Economy of effort is achieved by each group member examining several documents.

The group members attempt to take the standpoints of the recipients establishing:

a the feelings that the documents or letters are likely to arouse;

b the impression they give of teaching as a profession;

c the quality of presentation;

d their lucidity;

e the expectations of parental response latent in them;

f their effectiveness as inducements for parents to co-operate and give support to the school.

3.2 Individuals report back and key points are recorded on flip charts.

3.3 In groups of three or four, proposals are worked out for improving communication.

3.4 Then the whole group endorse or modify the recommendations for change.

4 Working with parents

4.1 Examine as a group the skills and training tutors will need if they are to be *effective representatives of the school working closely with parents.*

4.2 Describe carefully the circumstances in which they will do this. Within what structure will it take place?

4.3 Specify the likely content of these encounters.

4.4 As a group outline the content of six one-hour training sessions for tutors. What type of activity would be appropriate?

4.5 In pairs work out one of the training sessions in detail, paying especial attention to the introductory and final activities, and the involvement of tutors in decision-making and problem-solving exercises. Be prepared to explain and justify your procedures to the group, seeking helpful feedback and suggestions for improvement.

5 School and family

Relating the discussion to specific cases, try to determine how far the school can adapt to family circumstances without:

a imposing unacceptable burdens on already fully 'stretched' teachers;

b eroding achievement and order in the classroom;

c creating damaging conflicts of priorities for the teacher.

6 Parents and community

With the Parent Teacher Association, or any other relevant group, work out measures through which parents can help other parents and the wider community understand what is happening in the school and contribute to it. This should be more than fund-raising or supporting social occasions. Your aim should be working out a graduated, step-by-step plan covering three terms.

7 Parental involvement in learning about learning

7.1 As a group work out what knowledge and training should be given to parents to help them express constructively their interest in the student's progress at school.

7.2 In pairs work out a one and a half hour training session for parents, perhaps incorporating amongst other things:

a Homework in year 7.

b Management of time and supporting GCSE projects in Years 10 and 11.

c Coping with the tensions generated by GCSE and A-Level examinations.

d Dealing with their own anxieties about their child's academic progress.

8 Student involvement

8.1 As a developmental group debate the possibility of gradually instituting *year* councils in which students can raise matters that concern them.

8.2 Begin by assessing what you see as their advantages and disadvantages.

8.3 Explore the potential contribution of such year meetings to positive discipline and the growth of self-management and responsibility in students.

8.4 Consider also their potential use as 'early warning systems' which bring tensions and difficulties into the open before parents and governors feel compelled to raise them.

9 Whose viewpoint? Biased perceptions

9.1 Discuss the situation where a student gives biased and distorted views to his or her parents of what happens in school. Parents are also used as the reason for not doing homework. This is merely one example of the way in which the student constantly plays parents off against the school and *vice versa*. How would you gain the co-operation of the parents in dealing with the problem? How could this machiavellian student best be tackled?

Work in pairs, following this with group discussion.

9.2 How should parents' unwitting reinforcement of gender stereo-types about learning and potential careers be tackled? What part should tutor and parent meetings play in inducing necessary attitude change?

9.3 What stresses are created by the mutual judgements of parents and teachers. Begin by completing the blocks below:

Main criteria on which parents judge teachers	Main criteria on which teachers judge parents

Examine any discrepancies, concordances or possible sources of discord. Then ask what your analysis tells you about your concept of the teacher as a professional.

Next attempt to estimate the *motives* that each group will attribute to the other when dissonance and consequent tension arise. Proceed as before.

Motives likely to be attributed *to* teachers *by* parents	Motives likely to be attributed *to* parents *by* teachers

Discuss how awareness of judgemental tendencies on both sides helps you read situations more accurately, and therefore act constructively.

10 Loss and grieving

10.1 Identify the stresses which may be experienced by a student in the period before divorce or separation occurs and during the event. Produce general guidelines for coping to be employed by the tutor.

10.2 Discuss what you would find problematical in helping a tutor group cope with the death of a member. Work in pairs, then share ideas with the rest of the group. Then work out the structure and ground rules that you think would be helpful for tutors.

7 Relating counselling skills to careers education and guidance

Limitations

Of necessity, the discussion is too brief to take into account welcome developments in NVQs and the introduction of BTEC First programmes into sixth forms. Exciting work is being undertaken with industry – Warwick (Ed.) (1989) provides a stimulating overview. The challenge postulated by Europe is illuminated in Funnell and Muller (1991). Counselling skills and activities can support these exciting advances. Schools must apply self-concept theory, whilst understanding the conflicts and stresses of adolescent development. Doubt about oneself is paralleled by uncertainty about what one's future is to be. Counselling skills related to the vocational field will be concerned with practical activities which encourage self-knowledge and *informed* decision-making.

Life style

Developmental counselling helps the individual cope with the legitimate demands common to her or his culture and the social groups within it. One widespread expectation is that the adolescent will prepare herself or himself for working life. From the tutor's position, primacy should be given to three factors clearly linking self-perceptions to vocational development:

1. *Life style* The task is to assist the student to become aware of what will bring him or her satisfaction and a feeling of being engaged in a worthwhile enterprise within the world of work. Knowledge of the expanding range of choices available in a technological society has to be acquired so that wise decisions can be made. Put simply, the life style of a miner is different from that of a shop assistant. They are both different from someone working a continental shift system in a large factory or a member of the police force. All are different from the life

style of a milkman or woman. The life style of each will be acceptable, even desirable, to some individuals, and unsuitable, even repellent, to others. Note that occupational choices can never be totally free: it is choice within limits, although the limits may be wider than the individual supposes.

2. *Field* The occupational world can usefully be conceived as broad fields of activity, each integrated through a predominant activity or theme, eg the medical, computational or aesthetic fields. Within each field to which the individual is attracted for reasons of aptitude, personality and cultural values, many specific occupations exist.

3. *Level* Within a particular field, one may work at various levels of skill and responsibility, eg in the medical field the range would encompass senior consultant to mortuary attendant. Awareness of qualifications, willingness to undertake study and training, and to forego immediate rewards and satisfactions are factors germane to consideration of level.

The three – life style, field and level – form the basic framework for counselling activities concerned with career development. But as in 1974 it still seems necessary to question what is meant by a 'career'. Traditionally, it implied steady progress and advancement resulting from long term planning, but many of our students will occupy jobs as and when they can get them. They will reach maximal earning capacity early in life, whilst their work responsibilities will be limited. Careers education activitiesmay have over-stressed the intrinsic satisfactions of work, although students more realistically focus on pay and fringe benefits. The emphasis on intrinsic satisfaction *may* reflect the middle class concept ofcareer, and incorporate teachers' assumptions about what is desirable. *Curriculum Matters 10* (1988) helpfully avoids such evaluation by equating career with the 'variety of occupational roles' undertaken throughout working life. This descriptive rather than evaluatory approach underlies this chapter.

In common with many others, this discussion will emphasise choice and rationality in the activities. Yet in practice, the most potent theory of career choice may be accident theory. Many students will, in spite of our efforts, decide impulsively and on emotive factors. Vocational choice may still, despite the massive efforts of recent years, be a largely unplanned, haphazard or opportunistic affair for many adolescents. This is no justification for throwing in the towel; rather we should ensure careers education is a long-term activity related to every subject.

The experience of two major recessions means that those offering careers counselling and careers education have to face difficult questions. Many young people obtain their first job near home. If local unemployment is high, one response may be for careers counsellors to intensify the time and effort spent in developing pupils' job-search and self-presentation skills. This may equip people better to compete in the job market, but it does not make more jobs available. Careers staff have to be realistic without being defeatist: the forces which erode young people's self-respect and motivation if they remain unemployed must be anticipated and, if possible, strategies devised to combat them. Hard questions have to be faced: Is any job better than no job? The broader underlying questions are about values: if exchange relations are at the heart of social solidarity, what do the unemployed have to exchange?

The student's self-picture

Developing a satisfying occupational life style requires one to know oneself. Two fundamental questions have to be tackled during the student's secondary school career: 'Who am I?' and 'What am I to be?'. These twin lines of self-exploration form the foundation for positive mental health in adult working life. They illustrate the link between sharpening identity and vocational choice. If the student's self-knowledge is distorted or inadequate, she or he will be handicapped in making vocational decisions. The effective tutor will appreciate the significance of the second question. 'What am I to be?' is a very different question from 'What am I to do?'. The latter highlights the task, underplaying personality and life style with which the tutor taking a developmental stance will be concerned.

Super (1957) still offers the most developmentally relevant theory of vocational choice. In choosing an occupation he believes the adolescent, more or less consciously, to be translating her or his self-picture into reality. At the risk of over-simplifying, it seems that the job chooser is required to say, fairly explicitly, 'I am that sort of person'. Much therefore depends on the efficiency of provision of both self-exploratory and work-related activities by the school. Tutors must realise that their task is not to provide answers, but to help students raise meaningful questions, providing experiences through which they can find satisfying answers.

Perhaps the above conceals the possibility that choice may equally well be shaped by what the student is not, rather than what he or she is. We are all probably clearer about the negatives than the positives; about what we will not do, rather than what we will. We would not become accountants, butchers or clerks because we do not see ourselves as that kind of person. Realistically, many adolescents tend to select from what is available after the impossible and the distasteful have been eliminated. This makes it imperative that those offering counselling understand the student's perceptions of an occupational group. He or she may attribute to its members characteristics which are unreal, eg the armed services may be seen as generally belligerent. Activities must afford opportunity for evaluating such distorted stereotypes.

Reality suggests that factors other than self-image influence career choice. Economic structure dictates choices, eg the proportion of professional careers to relatively unskilled jobs. We cannot assume universality of values: more than a few adolescents see planning for their futures as neither desirable nor necessary. Some individuals have learned to depend on controls and directon from others. For some, the processes influencing choice are largely intuitive and unverbalised. Somehow, they have insulated themselves against the opportunities for rational self-understanding in guidance.

Choice is always within limits. Students may not be aware of constraints, but on the other hand the possibilities may be greater than the individual supposes. Ginzberg *et al* (1971) show that eventual career choice is preceded by a process: stimulating self-awareness and probing reality critically, building a fund of information for use in decision-making. Information is essential, but students have to be trained to assess and apply it.

It should be clear that tutor work should incorporate activities through which a student develops a perspective about herself or himself in relation to the world of work. As a developmental process it is liable to fluctuations in the rate of development similar to physical or emotional growth. The tutor is alert to retarded and impaired vocational development. Retarded vocational growth is where reactions and decisions are being unduly influenced by a factor usually predominant at an earlier age, eg glamour or excitement. Impaired vocational choice includes over-reliance on one factor such as aptitude without reference to interest and personality. Inflated aspirations unrelated to ability provide another form. Desires may incorporate immaturity and reflect maladjustment. Irrationality is high: goals are changed frequently, being determined by current mood. The student may be susceptible to parental attempts at imposing their frustrated ambitions, or pressures to conform to family patterns of work, eg where there is a long established country general practice, and the student is the only son or daughter. Personal counselling is necessary in the above situations; group counselling could be damaging, submitting the student to suggestions from peers who are unaware of the complications.

It should be stressed that students cannot fully profit from knowledge of the world of work until reasonable self-knowledge has been acquired. Hence the importance of self-appraisal in year seven. The objective is to afford students a chance to scrutinise such dichotomies and become aware that the distinctions are not so clear-cut as appears at first sight. A list of jobs is constructed from which students select those they believe to be mainly about working with people; those primarily orientated to machines, scientific instruments etc, and those to do with ideas. Partners then explore their likes and dislikes about the jobs placed under each heading. Questions can be raised about the validity of these distinctions, eg Does working with people sometimes require the use of machines? Computer-assisted guidance programmes can be useful here, incorporating much of the material found in interest tests. Follow-up discussion could pay critical attention to the topic of 'people versus things'. Broad preferences such as the orientation either to work primarily with people or things need careful discussion. Awareness of such preferences has to be followed by probing and assessment of their potential consequences, eg some who work in the helping professions are too drained to relate as they should to their own families. The clarifying of self and its matching with the occupational world is more complex than appears at first sight. Is a false or façade self operating? An individual may appear self-aware, but be unaware that this is the product of unusually strong family expectations, long-term conditioning and evaluations. A self has been imposed rather than acquired. Many of the forces shaping self-analysis *and* vocational decisions are largely intuitive, evading rational scrutiny. Constant debate and exploration are necessary to help the individual grasp opportunities to control his or her fate.

It is easy to talk as if the self is unitary, when as Wall (1948; 1968) argues, adolescents are building up a number of *selves*. Dissonance, even conflict, exists as much as concordance between these groupings of self-related constructs. Let me illustrate. If the philosophical or 'world view' self contains altruism as a predominant element, but for reasons of aptitude the student is attracted to an area of commerce where ruthless competition is the norm, potential for conflict between philosophical and vocational selves is obviously great. If a male perceives sharp and rigid divisions between masculine and feminine behaviours, and yet is drawn for reasons of availability to work in nursing or hotels – which he categorises as both feminine and servile – complicated adjustments have to be made. These illustrations taken from my counselling, highlight the need to build such tensions into exercises and discussions.

Unwillingness to make a choice may occasionally be a reaction to a philosophical self which defines its holder as a pawn unable to make any impact on the course of events. Topics for inclusion in the counselling activities should look closely at notions of success. Its nature and personal meaning should be clarified. Differences between desired success and expectations of what will occur spark off insights, and are the first step in interrupting self-defeating patterns of behaviour. Over-reliance on luck as an explanation of success, or blind reliance on effort as ensuring it should be challenged. The need to question assimilation of parental beliefs about nepotism in the work place indicate the variety of topics essential to self-development in the vocational self.

Field and level

Taken together, field and level provide a structure for many counselling activities. As mentioned earlier, field refers to the general characteristics of an occupation: eg computational, scientific, literary, persuasive. It is a broad area of human endeavour to which a student is attracted by both aptitude and personality. Level is about the student's aspirations within the field or fields of particular interest to her or him. It is concerned with the willingness to invest time and energy in pursuit of qualifications and training. Neither field nor level are unproblematical. Unrealistically high or low levels of aspiration occur even within a field suited to the student. Tensions arise when the student's proposed level of aspiration differs from that expected or desired for her or him by parents. Unrealistically high vocational aspirations held by the student often have a complex aetiology or serve widely differing functions – evasion of reality or self-punishment where the student foredooms himself or herself to continuous struggle and inevitable frustration. Tutors are then in a quandary: they wish to interrupt pursuit of an impossible goal, but fear intervention will cause damage to self-respect. One solution is to imbed such dilemmas into case histories for students to consider; another is systematically to train them in working out the probabilities of success and failure, encouraging them to apply the thinking in their own lives.

Field and level can be used as a tool for analysing vocational problems in counselling. If level of aspiration seems right, but the field is unrelated to interests and aptitudes, then undue parental and peer influence may be operating. Equally, idiosyncratic and unquestioned perceptions of either the selected or rejected field, or both, may need challenging.

Especially wearing are the students who try to evade responsibility for their own decisions through over-reliance on others. Their desire to be told what to do – usually to put the adviser in the wrong because they misuse the advice – extends to computer-assisted guidance. One has to resist their seductive helplessness and insist they use the one-step-at-a-time approach described earlier. They usually want a blanket prescription for action which, of course, is unlikely to work.

Able adolescents may need support in coping with a tendency well described by Tyler (1958). They feel compelled to become everything that they could be, resisting any attempt to encourage dropping or restricting possibilities. Yet they have to exclude some alternatives, deny some ambitions or reduce them to the status of hobbies. If they are not careful, they vacillate in approach/approach dilemmas. The alternatives are equally possible and attractive because of their ability. Their intelligence will usually release them: but intelligence and maturity are not necessarily concomitant. Students can, of course, be trapped in choice situations where the alternatives are equally unattractive.

Stereotypes and wider issues

Vocational development must be a process covering all the secondary years. Self-appraisal is at the heart of this many-faceted activity. Discussion topics range widely, eg balanced reflection on family perceptions of employment or the values relevant to future occupational roles. The career implications of subject choice is an obvious topic: not so palpable is the need for student identification of what they are learning which will be of value in the world of work. Attitudes, coping techniques, methods of dealing with loss of face or frustration are examples of cross-curricular leaning relevant to vocational development. For the teacher the question is, 'How can I through my subject prepare students for a changing world?' (Adapted from IFAPLAN, Brussels.) This should be debated vigorously by tutors in conjunction with students. Only this joint involvement will bring the sense of vitality and purpose needed to cope with the demands of industrial and social change.

Occupational stereotypes cannot be left unchallenged. They arc conventional and usually over-generalised beliefs about the nature of the job, and of those doing it. Content of occupational stereotypes is positive or derogatory, although the latter usually dominates. Teachers, police, clergy and lawyers seem particularly prone to be the object of stereotypes incorporating misconceptions and heavily loaded with prejudice. Stereotyping extends to subjects: students unthinkingly use them to judge areas of learning. A simple activity opening up the topic by discussing the familiar follows.

Discuss in groups of four:

What kind of person is good at:

- physics
- PE
- art
- mathematics
- French?

Then the tutor challenges their views by asking, 'Is there really a special kind of person or not? What evidence have you?' Class discussion follows.

Students can be given a job title, eg plumber, booking clerk or nurse. They write down the characteristics they associate with workers in that job. In groups of three each in turn tells the others what she or he has written. The other two then question him or her about the validity of what was written and if possible produce counter evidence.

Curriculum Matters 10 provides a comprehensive overview of careers education. It stresses the need for informed decision-making after methodical investigation of possibilities. Readers are referred to Chapter Three for a fuller discussion of decision-making. Yost and Corbishley (1987) produce a useful outline of the steps needed to make a career decision. It has been adapted and condensed to fit the situation of the adolescent at school in year 11 and in the sixth form:

1. *Self-understanding* – a process beginning in year seven and expanded in a planned way in later years.

2. *Making sense of data related to self exploration.* This is achieved through discussion and activities involving the individual and peers in mutual evaluation and formative assessment. (The discussion in Chapter Four on formative assessment should be helpful.)

3. *Identifying alternatives* – on the basis of life style, field and level the student identifies possible careers.

4. *Obtaining occupational information.* Possibilities are arranged in an order of priority. The benefits and costs of each are assessed as fully as possible.

5. *Making a choice.* Discussion with parents and interested adults, especially the careers officer, is essential to allow the student to check the wisdom of the choice.

6. *Making plans to reach goals*, anticipating any difficulties and taking measures to deal with them.

The italicized portions are taken from Yost and Corbishley (1987) although the wording has been slightly modified. Noteworthy in *Curriculum Matters 10* is the insistence on the importance of preparation of contingency plans. This is crucial in years ten, 11, and later, as choices crystallise. The skill of thinking in this way is part of preparation to be a creative, responsible worker. Schools do not condition students to become the passive recipients of managerial non-wisdom. They prepare them to be responsible workers who use their critical faculties constructively in problem solving. Dale (1985) and Roberts (1984) remark on the difference between preparing adolescents for obtaining a job, and stimulating the styles of thinking and problem solving essential to being an effective employee in an industrial world which demands versatility. Ansoff (1984) reminds us that turbulence in the economic and industrial climate is liable to turn past strengths into weaknesses. It is fatal to rely on past solutions when they are no longer competent guides to future action. Imaginative thinking which begins with recognition of potential contingencies, and breeds the flexible mental set to deal with them must be encouraged in careers guidance. The sensitivity in responding to scarcely visible signs of emerging problems – and of reading the signals accurately – is what we should be struggling to produce in student guidance. We would be lacking in social responsibility if we succumbed to pressures to send out into the world of work young people who look to the past, and who have limited perceptions of work skills more appropriate to the Victorian era than a post-industrial society. Much current talk debases the nature of skills, trivialising the task of the educator. Our job is to tackle the 'mentality filters' which restrict students' capacity to cope with rapid change.

In recent years it has been disturbing to note that the long run output of pastoral work may contradict our declared desire to facilitate responsible autonomy. Pastoral 'systems' restricted to emotional first aid, administration of trivial disciplinary reprimands and after-the-event reactions rather than preventive work may be reinforcing passivity and dependence and allocating deviant identities rather than building initiative and enterprise. The nature of success, the conditions in which it flourishes, and the use of productive tensions between co-operation and competition should be key areas in career counselling. Both competition and co-operation as behaviours are ethically neutral: it is the uses to which they are put that are more loaded. One can compete to out-perform other individuals or groups in altruistic activities. Perhaps this comes close to arguing that the end justifies the means, but there appears to be little evidence that constructive competition is inconceivable. One can co-operate with others in group situations to compete with other groups in achieving a standard of excellence. It is naïve to think in terms of 'winner take all' as inevitable in competition. Co-operation is used to raise group members' levels of competence so that all may eventually strive to achieve at their highest possible level in situations where competition is essential.

General approaches to activities

Activities should incorporate the interaction between co-operation and competition mentioned above. Small groups' members co-operate to achieve the task, comparing their results with those of others. Competition between small groups to contribute to some corporate task such as a careers exhibition is merely one example. Standpoint-taking has to be developed *and* applied in activities. The worker who fails to appreciate the views of her or his colleagues, superiors or employer will be handicapped through inflexibility. Certainly he or she will have limited capacity to anticipate contingencies. Inability to take standpoints reduces the likelihood of early detection of resentment, tensions and feelings of being manipulated.

The counselling task is to help the student understand the constraints that will reduce her or his efficacy as a future worker, eg blindly-held beliefs that they cannot master certain skills or that certain goals are not for them. Safety is sought through setting low targets, almost as if they were presenting themselves as incapable. These behaviours are purposeful strategies which function to defend their users against threats to a fragile sense of self-esteem by helping them avoid unwelcome vulnerabilities in competition and threat of failure.

All the information and activity will be of little use if they are not helped to understand these mechanisms. An earlier argument can now be restated: 'If there are processes at work in the adolescent's life which reduce his or her potential as a worker and constrain realistic ambitions unnecessarily, it is imperative that counselling confronts them.' The students just mentioned would have to see that they are motivated more by fear of failure and the need to avoid risk than by desire for success. They would have to recognise the wasteful expenditure of energy inherent in their behaviours. Tutors will meet students who have assimilated parental limitations on achievement: they must be aided to see that not only are their aspirations legitimate, but capable of achievement.

One meets frequent references to the growth of an 'underclass' in British society who are deprived and excluded from the rewards available to the majority. For them traditional emphases of careers education are irrelevant. They will be in and out of jobs in rapid succession, remaining only loosely attached to the occupational world. Most will be impervious to the views and sanctions of management. In many ways their behaviour in school is good preparation for a life of minimal satisfactions and survival through evasion. Yet we have a duty to help them without patronage or dishonest manipulation of facts. They know more than some of us about economic and social reality. The counselling component in TVEI and CPVE will have to be strengthened and adapted to their needs. Studies of the development of conscience and moral behaviour agree that self-respect is essential for responsible behaviour. These adolescents are bombarded with experiences which reduce self-respect, except within their peer group to which they probably affiliated strongly and defensively from the early years of schooling. Peer support and counselling will have to be utilised. (Hamblin, 1986 offers some help with this.) Emphasis will have to be on small group work where, in the presence of peers, students have to explain, justify and trim their ideas to meet new evidence and alternative standpoints coming from sources that possess credibility for them. The use of peer judges as evaluators is crucial; tensions and minor explosions will almost certainly occur but so does something useful. Occupation of the peer judge role is often the first step in modifying the student's views.

Self-assessment begins in year seven. Efforts should be made to link self-assessment for RoA and careers education. From year seven – before enthusiasm wanes – students should be given the experience of interviewing parents, relatives and family friends about fairly precise aspects of work, eg what the worker does in a typical day, enjoyable or tedious elements. They should present their findings to the form. The technique can, over the years, be elaborated into the presentation of simulations as described in Chapter Three. Students could investigate occasions when adults they know felt particularly satisfied with their work. The reasons for the satisfaction and its frequency should be assessed. Individuals or partners present their findings using tape recordings, posters, etc and launch small group discussions followed by general discussion. Herzberg (1968) offers cogent guides to topics for investigation in his findings that five factors are prime as determinants of job satisfaction:

1. The sense of achieving something worthwhile;

2. Recognition (from whom and for what will have to be made explicit);

3. The nature of the work itself;

4. The responsibilities undertaken by the post holder;

5. Opportunities for advancement.

From the outset imagination should play an important part. For example, students could describe what they believe to be the peak satisfactions of selected jobs. Comparison of perceptions with those of others follows. Year ten students could corroborate or change their beliefs through observation and interviews during work experience. Sources of dissatisfaction should be treated similarly.

In the later years close attention should be paid to authority relationships in work. This can be linked with other areas of tutorial activity which equip young people responsibly to question the credentials of alleged experts in an increasingly technological society. If family messages about work carry insinuations of manipulation and exploitation by managers, then counselling activities should evaluate their reality, challenging them if necessary. This leads to wider inquiry into the nature of working relationships. Social distance between groups of workers, age and gender in composition of working groups, and the ethos of the firm fostered as part of company policy merit scrutiny. Older students will see the implications of the possibility that identical actions will have different meanings in a school marked by openness and a collegiate approach and one permeated with threat, suspicion and distrust. Industrial and other organisations are similarly influenced. Careers education which does not encourage understanding of such factors could justly be queried as intellectually bankrupt.

Themes for specific years

Challenging gender stereotypes about work roles begins in year seven when the transition from primary to secondary creates a willingness to revise ideas. Small group work should examine students' beliefs about the abilities of the sexes. In activities it is important to encourage both sexes to question traditional views of women's role in work. Guests should be invited to tutor periods, questions being prepared in advance. This preparatory work is extremely valuable when conducted in small groups where students sharpen their questions and have to justify them. Incidentally, this increases the probability of efficient assimilation and processing of the answers. Ideas are then listed on the blackboard, the form selecting what will be asked of the guest, and the sequence of asking decided.

Year eight might usefully begin by thinking about values. The 'ladder' technique has stimulated many good discussions. The ladder is drawn on the board, along with a list of various qualities, eg interesting tasks, good pay, chance of promotion, pleasant workmates. The tutor starts to arrange qualities on the ladder according to the form's ideas. Then a duplicated form with qualities and the ladder is issued. Students then explain and justify their order of priority in groups of three or four. Discussion of the results with the whole form participating ends the session.

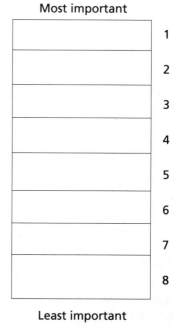

Figure 7.1 *The values ladder*

Sorting situations within work into 'liked', 'disliked' or 'uncertain' groups again sharpens awareness. There is no need for cards; it can be done from the blackboard or a transparency. Typical situations would be using a computer, answering the telephone, dealing with a complaint, working on a lathe or power machine, driving a fork lift. Small group discussions allow misconceptions to be corrected without loss of face. It has proved useful to get the form to produce the ideas for the situations sort. They are grouped under, 'I would like this', 'I would not like this' and 'Not sure'. Students then discuss the two most liked and the two most disliked with a partner. They then turn their attention to those about which they were uncertain. Contrasts are important, adding vitality to the activities. On the one hand, pictures of glamour based occupations could be collected. Students then look at the impact of chance, the factors which put individuals into favour or destroy popularity, the nature of rewards, snags and difficulties. Tutors should avoid a Cassandra approach: students' good sense will lead to realistic evaluation. On the other hand, students should study with the aid of parents easily accessible occupations, eg fire officer, road worker or office worker. Small groups then give simple presentations to the form with audience participation in finding solutions, eg 'How does the milkman or woman deal with the person who is never at home when the bill has to be paid?'.

Imagination has a part to play. Students record an imaginary interview with the workers, exercising their skills of standpoint-taking. They play them to the form, inviting comments, amongst other things, on accuracy. Critics have to produce evidence to justify their quibbles. There are several variations on this theme: describing a job as if they were the worker, or taping imaginary interviews with the manager of a small enterprise and with somebody who has just left school to work in the firm and is making initial adjustments. Guidance and stimulation of ideas will be necessary, but older students engaged in CPVE and TVEI can be enlisted as helpers.

Subsidiary objectives include gaining an appreciation of the changes in work during this century. This includes technical change as well as improved conditions. Even in one person's lifetime the change has been enormous te writer left school at 14 to work 44 hours a week in a factory; at 16 it went up to 48 hours. Pensioners can be asked about conditions, eg hours of work, holidays, supervision and fringe benefits, comparing them with those existing when they retired. Tutors should let the group think about the existence of nostalgia, romanticism and exaggeration in these reports.

Economic awareness begins with management of pocket money and saving for Christmas and holidays. One head uses a year seven school trip as the starting point. Money taken by students is restricted. On the first evening they go to the cinema and are allowed to spend freely. Next morning, students assess what they have left and work out their daily expenditure. The wisdom of buying several cans of drink and large ice creams is questioned. Rueful expressions show that the message is getting home. This then leads into a package of activities on saving and keeping to a budget.

Year nine's theme is success. It is the year when dissociation from school is evident in a sizeable group of students. A vigorous programme on success acts as an antidote to apathy. Successes pupils would like are compared with what they predict they will achieve. Ways of closing the gap are examined. Links with classroom experience are made: students look at beliefs about the cause of success in school. They proceed to look at success in work, assessing the qualities valued by employers and fellow workers. Sixth form students can lead discussions and activities on the career relevance of subjects.

Careful sampling of the range of occupations available in the locality can form the basis for visits. Note that the whole form need not attend: a well-briefed small group visits, and constructs a presentation on it, using audience participation as much as possible. Individuals shadow a worker for the day. They report back to the form who have prepared questions under the guidance of an older student. This leads to assessment of oneself as a potential worker. The form abstracts the qualities of a good worker from the experiences described above to construct a simple profile. They apply it to themselves, writing a brief report on themselves. Accuracy is checked through group work.

Standpoint-taking should figure largely in activities for years nine and ten. Small groups prepare playlets and recordings on accidents, crises, challenges and tensions which reveal the existence of different viewpoints. A strike or the challenge to deliver a major contract in the required time provide examples. More precise comparisons can be made of the teacher's job as seen by the teacher herself or himself, a student and a parent. The form divides into three to specify the perceptions held by each person. They describe them, holding a general debate on the significance of discrepancies and concordances.

The police officer's job can be investigated from the viewpoint of wife or husband, son or daughter, the person next door, and the constable, sergeant or inspector himself or herself. Aspects of life style, restrictions on friends and social activities or the impact on the partner of moving and isolation may surface. The impact on son or daughter is studied: to be a police sergeant's son or daughter in a small country town can create vulnerability, even a sense of threat.

The need to match job demands with personality and aptitudes reminds us of the old concept of 'occupational and psychological talk' (Starishevsky and Matlin, 1968). A simple application is shown in Figure 7.2.

Figure 7.2

	LIKE ME	NOT LIKE ME
A hairdresser should be:		
1 Polite	☐	☐
2 Able to understand the customer's viewpoint	☐	☐
3 Patient	☐	☐
4 Have a good sense of humour	☐	☐
5 Ready to learn etc	☐	☐
A lawyer should:		
1 Have good verbal ability	☐	☐
2 Be able to anticipate the reactions of others	☐	☐
3 Remain calm under pressure	☐	☐
4 Have persuasive skills	☐	☐
5 Be methodical and precise	☐	☐

If the match is strong, students could investigate the occupation further. But it should be made clear that such exercises are intended primarily to make them think more deeply about the links between personality and the demands of a job. Year ten students returning from work experience contribute well to these discussions.

Hopson, who has done so much excellent work in careers education, produced an aid to assessment of an occupation – SPEEDCOP. It is also a helpful framework for observation and questioning in work experience. In presenting it, I have modified the content slightly.

Surroundings Is the workplace, for example, noisy, dirty, hot? Does it involve offensive odours which cling to hair or clothing?

Prospects Is it a contracting or expanding occupation? Are new technological and commercial developments probable which will lead to new careers?

Entry and training What qualifications are required? What is the preferred age of entry? Is there a conflict between the training offered by the firm and staying on for A-Levels and other sixth form qualifications?

Effects Does it, for example, restrict social life through the hours worked? Is geographical mobility a requirement?

Description What are the main tasks? Is variety or routine the norm? Is the individual required to work alone or as a member of a team? What responsibilities have to be accepted?

Conditions What are the rates of pay; do they compare favourably with other jobs at approximately the same level? Is there long-term security or risk of redundancy? What fringe benefits are available, eg social clubs, pension plans, mortgages at preferential rates?

Organisation Is it large or small; dispersed or concentrated on one site? What image does it have with the public, eg Marks and Spencer's name evokes integrity.

People Who are the customers or clients? What are their general characteristics, economically and socially? What is the composition of the work group in terms of age, gender, and time of service with the organisation?

Speedcop has many uses for assessment of visits and work experience. It can be particularly helpful in providing a yardstick for measuring students' aspirations and satisfactions.

Students should be taught the skills of observation and constructive questioning if visits and work experience are to have full educational value. Hamblin (1986) argued that students should be taught the skills of counselling, and how to apply them in interaction with others, especially those involved in clarifying and exploring the problem. To establish communication students should know how to use open questions and send signals of acceptance. Listening for discrepancies between statements and detecting differences between what people say they do and what happens in practice is also essential.

Discussion of the student's role will include helping them understand the constraints and limits on behaviour operating in a work situation, accepting that routines and procedures have to be followed. There should be no premature evaluation of them: their avowed purposes and actual effect can be discussed later. The greater elasticity of school rules compared with those of industry, and the significance of sanctions such as verbal and written warnings, raise matters important in making successful transition from school to work. Rewards and frustrations should figure prominently in observation. How do people cope with the latter, and what value is placed on the rewards by those who receive and those who allocate them? The perceptions of the two groups will be very different. Adolescents are highly sensitive to loss of face: it will be enlightening for students to observe the situations and forms it take in work, and the methods of dealing with it. Observation of the beliefs and behaviours of sub-groups – workers, supervisors and senior management – about each other's purposes, and their ideas of the best way of doing things, leads to illuminating insights into behaviour in organisations.

Training in interview skills is the next step. This applies not only to the obvious skills of dressing appropriately, and finding out about the firm's objectives and its product, but the skills of reading the signals sent by the interviewer. Some personnel officers feel that interviewees are insensitive, failing to respond to cues or see the intent of questions. Sending a positive picture of oneself is not deceit: it is applying one's intelligence in *asking* questions which show that the issue has been grasped, and that the interviewee is capable of dealing with it.

In my work with young people it seems that problems of role adjustment and relationships largely account for stress in the first job. Failure to manage the social and psychological adjustments can cause young people to abandon their first job even when they recognise that they are unlikely to get another. Study of the relationships between different age groups and between the sexes as part of work experience is useful preparation. This should be extended through decision-making exercises which allow exploration of 'triggers for trouble' in work, eg an older and well-established worker encourages you to flout safety regulations on the flimsy, yet persuasive, basis that 'everybody here does it'. How would you cope? Alternative lines of action are worked out, evaluated, and then tried out in role play. The objective is to create awareness, extend the individual's potential repertoire of behaviour, and equip her or him to make thoughtful decisions taking costs and consequences into account.

Year 11 in practice is a two-term year. GSCE assignments and revision eat away the time available for other areas of guidance. Decision-making can be deepened through the involvement of parents. Parents can be invited in to talk about their work; key decisions they make; troublesome and anxiety-producing factors. Concrete situations are then presented, partners or small groups working at their resolution. Feedback is given to the parent who examines proposed actions, highlighting unrecognised costs and ignored complexities.

Students think of 'being interviewed by the careers officer'. He or she is seen as dominating, with most of the input coming from the adult. The student's task is to answer appropriately. Just as RoA require students to raise, rather than solely answer, questions, so there is great profit to be gained from the form interviewing the careers officer in depth. Once his or her functions and expertise have been clarified, attention turns to effective preparation for the individual interview with her or him. Suggestions are proffered, but the form debates, rather than passively acquiesces. This preparation is usefully linked with self-appraisal exercises in which the individual writes a report on himself or herself as if she or he were a potential employer. These reports are then scrutinised for accuracy or evidence of selective omissions and self-deception in a group of trusted friends.

Some preparation for transition difficulties in the first six months of work can be done in year 11. It cannot wait until the sixth form: the students who need guidance most are often those not proceeding to sixth form or tertiary college. The situations set out below embody some of the reported stress situations which undo young workers. If left unchallenged, they can lead to disenchantment and the blunting of enthusiasm for the job. Equally important: it is not sensible to invest effort in building self-esteem during the student's schooling, but fail to anticipate self-eroding incidents during a peculiarly vulnerable period – the first six months of work. The following recur often enough to merit special attention:

1. Coping with the initial joking and testing out that are the lot of a new entrant to an established working group. Clumsily aggressive reactions or display of discomfiture will lead to crude labelling as a 'bighead' or 'whinger' that will not easily be discarded. Labelling processes in working groups are stronger and more vicious than anything of which the secondary school has been accused.

2. Maintaining aspirations to maintain standards of excellence or achieve promotion when the individual is set within a working group where the norms focus around 'avoiding being done down' and 'doing as little as possible for as much as possible'. Management is seen as 'them' against 'us', leaving little opportunity for assimilation of managerial objectives.

3. Dealing with contradictory supervisors or immediate authority where the habitual response to problems is to apportion blame irrationally to others.

4. Dealing with the first major error. The importance of dealing with this competently, and using it as an opportunity to enhance credibility, should be studied carefully. The impression created by the young worker's reactions, and their likely influence on superiors' future judgements illustrate the issues to be discussed.

5. Tensions with workmates should be recognised as a major factor in work adjustment. Young people have to learn how to deal with the colleague who is always occupied elsewhere at the moment when hard work is required. Some conveniently self-declare themselves as sick

during periods of high pressure. The temptation of 'If she/he can get away with it, then I will' is typical of the points which get to the heart of the problem.

6. The young worker is likely to act as a buffer between the clients/customers and older uncooperative or well-established staff members. They feel trapped in a force field which is negative. Any action they take appears liable to provoke criticism. Simple exercises show potential ways of coping, restoring the sense of efficacy.

7. False accusations cause conflict to escalate if not handled wisely. Aggressive reactions strengthen the accuser's belief that the young person is guilty. If the accused is abusive, then she or he may be disciplined, even dismissed, for that rather than the alleged offence. The seriousness of a verbal warning may escape the young worker who has experienced many in his or her school career.

8. There is an implicit etiquette in industry and commerce: all the more powerful because it operates under the surface. Exploration of it is crucial if young people are not to activate suspicion, putting themselves at risk in the future. To bypass one's immediate supervisor to complain to a higher level of management probably means that one is listened to, but that manager is also asking, 'Do I have a trouble-maker here?'.

9. It is useful to simulate answering the telephone under noise or using a caculator or computer with people asking the worker questions or distracting them. Feelings and ability to cope are diverse, meriting close consideration of their consequences.

Sixth form work should examine the leadership skills needed to create the climate for calling out the best in others and productive teamwork. Discussion groups employing counselling skills should prepare the 16- to 19-year-olds for creative managerial interaction with colleagues. Topics should include what prevents one from 'reading' a situation accurately. The parts played by insecurity or prejudice will be only two of the factors highlighted. Students will need to examine the way in which they attribute negative or positive motivation to others in a variety of situations. Awareness of the criteria used in judging someone – age, race and social class – are viewed as possible sources of distortion; beliefs about the nature and purpose of criticism and subsequent reactions offer a glimpse of what has proved useful. Relevant material can be found in *Guidance 16–19*. The objective of making counselling a joint enterprise between students and staff will be achieved when we equip the 16–19 age group with the skills laid out in this book.

Activities

1 Work visits and experience:

1.1 In groups of four:

a Discuss the place of visits to local industries in your careers education and guidance programme. Consider the possibility and uses of visits in years eight and nine, the need to sample the range of occupations available.

b Look at alternatives to visits by the whole group, eg visits by a small group who present their finding to the tutor group using tape recordings, etc, the shadowing of a different worker by three or four students who then combine to prepare a presentation on the workers shadowed.

As a group prepare recommendations for the use of visits in years seven to 11.

1.2 As a group consider the possibility that students will meet opinions and have experiences that contravene the school's efforts to combat gender stereotypes. Identify the sources and nature of these forces; consider how you will help students deal with them.

1.3 **a** Examine critically the objectives of work experience. Debate whether or not students can really occupy a work role. If not, specify as precisely as possible its purposes and the degree to which they are achieved.

b Evaluate your current preparation of students for work experience. (Groups of four.)

- Does it offer training in observational and recording skills?

- Is attention drawn to what the placement values in its workers?

- Is attention directed to collection of feedback about themselves and assessment of their strengths and weaknesses? It may be particularly important to direct attention to what makes the individual acceptable or unacceptable in the working group.

As a group prepare recommendations for change based on the small group findings.

1.4 In small groups consider the adequacy of follow-up to work experience. Is sufficient attention paid to:

- unrealistic perceptions of interest or boredom of the job;

- differences between the discipline of the work place and that of school;

- gaining a balanced perception of the stresses of the job?

Then as a whole group:

a Develop an evaluatory schedule to be used by students after work experience;

b Outline a module of activities concerned with preparation and follow-up of work experience.

Topics to be included are:

- An imaginative assessment of what it would feel like to go to the placement as one's first job.

- The rewards available for hard work.

- The treatment of mistakes or indifferent performance.

- How workers are assessed. What do they know about staff appraisal and its purposes?

2 Interview training

2.1 As a whole group 'brainstorm' ideas for a package of activities on interview training. Submit them to critical scrutiny.

2.2 Select four or five topics you consider would form a short interview package.

2.3 In pairs, work out a training session for a form, relating it to the tutor time available in your school. If necessary, each topic can be spread over two or more sessions.

2.4 Construct an activity which asks students to assess the significance of statements and the underlying expectations of interviewers who make them. Examples are:

'If you found you were the only woman/man . . .?'

'How do you think other people would describe your ability to . . .?'

'I wonder if you would find it easy to . . .?'

'Do you think you will stay in the post?'

'Are there any questions you would care to ask me?'

3 Case histories for tutor training

3.1 Construct case histories describing students experiencing difficulties in vocational development. If possible, include examples of:

a Unrealistic aspirations – both riskily high and unduly low.

b The consequences of succumbing to parental pressures to fulfil their ambitions for the student.

c Vulnerability to gender based prejudices which led to abandonment of a promising career.

d Difficulties created by immaturity or personality maladjustment.

3.2 When the description has been completed, construct decision-making or problem-solving activities related to the case.

4 Constructing modules of activities

4.1 Vocational guidance and development is a process throughout the student's secondary career.

a *It involves self-knowledge*: learning about strengths, weaknesses, prejudices, etc. This self-knowledge is used to sharpen perceptions of what will be a satisfactory life style. It can be linked with self-assessment procedures in RoA.

b Each year should extend awareness of the careers lying within the broad fields of vocational activity to which individuals are attracted. Students assess the level at which they will work and their willingness to invest in training and study.

c Consideration of the nature and results of change are part of the programme.

4.2 The programme should embody continuity and observable progression. What is done in one year should extend what was done in the preceding year, also preparing for what will be done in the succeeding year. The progression should be clear to students, avoiding the situation in pastoral work where students react with, 'But we've done it before', or tenth year students complain of boredom caused by endless versions of 'Me and my friends'.

4.3 The first step is gathering topics under broad headings, eg economic awareness, self-assessment, investigating the world of work, or problem areas, eg occupational and gender stereotypes. Links with what is happening in RoA and other curriculum areas should be explored to avoid unnecessary replication. Topics should then be allocated to each year group, and set out on large sheets of paper, making evident the progressive steps and extension of knowledge and skill.

4.4 Those concerned with particular years then develop a module of activities suited to what they see as the needs of students and as manageable by staff. Attention should be given to:

- the sequence of topics;

- structure of the sessions: clear objectives must be given to students; the final section must indicate ways in which students can apply the experience or knowledge, also relating it where possible to other curriculum areas.

A productive method is working in pairs to develop the session. Then the pair meet another pair to whom they explain their activity, seeking helpful feedback for improving or extending it. The process is repeated by the other pair.

Students can be involved in testing out the activities and invited to make suggestions for other activities. Where they have actually developed their own activities, not only have they been realistic, they have demonstrated real commitment to careers education. The group should consider ways in which students can take a participant role in developing activities and acting as helpers in the guidance programme.

4.5 For older students a series of activities could be centred around crisis points in an occupation, eg a nurse on her first night duty on the understaffed ward.

5 Constraints

5.1 The emphasis will be on small group activities involving decision making, standpoint taking, problem solving and sharing of ideas between groups. Partner work is used to allow students to explain and justify their ideas. Peer judges can be used to evaluate small group activity: the position of peer judge being systematically allocated.

5.2 The excessive use of questionnaires should be avoided. Over-use leads to the 'so what?' response in students. Any written work must meet the standards operating elsewhere in the school.

5.3 Judicious use of role play and simulation is essential. A gradual introduction and planned extension of skills monitored by the drama or English departments is necessary if a key educational tool is to have credibility with students.

5.4 As with all guidance and counselling activities the underlying principle is education for responsibility based in building students' self-respect.

References

Adelson, J. (1980) (Ed.) *Handbook of Adolescent Psychology*, New York: Wiley.

Ainscow, M. and Florek, A. (1989) (Eds) *Special Educational Needs: Towards a Whole School Approach*, London: Fulton.

Allport, G. (1935) 'Attitudes'. In Murchison, C. (Ed.) *A Handbook of Social Psychology*, Worcester, Mass: Clark University Press.

Allport, G. (1955) *Becoming*, New Haven: Yale University Press.

Allport, G. and Postman, L. (1945) 'The Basic Psychology of Rumor'. Reprinted in Maccoby, E., Newcombe, T. and Hartley, E. (Eds) *Readings in Social Psychology*, London: Methuen.

Ansoff, H. (1984) *Implementing Strategic Management*, Englewood Cliffs, N.J.: Prentice Hall.

Ashforth, D. (1990) *Records of Achievement in the Market Place*, Windsor: NFER.

Atkinson, G. (1975) *Effective Negotiator! Practical Guide to the Strategies and Tactics of Conflict Bargaining*, Negotiating Systems Publications.

Atkinson, J. and Feather, N. (1966) *A Theory of Achievement Motivation*, New York: Wiley.

Bales, R. (1970) *Personality and Interpersonal Behaviour*, New York: Holt, Rinehart and Winston.

Bandura, A. (1969) *Principles of Behaviour Modification*, New York: Holt, Rinehart and Winston.

Bandura, A. (1971) 'Effecting Changes Through Participant Modelling'. In Krumboltz, J. and Thoresen, C. (Eds) *Counseling Methods*, New York: Hart, Rinehart and Winston.

Bandura, A. (1977) *Social Learning Theory*, Englewood Cliffs, N.J.: Prentice-Hall.

Bandura, A. (1977) 'Self-Efficacy: Toward a Unifying Theory of Behavioural Change', *Psychological Review*, 84, pp. 191–215.

Bandura, A., Ciaffi, D., Taylor C. and Brouillard, M. (1988) 'Perceived Self-Efficacy in Coping with Cognitive Stressors and Opioid Activation', *Journal of Abnormal and Social Psychology*, 55, pp. 479–488.

Banks, O. and Finlayson, D. (1973) *Success and Failure in the Secondary School*, London: Methuen.

Bartlett, F. (1932) *Remembering*, Cambridge: Cambridge University Press.

Bateson, C., Jackson, D., Haley, J. and Weakland, J. (1956) 'Toward a Theory of Schizophrenia', *Behavioural Science,* 1. pp. 251–264

Besag, V. (1989) *Bullies and Victims in Schools*, Milton Keynes: Open University.

Birney, R., Burdick, H. and Teevan, R. (1969) *Fear of Failure Motivation*, New York: Wiley.

Blocher, D. (1966) *Developmental Counselling*, New York: Ronald Press.

Bower, E. (1969) 'Primary Prevention of Mental and Emotional Disorder: A Frame of Reference'. In Clarizio, H. *Mental Health and the Educative Process*, Chicago: Rand McNally.

Bowlby, J. (1961) 'Processes of Mourning', *International Journal of Psycho-Analysis*, Vol. 44.

Bowlby, J. (1961) 'Childhood Mourning and its Implications for Psychiatry', *American Journal of Psychiatry*, Vol. 188, pp. 481–497.

Breakwell, G. (1990) *Interviewing*, Leicester: British Psychological Society and Routledge.

Brehm, J. and Cohen, A. (1962) *Explorations in Cognitive Dissonance*, New York: Holt, Rinehart and Winston.

Broadfoot, P., James, M., McMeeking, S., Nuttall, D. and Stierer, B. (1988) *PRAISE Report*, London: HMSO.

Bruch, H. (1974) *Eating Disorders*, London: Routledge and Kegan Paul.

Burchell, H. and Millman, V. (1988) (Eds) *Changing Perspectives on Gender*.

Buss, A. (1980) *Self-Consciousness and Anxiety*, San Francisco: Freeman.

Chernin, K. (1986) *The Hungry Self*, London: Virago.

Chandler, E. (1980) *Educating Adolescent Girls*, London: Unwin.

Cooley, C. (1922) *Human Nature and the Social Order*, New York: Scribner.

Cox, M. (1978) *Coding the Therapeutic Process*, Oxford: Pergamon.

Cox, M. (1978) *Structuring the Therapeutic Process*, Oxford: Pergamon.

Crisp, A. (1980) *Anorexia Nervosa*, London: Academic Press.

Curle, A. (1972) *Mystics and Militants*, London: Tavistock.

Dale, R. (1985) *Education, Training and Employment: Towards a New Vocationalism*, Oxford: Pergamon.

Dennison, B. and Kirk, R. (1990) *Do, Review, Learn and Apply*, Oxford: Blackwell.

Department of Education and Science (1988) *Careers Education and Guidance from 5 to 16, Curriculum Matters 10*, London: HMSO.

Department of Education and Science and Welsh Office, (1989) *The Elton Report: Discipline in Schools*, London: HMSO.

Douvan, E. and Adelson, J. (1966) *The Adolescent Experience*, New York: Wiley.

Dryden, W. (1989) (Ed.) *Key Issues for Counselling in Action*, London: Sage.

Dryden, W., Charles-Edwards, D. and Woolfe, R. (Eds) (1989) *Handbook of Counselling in Britain*, London: Tavistock/Routledge.

Dweck, C. and Licht, B. (1980) 'Learned Helplessness and Intellectual Achievement'. In Garber, J. and Seligman, M. (Eds) *Human Helplessness*, New York: Academic Press.

Egan, G. (1986) *The Skilled Helper*, (3rd Edn), Pacific Grove, Calif: Brooks/Cale.

Erikson, E. (1959) 'Identity and the Life Cycle: Selected Papers', *Psychological Issues, 1*. New York: International University Press.

Erikson, E. (1968) 'Womanhood and the Inner Space'. In *Identity, Youth and Crisis*, London: Faber and Faber.

Festinger, L. (1957) *A Theory of Cognitive Dissonance*, Evanston, Ill.: Harper, Row Peterson.

Fidler, B. and Bowles, G. (1989) (Eds) *Effective Local Management of Schools*, London: Longman.

Fiehn, J. In Best, R. and Rabbet, P. (Eds) (1989) *Whole Person: Whole School; Bridging the Pastoral/Academic Divide*, London: School Curriculum Development Committee.

Fishbein, M. (1967) (Ed.) *Readings in Attitude Theory and Measurement*, New York: Wiley.

Flavell, J. (1963) *The Developmental Psychology of Jean Piaget*, Princeton, N.J.: Van Nostrand.

Flavell, J. (1968) *The Development of Role-Taking and Communication Skills in Children*, New York: Wiley.

Frenkel-Brunswik, E. (1958) 'A Study of Prejudice in Children', *Human Relations*, 1, pp. 295–306.

Funnell, P. and Miller, D. (1991) *Vocational Education and the Challenge of Europe*, London: Kogan Page.

Galloway, D. (1990) *Pupil Welfare and Counselling*, London: Longman.

Garber, J. and Seligman, M. (1980) *Human Helplessness*, New York: Academic Press.

Garforth, D. and McIntosh, H. (1988) *Profiling: a User's Manual*, Cheltenham: Stanley Thornes.

Gaudry, E. and Spielberger, C. (1971) *Anxiety and Educational Achievement*, Sydney: Wiley.

Gergen, K. (1971) *The Concept of Self*, New York: Holt, Rinehart and Winston.

Ginzberg, E. (1971) *Career Guidance*, New York: McGraw-Hill.

Glasser, W. (1969) *Schools Without Failure*, New York: Harper and Row.

Gordon, C. and Gergen, K. (1968) *The Self in Social Interaction*, New York: Wiley.

Gorer, G. (1965) *Death, Grief and Mourning in Contemporary Britain*, London: Cresset.

Grinder, R. (1978) *Adolescence*, (2nd Edn), New York: Wiley.

Hamblin, D. (1974) *The Teacher and Counselling*, Oxford: Blackwell.

Hamblin, D. (1981) *Teaching Study Skills*, Oxford: Blackwell.

Hamblin, D. (1983) *Guidance: 16–19*, Oxford: Blackwell.

Hamblin, D. (1984) *Pastoral Care: a Training Manual*, Oxford: Blackwell.

Hamblin, D. (1986) *A Pastoral Programme*, Oxford: Blackwell.

Hamblin, D. (1989) *Staff Development for Pastoral Care*, Oxford: Blackwell.

Handy, C. (1984) *The Future of Work*, Oxford: Blackwell.

Hargreaves, A. (1979) 'Strategies, Decisions and Control: Interaction in a Middle School Classroom'. In Eggleston, J. (Ed.) *Teacher Decision-making in the Classroom*, London: Routledge and Kegan Paul.

Hargreaves, D., Hester, S. and Mellor, F. (1975) *Deviance in Classrooms*, London: Routledge and Kegan Paul.

Hastings, N. and Schwieso, J. (1987) *New Directions in Educational Psychology: 2. Behaviour and Motivation in the Classroom*, Lewes: Falmer.

Heider, F. (1958) *The Psychology of Interpersonal Relations*, New York: Wiley.

Herzberg, F. (1968) *Work and the Nature of Man*, London: Staple Press.

Hessey, P. and Blanchard, K. (1977) *Management of Organizational Behaviour: Utilizing Human Resources*, (3rd Edn), Englewood Cliffs, N.J.: Prentice-Hall.

Hitchcock, G. (1986) *Profiles and Profiling*, London: Longman

Hitchcock, G. (1988) *Education and Training, 14–18: a Survey of Major Initiatives*, London: Longman.

Hollander, E. (1964) *Leaders, Groups and Influence*, New York: Oxford University Press.

Holly, P. (1987) *The Dilemmas of Low Attainment*, London: FEU.

Hopson, B. and Hopson, C. (1973) *Exercises in Career Development*, Cambridge: CRAC.

Horrocks, J. and Jackson, D. (1972) *Self and Role*, Boston: Houghton Mifflin.

Howard, D., Nance, D. and Myers, P. (1987) *Adaptive Counselling and Therapy*, San Francisco: Jossey-Bass.

Inhelder, B. and Piaget, J. (1958) *The Growth of Logical Thinking from Childhood to Adolescence*, New York: Basic Books.

Insko, C. (1967) *Developmental Therapy*, San Francisco: Jossey-Bass.

Ivey, A. (1986) *Developmental Therapy*, San Francisco: Jossey-Bass.

Jahoda, M. (1958) *Current Concepts of Mental Health: A Report; Joint Commission on Mental Illness and Health:* Monograph Series No. 1, New York: Basic Books.

James, C. and Young, J. (1989) 'Case Study: Equal Opportunities through the Hertfordshire TVEI Project', In Burchell, H. and Millman, V. (Eds) *Changing Perspectives on Gender*, Milton Keynes: Open University Press.

James, W. (1910) *Psychology: The Briefer Course,* New York: Holt

Janis, I. (1972) *Victims of Groupthink,* Bosston: Houghton Mifflin.

Janis, I. (1982) *Groupthink: Psychological Studies of Policy Decisions and Fiascos,* (2nd Edn), Boston: Houghton Mifflin.

Jones, A. (1987) *Leadership for Tomorrow's Schools,* Oxford: Blackwell.

Jones, E. and Thibaut, J. (1958) 'Interaction Goals as Bases of Inference in Interpersonal Perception', In Taguiri, R. and Petrullo, L. (Eds) *Person Perception and Interpersonal Behaviour,* Stanford: Stanford University Press.

Katz, D. (1960) 'The Functional Approach to the Study of Attitudes', *Public Opinion Quarterly,* 24. pp. 186–195

Kearns, J. (1989) 'Case Study: Issues of Gender in the Inner London Education Authority Profile and London Record of Achievement Scheme', In Burchell, H. and Millman, V. (Eds) *Changing Perspectives on Gender,* Milton Keynes: Open University Press.

Kelly, G. (1955) *The Psychology of Personal Constructs,* New York: Norton.

Klein, D. (1960) 'Some Concepts Concerning the Mental Health of the Individual', *Journal Consulting Psychology,* 24, pp. 283–293.

Kohlberg, L. (1976) 'Moral Stages and Moralization' In Lickona, T. (Ed.) *Moral Development and Behaviour,* New York: Holt, Rinehart and Winston.

Kolb, D. (1984) *Experiential Learning,* Englewood Cliffs, N.J.: Prentice Hall.

Krumboltz, J. (1966) (Ed.) *Revolution in Counseling,* Boston: Houghton Mifflin.

Kubler-Ross, E. (1970) *On Death and Dying,* New York: MacMillan.

Lazarus, R. (1966) *Psychological Stress and the Coping Process,* New York: McGraw Hill.

Lazarus, R. and Folkman, S. (1984) *Stress, Appraisal and Coping,* New York: Springer Verlag.

Levine, J. and Wang, C. (1983) (Eds) *Teacher and Student Perceptions: Implications for Learning,* Hillsdale, N.J.: Erlbaum Associates.

Levitt, E. (1968) *The Psychology of Anxiety,* London: Staples.

Lewin, K. (1947) 'Frontiers in Group Dynamics: Concept, Method and Reality in Social Science; Social Equilibrium and Change', *Human Relations,* 1, No. 1, June, pp. 5–41.

Licht, B. and Dweck, C. (1983) 'Sex Differences in Achievement Orientations'. In Marland, M. (Ed.) *Sex Differentiation and Schooling,* London: Heinemann.

Lieberman, M., Yalom, I. and Miles, M. (1973) *Encounter Groups: First Facts,* New York: Basic Books.

Lindsay, G. (1983) *Problems of Adolescence in the Secondary School,* London: Croom Helm.

Livson, N. and Peskin, H. (1980) 'Perspectives in Adolescence from Longitudinal Research'. In Adelson, J. (Ed.) *Handbook of Adolescent Psychology,* New York: Wiley.

Lorac, C. and Weiss, M. (1981) *Communication and Social Skills,* Exeter: Wheaton.

Lowe, P. (1988) *Responding to Adolescent Needs: A Pastoral Care Approach,* London: Cassell.

Maccoby, E. and Jacklyn, C. (1975) *The Psychology of Sex Differences,* London: Oxford University Press.

Mandler, G. and Sarason, S. (1952) 'A Study of Anxiety and Learning', *Journal Abnormal and Social Psychology,* New York: Wiley.

Marcia, J. (1980) 'Identity in Adolescence'. In Adelson, J. (Ed.) *Handbook of Adolescent Psychology,* New York; Wiley.

Martin, J. (1987) *Cognitive Instructional Counselling,* London, Ontario: Althouse Press.

Maslow, A. (1970) *Motivation and Personality,* (2nd Edn), New York: Harper and Row.

Matza, D. (1969) *Becoming Deviant,* Englewood Cliffs, N.J.: Prentice Hall.

McCandless, B. and Trotter, R. (1977) *Children: Behavior and Development,* (3rd Edn), New York: Holt, Rinehart and Winston.

Mead, G. (1925) 'The Genesis of the Self and Social Control', *International Journal of Ethics,* Vol 35, No. 3, pp. 251–273.

Mearns, D. and Thorne, B. (1988) *Person-Centred Counselling in Action,* London: Sage.

Ments, M. (1983) *The Effective Use of Role Play,* London: Kogan Page.

Miller, J. cited in Adelson, J. (1980) *Handbook of Adolescent Psychology*, New York: Wiley.

Miller, N. (1952) 'Comments on Theoretical Models Illustrated by the Development of a Theory of Conflict Behavior', *Journal of Personality*. 20, pp. 82–100.

Mittler, P. (1988) Introduction in Lowe, P. *Responding to Adolescent Needs: A Pastoral Care Approach*, London: Cassell.

Morton-Williams, R. and Finch, S. (1968) *Enquiry 1*, Schools Council, London: HMSO.

Munby, S., Phillips, P. and Collinson, R. (1989) *Assessing and Recording Achievement*, Oxford: Blackwell.

Munro, A., Manthei, R. and Small, J. (1983) *Counselling*, London: Routledge.

Musgrove, F. (1971) *Patterns of Power and Authority in English Education*, London: Methuen.

Myers, D. (1982) 'Polarizing Effects of Social Interaction'. In Brandstetter, H., Davis, J. and Stocker-Kreichgauer, G. (Eds) *Group Decision Making*, New York: Academic Press.

Natale, S. (1972) *An Experiment in Empathy*, Slough: NFER.

National Curriculum Council (1990) 'Curriculum Guidance 6'. *Careers Education and Guidance*, Skeldergate, York.

Nunnally, E., Chilman, C. and Cox, F. (1988) (Eds) *Troubled Relationships: Families in Trouble Series*, Vol. 3, London: Sage.

Osborn, A. (1963) *Applied Imagination*, (3rd Edn), New York: Scribner.

Osgood, C., Suci, G. and Tannenbaum, P. (1957) *The Measurement of Meaning*, Urbana: University of Illinois Press.

Parkes, C. (1972) *Bereavement*, London: Tavistock.

Parsons, T. (1957) *Economy and Society*, Illinois: Free Press.

Pendleton, D. and Hasler, J. (1983) (Eds) *Doctor-Patient Communication*, London: Academic Press.

Petty, R. and Cacioppo, J. (1985) *Communication and Persuasion: Central and Peripheral Routes to Attitude Change*, New York: Springer-Verlag.

Phares, E. (1976) *Locus of Control in Personality*, Morriston, N.J.: General Learning Press.

Phillips, B. (1978) *School Stress and Anxiety*, New York: Human Sciences Press.

Piaget, J. and Inhelder, B. (1958) *The Growth of Logical Thinking from Childhood to Adolescence*, New York: Basic Books.

Premack, D. (1959) 'Toward Empirical Behaviour Laws: 1. Positive Reinforcement', *Psychological Review*, 66, pp. 219–233.

Pruitt, D. (1981) *Negotiation Behaviour*, New York: Academic Press.

Ravenette, A. (1967) 'Everyone His Own Scientist', Newsletters, Association of Educational Psychologists.

Reddin, W. (1970) *Managerial Effectiveness*, New York: McGraw-Hill.

Roberts, K. (1984) *School Leavers and Their Prospects*, Bletchley: Open University.

Rogers, C. (1942) *Counseling and Psychotherapy*, Boston: Houghton Mifflin.

Rogers, C. (1951) *Client Centered Therapy*, Boston: Houghton Mifflin.

Rogers, C. (1971) *Encounter Groups*, London: Allen Lane.

Rokeach, M. (1960) *The Open and Closed Mind*, New York: Basic Books.

Rokeach, M. (1968) *Beliefs, Values and Attitudes*, San Francisco: Jossey-Bass.

Roland, E. and Munthe, E. (1989) *Bullying: An International Perspective*, London: Fulton.

Rose, S. and Edleson, S. (1987) *Working with Children and Adolescents in Groups*, San Francisco: Jossey-Bass.

Rosenberg, B. and Sutton-Smith, B. (1972) *Sex and Identity*, New York: Holt, Rinehart and Winston.

Rotter, J. (1966) 'Generalized Expectancies for Internal versus External Control of Reinforcement', *Psychological Monographs*, 80, No. 1, Whole No. 609.

Rotter, J., Chance, J. and Phares, E. (1972) *Applications of a Social Learning Theory of Personality*, New York: Holt, Rinehart and Winston.

Ruebush, B. (1966) 'Conceptual Issues, Major Theoretical Approaches, Methodology, Behavioural Correlates of Anxiety'. In Stevenson, H., Kagan, J. and Spiker, C. (Eds) *Sixty second Year Book, National Society for the Study of Education, Part One*, Chicago: Chicago University Press.

Sapir, E. (1930) 'Communication'. In *International Encyclopedia of the Social Sciences*, (1st Edn), New York: Macmillan.

SCET (1988) *Self-Supported Study in Scotland*, TVEI/Learning System Unit: Scottish Council for Educational Technology.

SCRE (1977) *Pupils in Profile*, London: Hodder and Stoughton.

Seligman, M. (1975) *Helplessness: On Depression, Development and Death*, San Franciso: Freeman.

Shaw, M. (1981) *Group Dynamics*, (3rd Edn), New York: McGraw-Hill.

Sherman, M. (1979) *Personality: Inquiry and Application*, New York: Pergamon.

Spielberger, C. (1966) (Ed.) *Anxiety and Behaviour*, New York: Academic Press.

Spivack, G., Platt, J. and Shure, M. (1976) *The Problem-Solving Approach to Adjustment*, San Francisco: Jossey-Bass.

Stanworth, M. (1982) *Gender and Schooling*, London: Hutchison.

Starishevsky, R. and Matlin, N. (1968) 'A Model for the Translation of Self Concepts into Vocational Terms'. In Hopson, B. and Hayes, J. (Eds) *The Theory and Practice of Vocational Guidance*, Oxford: Pergamon.

Stewart, I. (1989) *Transactional Analysis Counselling in Action*, London: Sage.

Sumner, R. and Warburton, F. (1972) *Achievement in Secondary School*, Slough: NFER.

Super, D. (1957) *The Psychology of Careers*, New York: Harper and Row.

Sunderland, M. (1983) 'Anxiety, Aspirations and the Curriculum'. In Marland, M. (Ed.) *Sex Differentiation and Schooling*, London: Heinemann.

Thomas, G. and Feiler, A. (1988) *Planning for Special Needs*, Oxford: Blackwell.

Thomas, J. (1973) *Self-Concept in Psychology and Education*, Slough: NFER.

Thompson, S. and Kahn, J. (1970) *The Group Process in Helping Technique*, Oxford: Pergamon.

Trower, P., Casey, A. and Dryden, W. (1988) *Cognitive-Behavioural Counselling in Action*, London: Sage.

Truax, C. and Carkhuff, R. (1967) *Toward Effective Counselling and Psychotherapy*, Chicago: Aldine.

Turner, R. (1971) 'Role-Taking: Process Versus Conformity', In Rose, A. (Ed.) *Human Behavior and Social Processes*, London: Routledge and Kegan Paul.

Tyler, L. (1958) 'Theoretical Principles Underlying the Counseling Process', *Journal Counselling Psychology*, 5, pp. 3–10.

Tyler, L. (1969) *The Work of the Counselor*, New York: Appleton-Century-Crofts.

TVEI (1990) *Developments 10: Flexible Learning*, Sheffield: The Training Agency.

Wall, W. (1948) *The Adolescent Child*, London: Methuen.

Wall, W. (1968) *Adolescence in School and Society*, Slough: NFER.

Warwick, D. (1989) (Ed.) *Linking Schools and Industry*, Oxford: Blackwell.

Waterhouse, P. (1990) *Flexible Learning*, Bath: Network Press.

Watkins, C. and Wagner, P. (1987) *School Discipline*, Oxford: Blackwell.

Weiner, B. (1972) *Theories of Motivation*, Chicago: Markham.

Weiner, B. (1980) *Human Motivation*, New York: Holt, Rinehart and Winston.

Weiner, B. and Litman-Adizes, T. (1980) 'An Attributional, Expectancy Value Analysis of Learned Helplessness and Depression'. In Garber, J. and Seligman, M. *Human Helplessness*, New York: Academic Press.

Wolfendale, S. (1989) (Ed.) *Parental Involvement*, London: Cassell.

Yost, E. and Corbishley, M. (1987) *Career Counseling*, San Francisco: Jossey-Bass.

Name index

Subject index